GW00372796

THE FEMALE
SPECTATOR

Mrs ELIZA HAYWOOD.

Parmentier pinx: Vertue Sculp:

A portrait of Eliza Haywood
[Reproduced by Courtesy of the Trustees of the British Museum]

THE FEMALE SPECTATOR

BEING SELECTIONS FROM MRS ELIZA HAYWOOD'S PERIODICAL,
FIRST PUBLISHED IN MONTHLY PARTS (1744-6)

Edited with an Introduction
by

Gabrielle M. Firmager

Bristol Classical Press

Cover illustration: Frontispiece to Volume I of the first bound edition of *The Female Spectator*. [Reproduced by Permission of the British Library]

First published in 1993 by
Bristol Classical Press
an imprint of
Gerald Duckworth & Co. Ltd
The Old Piano Factory
48 Hoxton Square, London N1 6PB

© 1993 by Gabrielle M. Firmager

All rights reserved. No part of this publication
may be reproduced, stored in a retrieval system, or
transmitted, in any form or by any means, electronic,
mechanical, photocopying, recording or otherwise,
without the prior permission of the publisher.

A catalogue record for this book is available
from the British Library

ISBN 1-85399-209-7

Printed in Great Britain by
Cromwell Press, Melksham

CONTENTS

LIST OF SELECTIONS FROM *THE FEMALE SPECTATOR*

LIST OF ILLUSTRATIONS

ACKNOWLEDGEMENTS

I am much indebted to Jo Kemp for her researches on my behalf in Norfolk, and also to Jane Rowe, ex-Managing Editor of Bristol Classical Press, for her helpful suggestions and advice. I am grateful to the British Library and the British Museum Prints & Drawings Department for permission to reproduce the illustrations. I must also thank the editor of the *Huntington Library Quarterly* and the University of North Carolina Press for giving permission to quote from their publications. My greatest debt, however, is to Dr Mara Kalnins, without whose enthusiasm, constant advice and support this work would never have been undertaken.

A NOTE ON DATES

At the time *The Female Spectator* was published two calendars were in operation in this country. Until the end of 1751 the legal beginning of the year in Great Britain was 25 March, not 1 January, as in other countries in Europe, but to avoid confusion it was common practice to date letters and documents written from January to March in each year using both styles, for instance, 'January 12 1744-5'; that is, 1744 Old Style, 1745 New Style.

INTRODUCTION

The Mystery of Eliza Haywood

Apart from some literary historians, very few people nowadays have even heard of Eliza Haywood, yet in her day she was one of the most prolific and successful writers of popular fiction. She was also notorious, made so by Pope's malicious reference to her in *The Dunciad* in 1728:

> See in the circle next, Eliza plac'd;
> Two babes of love close clinging to her waste;
> Fair as before her works she stands confess'd
> In flow'rs and pearls by bounteous Kirkall dress'd.
> Pearls on her neck and roses in her hair,
> And her fore-buttocks to the navel bare.

> Alexander Pope, *The Dunciad* (1728) ll.149-54

In the following lines, a lewd contest between two booksellers, who vie for the favours of 'yon Juno of majestic size,/With cow-like udders and with ox-like eyes', 'Juno' was also assumed to be Mrs Haywood. After this reflection on her morals it is not surprising that Eliza Haywood should have taken steps to ensure that very little information concerning her life should be handed down to posterity. Indeed, her first biographer David Erskine Baker, writing in 1764 a few years after her death, stated that 'from a supposition of some improper liberties being taken with her character after death...she laid a solemn injunction on a person who was well-acquainted with all the particulars of it, not to communicate to any one the least circumstance relating to her'.[1] All that Baker could learn of her early life was that her father was in the mercantile way, that she was born in London and that at the time of her death in 1756 she was about 63 years of age. Most commentators on Eliza Haywood in this century have relied on the research of George Whicher who, in his monograph *The Life and Romances of Mrs Eliza Haywood* (New York, 1915), remarked that the

1

one resemblance she bore to Shakespeare was the obscurity which covered the events of her life. So effective was she that recent attempts to delve into her early life have merely tended to increase the mystery surrounding it.

Dr Whicher's researches into London Parish Registers led him to an entry dated 21 January 1689-90 referring to the christening of 'Elizabeth dau. of Robert ffowler & Elizabeth his wife' at St Peter's, Cornhill. Further entries showed 'Robert ffowler' to have been a hosier to his trade, but Dr Whicher could find nothing which positively identified Eliza Haywood as the daughter of Robert Fowler. However, he subsequently maintained that Elizabeth Fowler married a clergyman, the Rev. Valentine Haywood, fifteen years her senior, 'some time before or during 1711', for in December of that year a son, Charles, was christened at St Mary Aldermary Church in London. Although he could find no evidence of the actual marriage, he noted that Valentine Haywood held at that time a small living in Norfolk, and had recently been appointed lecturer of St Matthew's Church, Friday Street, London. Ten years later, in 1721, the Rev. Haywood inserted an advertisement in *The Post Boy* to the effect that his wife having 'eloped' a few weeks earlier, he was no longer responsible for her debts.

Upon what evidence Dr Whicher based his claim that Elizabeth Fowler and the Rev. Valentine Haywood were married is difficult to determine. The 'small living' in Norfolk was at Baconsthorpe, with Bodham, and the parish register of Baconsthorpe contains an entry referring to the marriage of 'Valentine Haywood, Rector of Baconsthorpe, singleman, and Elizabeth Foord, singlewoman, on June 11th, 1706, by Licence'. Elizabeth Foord certainly existed but she was the daughter of Charles and Abijah Foord, of Stepney. She was christened on 20 December 1685, at St Dunstan's Church, Stepney. Examination of Boyd's Index of Marriages, which only covers a few English counties, and in any case is incomplete, has yielded no evidence of a marriage between a woman named Elizabeth Fowler and a man called Haywood, although earlier references, notably the *Dictionary of National Biography* (1891 edition), also agree that Eliza Haywood was the daughter of a London tradesman named Fowler and that she contracted at an early age a marriage with a man named Haywood, who subsequently abandoned her and her two children.

Some confirmation of these facts can be found in an undated letter recently discovered in the Manuscript Department of the British Library, which has no indication of the name of the intended recipient, but which asks for patronage for the publication of a 'Tragedy', and is signed 'Eliza Haywood'. The writer claims that her maiden name was Fowler and that she is 'nearly related to Sir Richard of the Grange'. An 'unfortunate marriage' had reduced her to the 'melancholly necessity' of depending on her

Pen for the support of herself and two children, 'the eldest of whom is no more than 7 years of Age'. Although 'not personally known' to her correspondent, she concludes her letter by offering to wait upon him in person 'to know how far you can forgive this Presumption'. As Mrs Haywood's first 'Tragedy', *The Fair Captive*, was produced and printed in 1721, it seems likely that this letter was written about that time. Since she was prepared to meet her intended patron face to face it seems unlikely that she would reveal so much about herself without being able to substantiate her claim, if, as seems reasonable, the person to whom she was writing was also acquainted with 'Sir Richard of the Grange'. There was a Sir Richard Fowler living at that time at Harnage Grange, near Cound, Shropshire. He had married Sarah, the niece of Sir Hans Sloane, the eminent physician, to whom Mrs Haywood certainly applied for patronage on a later occasion. Richard's youngest sister Elizabeth, was christened at Cound in January 1692-3, but the possibility that she might have been our Eliza Haywood was ruled out when it was found that she died some time before 1728. Exhaustive research has not so far been able to establish any connection between Eliza Haywood and Sir Richard Fowler, but since his wife was Sir Hans Sloane's niece it seems a distinct possibility that Mrs Haywood's letter was addressed to that gentleman and that she was at least trading on her maiden name to establish some kind of rapport. The Shropshire Fowlers were an extensive and important family and it is possible that future enquiries may yet establish some kind of kinship.

In another undated letter recently found with no indication of the recipient and signed 'E. HAYWOOD', which seeks patronage for a book entitled *La Belle Assemblèe*, the writer refers to 'the Sudden Deaths of both a Father, and a Husband, at an age when I was little prepar'd to stem the tide of Ill fortune'.[2] How much credence can be given to this statement is difficult to determine, but *La Belle Assemblèe*, translated from the French by Eliza Haywood, was first published in 1724. However it is on record that Eliza Haywood was acting on the stage of the playhouse in Smock Alley, Dublin, during the season of 1715, as Chloe in Thomas Shadwell's adaptation of *Timon of Athens*. It is not beyond the bounds of possibility that during her time in Ireland she met and married a man called Haywood. Unfortunately many Irish records were destroyed in Dublin in 1922 (during the 'Troubles') and it seems unlikely that any evidence will emerge to support this theory.

For further clues to Eliza Haywood's early life the reader may be referred to the opening paragraphs of *The Female Spectator* wherein she confesses that she had never been a 'Beauty', was now no longer young, but that she had 'run through as many scenes of Vanity and Folly as the greatest Coquet of them all.— Dress, Equipage and Flattery were the Idols of my Heart'. Her life, she continues, 'for some Years, was a continued Round of what I then called Pleasure, and my whole Time engross'd by a Hurry of promiscuous Diversions'. However, 'when the too great Vivacity of my Nature became temper'd with Reflection',...'a thousand odd Adventures...now rise fresh to my Remembrance...and I find it easy to account for the Cause by the Consequence'. Whatever her origins, it was in 1719 that Mrs Haywood burst upon the London scene with the publication of her first novel, *Love in Excess; or, The Fatal Enquiry*, which became an immediate success.

Thereafter, Mrs Haywood settled down to earn her living by writing. She had found a good formula and exploited it to the full: her early novels were titillating tales of illicit passion and unrequited love, persecuted maidens and unrepentant rakes. Between 1720 and 1730 she wrote, besides plays and translations, thirty-eight works of her own composing. She was befriended by Aaron Hill, the poet and dramatist, and Richard Savage wrote verses in her honour, although he later turned against her and advised her to take in washing rather than write 'Novels of Intrigue, to teach young Heiresses the Art of running away with Fortune-hunters, and scandalising Persons of the highest Worth and Distinction'.[3]

It could be said that Eliza Haywood brought about her own downfall, and incurred Pope's fury, by producing in 1725 and in 1727 a couple of 'scandal novels': fictionalised exposés of well-known living persons, some of them Pope's friends. Apart from the verse from *The Dunciad* already quoted, Jonathan Swift reacted by describing her as 'a stupid, infamous, scribbling woman'.[4] The name of Eliza Haywood never again appeared on the title page of any of her works after the publication of *The Dunciad*, and for a time she seems to have taken to the theatre again. She had already written two or three not very successful plays and had acted in one of them – *A Wife to be Lett: A Comedy* – in 1723. During the 1730s she took part in several plays at the Little Theatre in the Haymarket under the management of Henry Fielding, with whom she does not appear to have been on particularly good terms (he had ridiculed her as 'Mrs Novel' in his play, *The Author's Farce* in 1730, and she later retaliated in *The History of Miss Betsy Thoughtless* in 1751).[5] Her only real success in the theatre was *The Opera of Operas*, written in 1733 in collaboration with the actor-playwright William Hatchett with whom she is said to have lived 'on terms of friendship',[6] based on Fielding's *Life and Death of Tom Thumb the Great*, and with music by Thomas Arne.

Eliza Haywood's next full-scale work of fiction appeared in 1736. Under the guise of a fairy tale, *The Adventures of Eovaii* was a barely concealed attack on the government headed by Sir Robert Walpole. After this she may have found it convenient to leave the country for a while, for there is a gap of some years before she returned to the fray, but by now she was employing a more moralistic and didactic tone in tune with the changing times – Richardson's *Pamela* had appeared in 1740. She was to produce several more reasonably successful novels between 1741 and 1756, the year of her death. Of these the most notable was *The History of Miss Betsy Thoughtless*, first published in 1751, which is generally regarded as the most carefully crafted of all her novels and which is still eminently readable today. It was also during this period of her life that Mrs Haywood turned journalist, launching *The Female Spectator* in May 1744 and continuing it until April 1746. After a lapse of some months she tried her hand again with *The Parrot, with a Compendium of the Times*, 'by the authors of *The Female Spectator*'. This was a weekly periodical which ran from August to October 1746, but was then abandoned and Mrs Haywood returned to novel-writing.

In *The Whitehall Evening Post: or London Intelligencer* for Tuesday, 24 February to Thursday, 26 February 1756, there appeared the following announcement:

> Yesterday Morning died, in the 60th Year of her Age, after a very severe illness of three Months, which she bore with great Fortitude and Resignation, Mrs. Eliza Haywood, the celebrated Authoress of some of the best moral and entertaining Pieces that have been published for these many Years. The great Hand she had in those elegant Productions the Female Spectator, and Epistles for the Ladies, together with her Histories of Miss Betsy Thoughtless, Jemmy and Jenny Jessamy, her Invisible Spy, and the Fortunate Foundlings, will ever remain as living Monuments of her Merit.

Eliza Haywood was buried in the churchyard of St Margaret's, Westminster (which is adjacent to Westminster Abbey), on 3 March 1756. There is no record of the commission of a gravestone, or of any memorial to her in the church, but according to the Churchwardens' Accounts her funeral cost 8s. 6d., a fairly average amount for that time. 2s. 6d. was allotted to the 'ground', 2s. 10d. was paid for the 'knell', 3s. for 'cloth' and 2d. for the parson. The graveyard of St Margaret's has been grassed over for many years and although a record was made of some of the stones beforehand there is nothing now to show just where Eliza Haywood was buried. She remains as tantalisingly elusive in death as in life.

After the advent of such literary luminaries as Fanny Burney and Jane

Austen, Mrs Haywood and all her works descended into oblivion, but she was in many ways a pioneer, and despite her treatment at the hands of her male contemporaries she emerges as a not inconsiderable influence upon the manners and morals of her time, and an early advocate for a more liberal attitude to the education of women.

The Historical Background

Although the date of Mrs Haywood's birth cannot at present be established with any certainty, if it can be assumed that she was born early in the last decade of the seventeenth century and that she certainly died in 1756, she would have lived through five reigns: that of William and Mary (1689-94), William alone (1694-1702), Anne (1702-14), George I (1714-27) and George II (1727-60). England in the time of George II was divided into two political parties, the 'Whigs' and the 'Tories', and at this point it may be useful to distinguish between the two factions. Both terms derive from packs of outlaws – the Scottish *whiggamores* were pack-saddle thieves, employed by Scottish Covenanters to aid them in their opposition to the governments of James I and Charles II, and eventually the term 'Whig' was attached to anyone who upheld the right to political and religious liberty. 'Tory' derives from Irish Catholic outlaws (*tóraidhe*) and, according to Lord Macaulay, 'the name was first given to Englishmen who refused to concur in excluding a Roman Catholic prince [that is, James II] from the throne'.[7] With the death of Queen Anne many Tories would have favoured a return to the Stuart dynasty in the person of the Old Pretender, James Edward (half-brother to Queen Anne), despite his adherence to the Catholic faith. Even so, Whig and Tory were much more loosely defined parties and far less disciplined than their Conservative, Liberal and Labour successors of the present day.

The Whig commitment to the Hanoverian succession put them in a powerful position *vis-à-vis* the Throne. Two years before the first appearance of *The Female Spectator*, Sir Robert Walpole, an astute and subtle politician and the first 'Prime Minister' (although the title originated as a term of abuse) to reside at Number Ten Downing Street, had resigned after having governed England for nearly 20 years. A squabble with Spain over the smuggling of slaves into Spanish plantations in the New World had resulted in war having been declared in 1739, much against Walpole's better judgement, and war with Spain meant war with France, as the two countries were linked by the Family Compact of 1733. Meanwhile Frederick the Great had precipitated the War of the Austrian Succession by seizing Silesia from the new Hapsburg Queen, Maria Theresa (popularly referred to as the Queen of Hungary). England offered help to the beleaguered Queen and so the chief combatants lined up: Prussia Spain and France against England and Austria.

In 1743 George II, accompanied by his younger son the Duke of Cumberland, left England to take part in the campaign. At the village of Dettingen, near Aschaffenburg on the River Main the two opposing forces clashed. The French cavalry charged; King George's horse bolted but he dismounted and, sword in hand, led his Hanoverian and British infantry into action against the French. They fled and many were drowned in trying to cross the river. It was a famous victory, and the last time an English king led his troops into battle. Two years later a still greater battle was fought in defence of the garrison town of Tournai, at the village of Fontenoy. The English troops, under the command of the Duke of Cumberland, were outnumbered almost two to one. For nearly four hours the English troops withstood attacks by cavalry, artillery and infantry until by nightfall the remnants were led to safety by the Duke. Although a defeat, it was regarded by the English populace as a glorious one. A few months later Cumberland withdrew his troops to England to fight the Young Pretender, Charles Edward and England played no further part in the War of the Austrian Succession.

From her other writings there appears to be little doubt about Mrs Haywood's political persuasions. In common with many of her contemporaries she looked back to the Age of Queen Anne as a 'Golden Age' and regarded the Hanoverian Georges with some contempt. Evidence for her political views can be found in her anti-Walpole satire *Eovaii* and the fact that she was prepared to act in Henry Fielding's anti-government satires, the last of which effectively closed many London theatres and introduced a form of censorship of theatrical performances by the Lord Chamberlain's Office which did not end until 1968. By the time she was writing *The Female Spectator*, however, Mrs Haywood appears to have adopted a more equivocal stance and despite her assurance in her opening pages of 'penetrating into the Mysteries of the Alcove, the Cabinet, or Field' very little intelligence regarding the momentous events of the day appears to have crept into the pages of her periodical. When taxed with this omission, however, she retorts that such topics came not within the province of *The Female Spectator* 'such as Armies marching — Battles fought, — Towns destroyed — Rivers cross'd, and the like', these being the concern of the daily press. She continues:

To check the enormous Growth of Luxury, to reform the Morals, and improve the Manners of an Age, by all confess'd degenerate and sunk, are the great Ends for which these Essays were chiefly intended'.

The Female Spectator: Publication and Critical Reception (from Early Reviews to the Present Day)

In the December 1744 issue of *The Gentleman's Magazine* the receipt of 'Book 8' of *The Female Spectator* was acknowledged in the following terms:

> Ye fair philosophers in virtue's cause,
> Conspicuous merit claims a just applause!
> Thrice worthy league! your gen'rous plan pursue,
> And take this tribute to your labours due:
> Were your great predecessor yet on earth,
> He'd be the first to speak your page's worth:
> There all the foibles of the fair you trace;
> There do you shew your sex's truest grace;
> There are the various wiles of man display'd,
> In gentle warnings to the cred'lous maid;
> Politely pictur'd, wrote with strength and ease,
> And while the wand'rer you reclaim, you please:
> Whether the fair, yet glows the blooming maid,
> Or a gay bride to hymen's porch is led
> Or matron busy'd with domestick cares,
> Or as a widow for her loss despairs,
> Learn'd in the weaker sex in every state,
> *You* shew a *judgment* more than *man*'s complete.
> Women, the heart of women best can reach;
> While men from maxims — you from practice teach.[8]

First issued in twenty-four monthly parts from April 1744 to May 1746, *The Female Spectator* is generally regarded as the first periodical directly aimed at a female readership to have been edited by a woman. There had been other attempts in this direction early in the eighteenth century, but they were either scurrilous (such as Mrs Delarivière Manley's *Female Tatler*, which was issued three times a week from July to November 1709) or not directly attributable to a woman. Based loosely on Addison's and Steele's original *Spectator* (1711-12) which, although it appeared daily rather than monthly, was presented as the work of a group of gentlemen from different walks of life, *The Female Spectator* was ostensibly the work of a club, this time of four women from slightly dissimilar backgrounds. As in the *Spectator*, they are introduced in the opening pages with a short account of themselves: *Mira, Euphrosine*, and a 'widow of quality'; but the Editor herself retains her anonymity and insists that she only is the 'Mouth'. It seems, however, to have been generally accepted that *The Female Spectator* was probably written almost entirely by Mrs Eliza Haywood, who after a somewhat questionable career as actress, poet, playwright, and author of many popular lurid romances, managed to recover a slightly tarnished reputation by devoting herself in the latter part of her life to reforming the manners and morals of a 'degenerate age' with an almost missionary zeal.

The first issue of *The Female Spectator* was advertised a few days beforehand in *The Daily Post* and *The General Advertiser*, to be published the following Tuesday, 24 April 1744. On the the day of publication both papers carried the following advertisement:

> *This Day is publish'd, Price 1s.*
> THE FEMALE SPECTATOR.
> BOOK I
> Printed and publish'd by T. Gardner, at Cowley's Head opposite St. Clement's Church in the Strand; and sold by R. Dodsley in Pall-Mall; M. Cooper in Pater noster Row; and all Booksellers in Town and Country.
>
> *N.B.* The Authors engag'd in this Undertaking propose publishing a fresh Pamphlet Monthly, under the above Title, not by Way of Subscription, or to tye any Person down to engage for a longer Time than is agreeable to themselves, every Publication being of itself a compleat Book: All that is therefore requested, is a favourable Reception of the *First*, on the Merits of which the *Succeeding Ones* must depend. The Design of it is to *promote the Practice of Virtue* in those who stand in need of such Excitements, by shewing the most amiable Examples of it; and to *reform those Errors in Conduct*, which, tho' perhaps trivial in themselves, frequently are productive of the most irreparable Misfortunes. And this, the Authors flatter themselves, will be done in so gay and inoffensive a Manner, as that None shall imagine themselves pointed at, while Many will be amended, and All agreeably amused.

On Friday May 24, *The General Advertiser* carried the following advertisement:

This day is published, And to be continued Monthly, Price 1s.
THE FEMALE SPECTATOR
BOOK II
Book I (which was published the Middle of last Month, and is now selling) having met with the general Approbation of all who have read it, the Authors take the Opportunity of assuring the Publick, that from the great Helps they continually receive from Persons whom they are not authorized to Name, there is not the least doubt, but that the same Spirit, which appears in the first Book, will run through the Whole of this Undertaking.

So far as is known, none of the individual issues still exist, but *The Female Spectator* was in fact so popular that when it ceased publication in 1746 the twenty-four individual issues were reissued at weekly intervals and the whole was then bound into four volumes (each containing six issues or 'books') which were subsequently reprinted a number of times until as late as 1775. Copies of all the editions published in the eighteenth century are still extant, mostly in the libraries of American universities, but the first edition is available in the British Library and Cambridge University library. The work was even translated into French in 1751 as *La Nouvelle Spectatrice*. Apart from the panegyric in the *Gentleman's Magazine* quoted above, no recognition of the popularity of *The Female Spectator*, or any critical review of it, has been found in contemporary publications, although knowledge of these is necessarily limited. However, *The London Magazine* did acknowledge in its Monthly Catalogue, under 'Entertainments and Poetry', the publication of Books 8 and 20. In May 1746 it announced publication of 'THE FEMALE SPECTATOR, Book 24th, and last, which compleats the Whole'.

The Female Spectator is generally recorded as appearing between April 1744 and May 1746, with two months omitted. The reason for the omissions can be found in the Burney Collection of newspapers in the British Library, where advertisements for it were printed in *The Daily Post* and *The General Advertiser* on the following dates:

Book I	April 24
II	May 25
III	June 19
IV	July 27
V	September 5
VI	October 9

VII	November 2
VIII	December 4
IX	January 5 (1745)
X	February 4
XI	March 5
XII	April 1

It would appear that in common with many authors Mrs Haywood occasionally had problems in meeting her deadlines. When Book VI was advertised on October 9 the following announcement also appeared:

> Note: The Encouragers of this Undertaking are desir'd not to bind up their Sets 'till about Christmas next, when there will be a Frontispiece, General Title, Dedication, and Index given Gratis.

For some reason no advertisements for books XIII and XIV in May and June 1745 have been found. However, the weekly periodical *The Westminster Gazette* commenced advertising books XV to XXIV on the following dates:

XV	July 20 (1745)
XVI	August 10
XVII	September 7
XVIII	October 19
XIX	November 2
XX	December 14
XXI	January 4 (1746)
XXII	February 1
XXIII	February 22
XXIV	May 31

Mrs Haywood, or perhaps her printer, was not averse to the unsolicited testimonial so beloved of advertisers in our own day. When Book X was published in February 1745 the advertisement in *The Daily Post* contained the following:

> I cannot help congratulating, not only the Fair Sex, but my own, in having, during these degenerate Times, in the FEMALE SPECTATOR, a polite and and elegant Advocate for Private Virtue, the true Foundation of that Public Spirit which my Labours have ever endeavoured to promote.
>
> See the Old England Journal, Jan 12, No. 92

The final advertisement, which appeared on Saturday, May 31, 1746, advised 'Those who have not compleated their Sets are desired to do so with all possible Expedition' and continued:

> The following are Encomiums conferr'd on this Work by some of the distinguish'd Judges, in Letters to the Printer, as — *That it is well adapted for improving the Morals, and refining the Taste;* — *Exalts the Ideas;* — *is a polite and elegant Advocate for private Virtue;* — *its Language clear and conspicuous;* — *its Stories affectingly related;* — *judiciously blended with Instruction and Entertainment;* — *an admirable Lesson for the Young and Unexperienced, &c.*

The individual monthly offerings varied in length between sixty and seventy pages of text, that is up to about 15 000 words in each issue. Each book tended to concentrate on a particular theme such as ingratitude, taste, gambling, the state of the theatre, and the accompanying anecdotes illustrated the views expressed in the opening essay. The entire output over two years was some 350 000 words, of which about one-fifth is presented here. An attempt has been made to extract a representative selection from the essays and stories to give an insight into the mores and manners of the eighteenth century as perceived by a woman.

Few comparisons can be made with modern women's magazines: there are no recipes, no household hints or dress and knitting patterns: these were not the concern of Mrs Haywood's readership (she actually advises young ladies of Fortune not to make so much use of the Needle: 'there are enough whose Necessities oblige them to live wholly by it, and it is a Kind of Robbery to those unhappy Persons to do that ourselves which is their whole support' [Essay 17, p. 151]). Yet there is one role which Mrs Haywood seems to have pioneered, that of 'agony-aunt'. Whether or not the letters were written by real correspondents or simply by herself, she dispenses advice to desperate lovers, distraught mothers and unhappy daughters, spiced with suitable stories to prove her point. In addition, having had what she terms 'an Education more liberal than is ordinarily allowed to Persons of my Sex', a recurring theme is a plea for a more enlightened attitude to education than was normally accorded to women at that time. Mrs Haywood was by no means the first woman to air these views (the writings of Mary Astell, in the late seventeenth and early eighteenth century, are a case in point) but her arguments are lively and succinct, and may well have reached a larger audience.

It was not until 1929 that *The Female Spectator* was partially resurrected, when Mary Priestley edited a slim volume of 'Selections from Mrs

Introduction

Heywood's [sic] *Female Spectator'*, with an Introduction by J. B. Priestley, who refers to the original editor as 'an Addison in petticoats'. These extracts tended, however, to emphasise the more frivolous aspects of Mrs Haywood's work, and the Introduction is more than a little patronising. Recently there has been an upsurge of interest in women writers of the eighteenth century, notably in Alison Adburgham's *Women in Print* (London, 1972), Dale Spender's *Mothers of the Novel* (London, 1986) Jane Spencer's *The Rise of the Woman Novelist* (Oxford, 1986) and, dealing in particular with Eliza Haywood, Mary Anne Schofield's *Quiet Rebellion, The Fictional Heroines of Eliza Haywood* (Washington, DC, 1982) and *Eliza Haywood* (Boston, 1985). All these works contain some appreciation of *The Female Spectator*. In addition, there have been two essays in American literary publications: '*The Female Spectator*, A Courtesy Periodical' by James Hodges (from *Studies in the Early English Periodical*, University of North Carolina Press, 1957) and Helene Koon's 'Eliza Haywood and the *Female Spectator*' (*Huntington Library Quarterly*, No. 42, 1978-9). In the last-mentioned study Ms Koon contends that although *The Female Spectator* has been 'ignored, patronised and mislabelled,...it occupies a unique place in the history of periodical literature'. While Addison and Steele (in the original *Spectator*) 'use male figures, Haywood uses females, portraying a world as different as if it had been created on another planet: attention is strictly devoted to women's affairs and men are only peripheral'.[9] Ms Koon also points out the lack of interest in child care, and suggests that Mrs Haywood's periodical reveals a 'depressing emptiness and a horrifying purposeless in the lives led by women of her time'. James Hodges, on the other hand, regards *The Female Spectator* as continuing a tradition of 'courtesy' or conduct books which had been in vogue for some considerable time. These books gave advice to both sexes on a variety of topics, 'concerning themselves with human conduct as a matter of practicality, rather than as a subject for mere speculation'. *The Female Spectator* similarly 'offers advice which is entirely practical in character and is based not upon any academic theorising about life but upon a real appreciation of its actual difficulties and problems'.[10] After commenting on a number of the essays and stories, and referring back to similar 'admonitory' essays such as those by Defoe, Addison, and Steele, Mr Hodges concludes with an apt assessment of Haywood's achievement:

> The sizable success of the paper among its readers has been followed by a journalistic vogue that continues even into the women's magazines and 'Advice' columns of the present century. Because of its commendable literary quality it holds a position of prominence in an

age which produced the best essay journals. It has a large historical importance as the first periodical designed solely for female patronage. But, in the end, the greatest value of the *Female Spectator* rests on its effectiveness as a medium of courtesy counsel for the proper behavior of ladies and would-be ladies of mid-eighteenth century England.[11]

Notes

1 Baker, David Erskine, *Biographica Dramatica* 'Originally compiled to the year 1764, continued thence to 1782 by Isaac Reed, R.A.S. and brought down to the End of November 1811 with very considerable Additions and Improvements by Stephen Jones' (London, 1812) 319-21.

2 Both letters referred to are given in full in the June 1991 issue of *Notes and Queries*, 181-3.

3 Whicher, George, *The Life and Romances of Mrs Eliza Haywood* (New York, 1915) 125-6.

4 Ibid. 115-16 n. 24.

5 Haywood, Eliza, *The History of Miss Betsy Thoughtless* (1751) vol. I 42 (Pandora, reprinted 1986).

6 See Marcia Heinemann, 'Eliza Haywood's Career in the Theatre' *Notes and Queries* (January, 1973) 9.

7 Lord Macaulay, *The History of England* (1848) vol. I, 193 (Everyman's Library, Dent, reprinted 1962).

8 *The Gentleman's Magazine* (December 1744) 669.

9 Koon, Helene, 'Eliza Haywood and the *Female Spectator*' *Huntington Library Quarterly*, No. 42 (1978-9) 45.

10 Hodges, James, '*The Female Spectator*, A Courtesy Periodical' *Studies in the Early English Periodical* (University of North Carolina Press, 1957) 154.

11 Ibid. 176.

A NOTE ON THE TEXT

Mrs Haywood's periodical was first issued in twenty-four monthly parts by T. Gardner at Cowley's Head, opposite St Clement's Church, in the Strand, from April 1744 to May 1746, with two months omitted (see Introduction pp. 10-11). Because of its continued popularity the individual issues were subsequently bound into four volumes each with a different frontispiece, general title page (all dated 1745), a dedication and an index.

The text for these selections is the first edition dated 1745, published by T. Gardner (from the copy held in the Newbury Library, Chicago). The original spelling and punctuation have been retained, but the following emendations have been made silently:

1 The printer's long '*f*' has been replaced by 's' throughout.

2 The convention of capitalising the first word of each paragraph has not been retained.

3 The convention of italicising proper names has been omitted in favour of Roman type. Italics have only been retained in quotations and where there is any special emphasis.

4. The convention of using single quotation marks at the beginning of each individual line in quoted letters to the Editor has not been retained.

5 Where the original text contains sentences which end in a colon and a long dash, the colon has been replaced by a full-stop.

6 Any *errata* at the end of a volume have been taken into the text.

7 Inadvertent printing and spelling errors have been corrected.

8 The essay titles have been supplied.

SELECTIONS FROM
THE FEMALE SPECTATOR

ເລ 1 ອອ

The Editor introduces herself...
and her 'Associates'

It is very much, by the Choice we make of Subjects for our Entertainment, that the refin'd Taste distinguishes itself from the vulgar and more gross: Reading is universally allowed to be one of the most improving, as well as agreeable Amusements; but then to render it so, one should, among the Number of Books which are perpetually issuing from the Press, endeavour to single out such as promise to be most conducive to those Ends. In order to be as little deceiv'd as possible, I, for my own part, love to get as well acquainted as I can with an Author, before I run the risque of losing my Time in perusing his Work; and as I doubt not but most People are of this way of thinking, I shall, in imitation of my learned Brother of ever precious Memory, give some Account of what I am, and those concerned with me in this Undertaking; and likewise of the chief Intent of the Lucubrations hereafter communicated, that the Reader, on casting his Eye over the four or five first Pages, may judge how far the Book may, or may not be qualified to entertain him, and either accept, or throw it aside as he thinks proper. And here I promise, that in the Pictures I shall give of myself and Associates, I will draw no flattering Lines, assume no Perfection that we are not in reality possess'd of, nor attempt to shadow over any Defect with an artificial Gloss.

As a Proof of my Sincerity, I shall, in the first place, assure him, that for my own Part I never was a Beauty, and am now very far from being young;

(a Confession he will find few of my Sex ready to make:) I shall also acknowledge, that I have run through as many Scenes of Vanity and Folly as the greatest Coquet of them all.—Dress, Equipage, and Flattery, were the Idols of my Heart.—I should have thought that Day lost which did not present me with some new Opportunity of shewing myself.—My Life, for some Years, was a continued Round of what I then called Pleasure, and my whole Time engross'd by a Hurry of promiscuous Diversions.—But whatever Inconveniences such a manner of Conduct has brought upon myself, I have this Consolation, to think that the Publick may reap some Benefit from it. —The Company I kept was not, indeed, always so well chosen as it ought to have been, for the sake of my own Interest or Reputation; but then it was general, and by Consequence furnished me, not only with the Knowledge of many Occurrences, which otherwise I had been ignorant of, but also enabled me, when the too great Vivacity of my Nature became temper'd with Reflection, to see into the secret Springs which gave rise to the Actions I had either heard, or been Witness of—to judge of the various Passions of the human Mind, and distinguish those imperceptible Degrees by which they become Masters of the Heart, and attain the Dominion over Reason.—A thousand odd Adventures, which at the Time they happen'd made slight Impression on me, and seem'd to dwell no longer on my Mind than the Wonder they occasion'd, now rise fresh to my Remembrance, with this Advantage, that the Mystery I then, for want of Attention, imagin'd they contain'd, is entirely vanish'd, and I find it easy to account for the Cause by the Consequence.

With this Experience, added to a Genius tolerably extensive, and an Education more liberal than is ordinarily allowed to Persons of my Sex, I flatter'd myself that it might be in my Power to be in some measure both useful and entertaining to the Publick; and this Thought was so soothing to those Remains of Vanity, not yet wholly extinguished in me, that I resolved to pursue it, and immediately began to consider by what Method I should be most likely to succeed. To confine myself to any one Subject, I knew could please but one kind of Taste, and my Ambition was to be as universally read as possible. From my Observations of human Nature, I found that Curiosity had, more or less, a Share in every Breast; and my Business, therefore, was to hit this reigning Humour in such a Manner, as that the Gratification it should receive from being made acquainted with other People's Affairs, should at the same Time teach every one to regulate their own.

Having agreed within myself on this important Point, I commenc'd Author, by setting down many Things, which, being pleasing to myself, I imagin'd would be so to others; but on examining them the next Day, I found an infinite Deficiency both in Matter and Stile, and that there was an absolute Necessity for me to call in to my Assistance such of my Acquaintance as were qualified for that Purpose.—The *first* that occurr'd to me, I shall distinguish by the Name of *Mira*, a Lady descended from a Family to which Wit seems hereditary, married to a Gentleman every way worthy of so excellent a Wife, and with whom she lives in so perfect a Harmony, that having nothing to ruffle the Composure of her Soul, or disturb those sparkling Ideas she receiv'd from Nature and Education, left me no Room to doubt if what she favour'd me with would be acceptable to the Publick.— The *next* is a Widow of Quality, who not having buried her Vivacity in the Tomb of her Lord, continues to make one in all the modish Diversions of the Times, so far, I mean, as she finds them consistent with Innocence and Honour; and as she is far from having the least Austerity in her Behaviour, nor is rigid to the Failings she is wholly free from herself, those of her Acquaintance, who had been less circumspect, scruple not to make her the Confidante of Secrets they conceal from all the World beside.—The *third* is the Daughter of a wealthy Merchant, charming as an Angel, but endued with so many Accomplishments, that to those who know her truly, her Beauty is the least distinguish'd Part of her.—This fine young Creature I shall call *Euphrosine*,[1] since she has all the Chearfulness and Sweetness ascribed to that Goddess.

These three approved my Design, assur'd me of all the Help they could afford, and soon gave a Proof of it in bringing their several Essays; but as the Reader, provided the Entertainment be agreeable, will not be interested from which Quarter it comes, whatever Productions I shall be favour'd with from these Ladies, or any others I may hereafter correspond with, will be exhibited under the general Title of *The Female Spectator*, and how many Contributors soever there may happen to be to the Work, they are to be consider'd only as several Members of one Body, of which I am the Mouth.

It is also highly proper I should acquaint the Town, that to secure an eternal Fund of Intelligence, Spies are placed not only in all the Places of Resort in and about this great Metropolis, but at Bath, Tunbridge, and the Spaw,[2] and Means found out to extend my Speculations even as far as France, Rome, Germany, and other foreign Parts, so that nothing curious or worthy of Remark can escape me; and this I look upon to be a more effectual Way of penetrating into the Mysteries of the Alcove, the Cabinet, or Field, than if I had the Power of Invisibility, or could with a Wish transport myself wherever I pleased, since with the Aid of those supernatural Gifts, I could still be in no more than one Place at a Time; whereas now, by tumbling over a few Papers from my Emissaries, I have all the

Secrets of Europe, at least such of them as are proper for my Purpose, laid open at one View.

I would, by no means, however, have what I say be construed into a Design of gratifying a vicious Propensity of propagating Scandal:—Whoever sits down to read me with this View, will find themselves mistaken; for tho' I shall bring real Facts on the Stage, I shall conceal the Actors Names under such as will be conformable to their Characters; my Intention being only to expose the Vice, not the Person.—Nor shall I confine myself to modern Transactions—Whenever I find any Example among the Antients which may serve to illustrate the Topick I shall happen to be upon, I shall make no scruple to insert it.—An Instance of shining Virtue in any Age, can never be too often proposed as a Pattern, nor the Fatality of Misconduct too much impress'd on the Minds of our Youth of both Sexes; and as the sole Aim of the following Pages is to reform the Faulty, and give an innocent Amusement to those who are not so, all possible Care will be taken to avoid every thing that might serve as Food for the Venom of Malice and Ill-nature. Whoever, therefore, shall pretend to fix on any particular Person the Blame of Actions they may happen to find recorded here, or make what they call a Key to these Lucubrations, must expect to see themselves treated in the next Publication with all the Severity so unfair a Proceeding merits.

And now having said as much as I think needful of this Undertaking, I shall, without being either too greatly confident, or too anxious for the Success, submit it to the Publick Censure.

From Volume I, Book I, 1-7

Explanatory Notes

1 Euphrosine: (or Euphrosyne) was one of the three sister goddesses (or Graces) of Greek and Roman mythology, regarded as bestowers of beauty and charm, and portrayed as women of exquisite beauty.

2 Bath, Tunbridge and the Spaw: Bath and Tunbridge (Wells) were (and still are) resorts famous for their mineral springs. The reference here to 'the Spaw' (an obsolete form of 'Spa') may refer to the Belgian town in the province of Liege, which was celebrated for its medicinal waters.

2

The Dangers of Masquerades
and Two Cautionary Tales

The great Encouragement these later Times afford to Luxury of every kind, can never be too much guarded against by those who are charged with the first forming of the Mind. Nature is in itself abhorrent of Vice; but the ingenious Contrivers of some of our modish Entertainments have found such ways to take off the Deformity, that there requires a more strong Discernment than Youth will ordinarily admit of, to distinguish it from Innocence.—The Glitter with which it is adorn'd strikes the Eye at a Distance, and you perceive not the Serpent within, 'till, by too near an Approach, you are in Danger of being infected with its Venom. It was not in Diversions, such as our modern *Masquerades* in Winter, and *Ridottoes al Fresco*[1] in Summer, that our Ancestors pass'd their Evenings; both which, agreeable as they may seem for the present to the Senses, have often given Source to the most bitter Agonies in the reflecting Mind.—They appear to me as a daring Attempt to invert the very Order of Nature, especially the former, which begins at those Hours when Recreations ought to cease, and encroaches on the Time we should be preparing for that Repose the Mind and Body stand in need of.—Those who escape the best, are sure to lose one Day from Life after every Masquerade; but others more delicate in their Constitutions contract Colds, and various Disorders, which hang upon them a long while, and sometimes are never got rid of.—Yet how severely treated would our young Gentlemen and Ladies think themselves, were they to be deprived of this elegant Entertainment, as they term it!—*What can be more innocent,* (say they) *than to see such a Number of People together, all dress'd in different Habits, some talking, some dancing, some gaming, and the Musick all the Time sweetly playing.—Then the Repartees among us so whet the Wit!*—

It is certain, indeed, that some great Families, who continue the whole

Winter in the Country, frequently have what they call a Masquerade at their Houses, to which all the neighbouring Gentry are invited, and nothing can be more agreeable than those kind of Entertainments.—Where a select Company are disguised so as not to be known for a Time to each other, a Round of Wit is perpetually played off, and affords Matter, by the pleasant Mistakes sometimes made, for Conversation afterwards; for where every one is obliged to pluck off his Mask, and own himself for what he is, as soon as the Ball is over, nothing will be said or done improper or indecent. But here it is quite otherwise, in these mercenary Entertainments, the most abandon'd Rake, or low-bred Fellow, who has wherewithal to purchase a Ticket, may take the Liberty of uttering the grossest Things in the chastest Ear, and safe in his Disguise go off without incurring either the Shame or Punishment his Behaviour deserves. But, besides being subjected to the Insults of every pert Coxcomb, who imagines himself most witty when he is most shocking to Modesty, I wonder Ladies can reflect what Creatures of their own Sex they vouchsafe to blend with in these promiscuous Assemblies, without blushing to Death.

A witty Gentleman of my Acquaintance, but somewhat wild, told me, he never was so much diverted in his Life as one Night, when he saw the greatest Prude in the Nation, after having been accosted with some very odd Expressions by one, who, doubtless, mistook her for another, ran as if to shield herself from his Importunities, to a certain *Fille de Joy*,[2] to whom he had given a Ticket, and cry out, *O, Madam, did you hear the filthy Creature?*

I could not forbear acknowledging the Ridicule this Lady incurr'd, was a just Punishment for her appearing in a Place so little conformable to the Austerity she profess'd in other Things, but at the same Time took this Opportunity of telling him, that I thought Women of Honour had little Obligations to him, or to any of those Gentlemen, who by making Presents of Tickets to such loose Creatures, introduc'd them into Company they otherwise would never have the Assurance to approach.—I added, that, in my Opinion, a greater Affront could not be put upon the Sex; and that it was also strangely impolitick to bring their Mistresses into an Assembly, where Chance might possibly engage them in Conversation with their own Wives or Sisters.

To these last Words he answer'd with a kind of a malicious Smile, *No Madam, we never give Masquerade Tickets to them.* Intimating, that it was not with the Approbation of the Men, that the Ladies of their own Family should frequent such Places; and therefore, if they happen'd to be affronted there, they must condemn themselves.

A Husband's Stratagem

This put me in Mind of an Acquaintance of mine, who is accounted a very good Husband, and in Effect is so, tho' he took somewhat an extraordinary Method to cure his Wife of a too great Passion she had express'd, on their first Marriage, for going to these nocturnal Revels. Notice was no sooner given of a Masquerade, than her Eyes sparkled with Joy, the Habit Maker was immediately sent for, and nothing was either talk'd or thought on, but the Dress she should wear on the approaching happy Night. Not but he was convinc'd, her Intentions were perfectly innocent, as she never desired to go without him, and even testify'd an Eagerness that he would participate of a Pleasure which had so many Charms for herself; but he was a Man who knew the Town, and the Dangers to which many Women had been expos'd in these Assemblies; besides, the Expence was what he could by no means relish, and fearing to draw on himself the Character of a churlish, or a jealous Husband, if he gave either of these Reasons for restraining her, he bethought himself of a Stratagem, which should render her avoiding going for the future entirely her own Act and Deed.

He caused, unknown to her, one of his intimate Friends to put on a Habit so exactly the same with that he wore himself, that being of a pretty equal Stature, they could not be distinguish'd from each other when the Masks were on. This Gentleman, in the midst of a Dance, slip'd into the Husband's Place, who immediately withdrew, and absconded 'till the Ball was over. The poor Lady, little suspecting the Deception, kept close to her suppos'd Spouse the whole Time, and when the Company broke up, was put by him into a Hackney Coach, which had Orders to drive to a Tavern in Pall-Mall.[3] She was a little surpriz'd at finding where she was; but thinking it a Whim of him, whom it was her Duty to comply with, suffer'd herself to be conducted into a Room, where he, plucking off his Mask, the Sight of his Face, and his desiring she would do the same, with some Expressions not very becoming the Person she had taken him for, so alarm'd and terrify'd her, that she gave a great Shriek.—The Husband, who had follow'd them in another Coach, came in that Moment, and found her ringing the Bell, calling for the People of the House, and for a Chair, that she might be carried home, the Gentleman struggling with her, and endeavouring all he could to prevail on her to unmask.—He so well acted his Part, that the Person who employ'd him was highly diverted, and had suffer'd the Farce to go on some time longer, had not the excessive Fright his Wife was in oblig'd him to put an End to it, which he did, by plucking off his Vizard, and taking her in his Arms, conjur'd her to compose herself; this Accident, said he, might have proved of ill Consequence indeed, had it not happen'd with my particular Friend.—I saw, and follow'd you with a Resolution to revenge the Affront I imagin'd offer'd to me; but I am now convinc'd it was all a Mistake on his Side, as well as your's.—See here, continu'd he, taking off his Wife's Mask, who it is you have gallanted, and were about to be so free with.

The Gentleman affected to start, and be very much amaz'd and asham'd of what he had done, begg'd his Friend's Pardon, and the Lady's, who he said he had accosted, as thinking her a fine Woman, and meeting with no manner of Repulse, but on the contrary, that she was very desirous of keeping as near to him as possible, and shunning all other Conversation, he had all the Reason in the World to flatter himself, she would be no less satisfy'd with his Company in another Place.—But, said he, I now perceive it was the likeness of Habits deceiv'd her, and that while I imagin'd I was gaining a Mistress, she doubted not but she was following a Husband.

This Adventure occasion'd a good deal of Merriment among them, but it had all the Effect my Friend wish'd it should have on his Wife.—The imagin'd Danger she had been in, and the real Terror it had given her, dwelt so much upon her Mind, that she resolv'd never more to set her Foot within a Place where Virtue and Reputation were liable to such Hazards.— He had the Discretion, however, to maintain inviolably the Secret of the Trick he had put upon her, which had it been so much as guess'd at by her, might, perhaps, have occasion'd a Resentment more to the Prejudice of his Peace, than the Continuance of that immoderate Love of an Amusement he did not approve could have been.

✻ ✻ ✻

The Sad Tale of Erminia

But of all who ever suffer'd by their Curiosity or Attachment to this dangerous Diversion, the Case of the Innocent Erminia was most truly pityable.

This young Lady, and her Brother, were the only Issue of a very happy Marriage, and both shar'd equally the Tenderness of their indulgent Parents.—They were educated in the strictest Rudiments of Piety and Virtue, and had something so innately good in their Dispositions, as made the Practice of those Duties, which to others seem most severe, to them a Pleasure.—The Family lived in the Country, and came not to London but once in two or three Years, and then stay'd but a short Time, 'till the young

Gentleman having finish'd his Studies at Cambridge, it was thought proper he should see more of the World, than he could possibly do in that retir'd Part. But, fearing he should fall into the Vices of the Age, in case he were left too much to himself, they resolv'd on removing to Town, in order to have him still under their own Eye.

Accordingly a House was taken in a certain Square, and the whole Family came up, and, not to seem particular, were oblig'd to live after the Manner People do in Town: Erminia was not now above Sixteen, and (as all new Faces are, if tolerably handsome) was extremely taken Notice of, yet was not her young Heart puff'd up with the least Pride or Vanity; and tho' she had all that Chearfulness which is the inseparable Companion of Innocence and Good-nature, yet did it never transport her so far as to take, or permit, any of those Liberties, which she saw some of her new Acquaintance make no Scruple of.

Soon after their Arrival Winter came on, and wherever either she or her Brother went, nothing was talk'd on but the Masquerade; neither of them had ever seen one, and the Eagerness they observed in others, excited a Curiosity in them.—Their Parents would not oppose the Inclination they express'd, and consented they should go together, but gave their Son a strict Charge to be watchful over his Sister, and never to quit Sight of her 'till he brought her home to them again.—Tho' this was an Entertainment unknown in England in their gay Time of Life, and, consequently, they were Strangers to the Methods practised at it, yet having heard somewhat of the Dangers, they repeated over and over the same Injunction to the young Gentleman, who assured them, he would take the same Care as if themselves were present.

Alas! he little knew how impracticable it was to keep his Promise; they were no sooner enter'd than both were bewilder'd amidst the promiscuous Assembly,—the strange Habits,—the Hurry,—the Confusion quite distracted their Attention.—They kept close to each other, indeed, for some Time, but were soon separated by a Crowd that came rushing between them, some accosting the Brother, others the Sister.—Those who talk'd to them easily found they were Strangers to the Conversation of the Place, and whispering it about, our young Country Gentry serv'd as Butts for the Company to level all the Arrows of their Wit against.

Erminia had lost her Brother for a considerable Time, and was encompassed by Persons of both Sexes, whose Mode of Speech was neither pleasing to her, nor did she know how to answer; at last the Sight of a Blue Domine,[4] which was the Habit he went in, revived her, and she ran to the Person who wore it, and catching fast hold of him, *Dear Brother,* (cry'd she) *let us go home, I have been frighted to Death by those noisy People yonder.—I wonder what Pleasure any body can take in being here.*

The Person she accosted made no Reply; but taking her under the Arm, conducted her out as she had desired, and went with her into a Hackney Coach. Little suspecting the Accident that had befallen her, she attended not to what Orders he gave the Coachman, and, glad to find herself out of a Place, which for her had so few Charms, entertain'd her suppos'd Brother with a Repetition of what had been said to her, 'till the Coach stopp'd at the Door of a great House. As it was not yet light, she distinguish'd it not from their own, and innocently jump'd out, and was within the Entry before she discover'd her Mistake; but as soon as she did, *Bless me,* (cry'd she) *where have you brought me, Brother?* She follow'd him, however, up Stairs, where he, pulling off his Vizard, discover'd a Face she had never seen before.

Never was Surprize and Terror greater than that which now seiz'd the Heart of this unfortunate young Lady:—She wept, she pray'd, she conjur'd him by every thing that is call'd sacred or worthy of Veneration, to suffer her to depart; but he was one, to whom had she been less beautiful, her Innocence was a sufficient Charm.—The more averse and shock'd she seem'd at the rude Behaviour with which he immediately began to treat her, the more were his Desires inflam'd, and having her in his Power, and in a House where all her Shrieks and Cries were as unavailing, as her Tears and Entreaties, he satiated, by the most barbarous Force, his base Inclinations, and for a Moment's Joy to himself, was the eternal Ruin of a poor Creature, whose Ignorance of the World, and the Artifices of Mankind, alone had betray'd to him.

The cruel Conquest gain'd, he was at a Loss how to dispose of his Prey; a thousand times she begg'd he would compleat the Villany he had begun, and kill the Wretch he had made; but this was what neither his Safety, nor perhaps his Principle, wicked as he was, would permit him to do.—He easily found she was a Girl of Condition, and doubted not but she had Friends who would revenge the Injury he had done her, could they, by any Means, discover the Author; he therefore, after having in vain endeavour'd to pacify her, and prevail on her to comply with his Desires of holding a secret Correspondence with him, compell'd her to let him bind a Handkerchief over her Eyes, that she might not be able to describe either the House, or Street where she had been abused; then put her into a Hackney Coach, which he order'd to drive into an obscure, dirty Lane, in the Strand, near the Water Side, where he made her be set down, and immediately drove away with all the Speed the Horses could make.

She no sooner found herself at Liberty, than she pluck'd the Bandage from her Eyes,—she cast a disconsolate Look about,—she knew not where she was; but the Sight of the Water at some little Distance from her, tempted her more than once, as she has since confess'd, to throw herself into it.—The Precepts of Religion, however, restrain'd her, and she wander'd backwards and forwards for some Time, uncertain what to do; at length she came to a more populous Place, and seeing a Chair, made herself be carried home, tho' with what Agonies of Shame and Grief is easier to imagine than describe.

The young Gentleman, her Brother, had all this Time been in the utmost Distraction; he no sooner miss'd, than he went in search of her round and round the Room, and through all the little Avenues that led to it, describ'd her Habit to the Servants, and ask'd if they had seen such a Lady; but all his Endeavours being fruitless, he ran home, flattering himself, that missing him, she was gone before.—Not finding her there, he flew back again to the Haymarket,—made a second Search, a second Enquiry, and that being ineffectual as the first, his Grief and his Despair was beyond all Bounds.—He truly lov'd his Sister, and doubted not but some very unhappy Accident had befallen her; but what involved him yet in greater Horrors, was how he should answer to his Parents his so ill acquitting himself of the Charge they laid on him concerning her.—Dreading their Reproaches, and even yet more the Agonies they would feel at seeing him return without her, he flew about the Streets like one totally depriv'd of Reason, 'till Day being far advanc'd, and every body he met staring at him as a Person whom Drink or Madness had render'd an Object of Derison, Shame, at last, got the better of his Vexations, and he ventur'd to encounter what was more dreadful to him than Death itself.

The anxious Parents could not think of going to their Repose 'till their dear Children were return'd in Safety; they had Apprehensions which they could not account for, none having dared to inform them, that Erminia was missing, or that her Brother, many Hours before, had call'd at the Door to ask if she was come, but when they now saw him enter with that confus'd and dejected Air, and found their Daughter was not with him, they both at once cry'd out, in a Transport of mingled Rage and Grief,—*Where is your Sister?—What is become of Erminia?—Dare you approach us without her?*

The condition this poor Youth was in, would be very difficult to express,—he trembled,—hung down his Head, and his flowing Eyes let fall a Shower of Tears upon his Breast, but had not Power to speak, 'till his Father, impatient of knowing even the worst that could befal, commanded him either to repeat what had happen'd, or that Instant leave his Sight for ever. *O Sir,* (then cry'd he) *what can I say,—My Sister is gone,—all my Care in obeying your Commands was vain, and I am wholly ignorant how this Misfortune happen'd.*

27

Scarce had he spoke these Words, when the ruin'd Maid appear'd.—
Father, Mother, Brother, all ran at once to catch her in their Arms, but the
Shock of returning to them as she now was render'd, work'd too power-
fully on the Weakness of her Spirits, to leave her in a Condition to receive
their Embraces, and she fell into a Swoon, in which she continu'd a long
Time, tho' they immediately undress'd, put her to Bed and used all
possible Means for her Recovery.

On the Return of her Senses, she fell into the most lamentable Complaints, but could not be prevail'd upon, while her Father and Brother were
in the Room, to reveal any thing of the Occasion. Her Mother observing
their Presence was a Restraint, desir'd them to withdraw, after which,
partly by Commands, and partly by Intreaties, but more by mentioning all
the Evils that her Imagination could suggest, at last the whole sad Secret
was reveal'd.

Never was so disconsolate a Family, and the more so, as they could by
no Means discover the brutal Author of their Misfortune; the Precautions
he had taken render'd all their Search in vain, and when some Days after
they prevail'd on Erminia to go with them in a Coach almost throughout all
London, yet could she not point out either the House or Street where her
Ravisher had carried her.

To fill the Measure of her Woes, a young Gentleman arriv'd in Town,
who long had lov'd, and had the Approbation of her Friends, and for whom
she also felt all of that Passion that can inspire a virtuous Mind; he had by
some Business been prevented from accompanying the Family in their
Removal, but was now come full of the Hopes of having his desires compleated, by a happy Marriage with the sweet Erminia.

Melancholly Reverse of Fate! instead of being receiv'd with open
Arms, and that chearful Welcome he had been accustom'd to, and had
Reason to expect, the most heavy Gloom appear'd on all the Faces of those
he was permitted to see; but Erminia no sooner heard of his Arrival, than
she shut herself up in her Chamber, and would, by no means, be prevail'd
upon to appear before him.—To excuse her Absence, they told him she
was indispos'd; but this Seem'd all Pretence, because the Freedom with
which they had always liv'd together, might very well have allow'd him
the Privilege of visiting her in her Chamber.—He complain'd of this Alteration in their Behaviour, and doubted not, at first, but it was occasion'd by
the Preference they gave to some new Rival.—The true Reason, however,
could not be kept so much a Secret, but that it was whisper'd about, and he
soon got a Hint of it.—How sensible a Shock it must give him may easily
be conceived; but he got the better of it, and after a very little Reflection,
went to her Father, told him the afflicting News he had heard, but withal

assur'd him, that as his Love for Erminia was chiefly founded on her Virtue, an Act of Force could not be esteem'd any Breach of it, and was still ready to marry her, if she would consent.

This Generosity charm'd the whole Family, but Erminia could not think of accepting the Offer;—the more she found him worthy of her Affections in her State of Innocence, the less could she support the Shame of being his, in the Condition she now was.—She told her Parents, that she had taken a firm Resolution never to marry, and begg'd their Permission to retire to an Aunt, who was married to an old Clergyman, and lived in one of the most remote Counties in England. Dear as her Presence was, they found something so truly noble in her way of Thinking, that they would not oppose it; and even her Lover, in spite of himself, could not forbear applauding what gave a thousand Daggers to his Heart.

Erminia in a short Time departed for her Country Residence; nothing was ever more mournful than the Leave she took of her Parents and Brother; but not all the Entreaties of her Lover, by Messages and Letters, could gain so far upon her Modesty, as to prevail on her to see him; she sent him, however, a Letter, full of the most tender Acknowledgements of his Love and Generosity, and with this he was oblig'd to be content.

From Volume I, Book I, 30-7 and 45-55

Explanatory Notes:

1 *Ridottoes al Fresco*: assemblies where the company is first entertained by music, then joins in the dancing, presumably in the open air.

2 *Fille de Joy*: a 'lady of pleasure', i.e., a courtesan, or prostitute.

3 **Pall-Mall**, then a highly fashionable street in St James's, SW1, which takes its name from a game something like croquet.

4 **Blue Domine**: (usually 'domino'), a kind of loose cloak with a small mask covering the upper part of the face, worn at masquerades by those not wishing to personate a character.

3

On the Conduct of Military Gentlemen

I remember, that some Years ago I heard a Lady say, she imagin'd it was owing to our long Peace, that every publick Place abounded so much with Coxcombs and Finikins; and that if we once came to have a War again, a more manly Air and Dress would be so much the Fashion, that those Gentlemen who stay'd at Home would naturally affect it, and exchange their foreign Silk Brocades for downright English Cloth.—Some Accidents in Life have since that Time broke off our Acquaintance, it would else have given me some Pleasure to rally her Mistake.—We are now engag'd in three Wars—threaten'd with Invasions—Popish Pretenders —Plots, and what not;—great Fleets are equipping;—huge Armaments getting ready;—pressing for Land and Sea Service;—our Fields are cover'd with Tents;—our Streets swarm with Soldiers;—in every Quarter we hear Drums beating—Trumpets sounding—nothing but military Preparations going forward; yet in my Opinion, our fine Gentlemen appear every whit as clean, as calm and unconcern'd as ever, except when they labour under the Want of any of those Commodities, the Interruption of our Commerce prevents from being imported; and then indeed they complain bitterly against the Times.—One who can endure no Cloaths that are not of the French Cut, cries, he is made a Monster by a Dunce of an English Taylor.—Another is poison'd with ill Scents, and dies for some fresh Orangerie and Bergamot;—a Third says, Pax on the Spanish War, and those that forced our late Minister into it; there is not a Bit of right Vermillion Paste now to be had!

How long this Over-Delicacy will continue, Heaven knows; but it is yet far from being extirpated;—even among the military Gentlemen, there are some, who being infected with it before they became so, find it an insuperable Difficulty to bring themselves to that Hardiness and Neglect of personal Ornaments, which suits with the Life of a Soldier.

A Person who has had great Dealings with the *Beau Monde*, and has

30

lately been oblig'd to deliver up her Books, on Account of a Statute of Bankruptcy awarded against her, one of the Assignees, who happens to be a particular Acquaintance of mine, took the Pains to transcribe, as a great Curiosity, the Copy of a Bill owing to her from a Gentleman now in the Army, and made me a Present of it;—as I am convinc'd all the Items in it are genuine, it afforded me a good deal of Diversion, and I believe will not be unacceptable to the Publick.

Cornet Lovely *Debtor* to Rebecca Facemend, June 6, 1743

For a Riding Mask to prevent Sunburn	1	1	0
For a Night Mask to take away Freckles	1	1	0
For 6 Pounds of Jessamin Butter for the Hair	6	6	0
For 12 Pots of cold Cream	1	10	0
For 4 Bottles of Benjamin Water	1	0	0
For 30 Pounds of perfum'd Powder	1	10	0
For 3 Boxes of Tooth-Powder	0	15	0
For a Sponge Tooth-Brush		2	6
For a Hair Tooth-Brush		1	0
For 6 Bottles of perfum'd Mouth-water	1	4	0
For a Silver Comb for the Eye-brows	0	5	0
For 2 Ounces of Jet Powder for ditto	0	18	0
For 4 Boxes of fine Lip-salve	1	0	0
For an Ounce of best Carmine	3	0	0
For 6 Bottles of Orange Flower-Water	1	10	0
For 12 Pounds of Almond Paste	6	6	0
For 2 Pounds of Bergamot Snuff	8	0	0
For 3 Bottles of Essence ditto	1	10	0
For 6 Pair of Dog-skin Gloves	1	10	0

Total 38   9   6

Such was the Ammunition this doughty Hero, it seems, took with him; the Loss of which, had it happen'd to have fallen into the Enemy's Hands, would probably have given him more Concern than the routing of the whole Army, provided his own dear Person had escaped without a Scar.

Frequent Campaigns however, 'tis to be hop'd, will wear this Effeminacy off, and the Example of others teach such new-fledg'd Warriors, that if they would soar to Glory, they must entirely throw aside all the softening Luxuries of their silken Youth.

Not that there is any Necessity that a Man must be a Sloven, because he is a Soldier, and neglect all the Decencies of Life to prove his attachment to his Vocation;—there is an Affectation in this also, as well as the other; and I should say that Officer, who, when he might have a good Tent to defend him from the Weather, chose to lie on the bare Earth, exposed to all the Inclemencies of the Air, had an equal Share of Vanity with him who had his Pavilion hung with Velvet and Embroidery;—to endure all the Toils and Hardships of the Field with Patience and Intrepidity,—to be fearless of Dangers, when the Duties of his Post commands, is highly laudable and emulative; but to run into them without a Call, and when Bravery can be of no Service, is altogether idle; and Courage in such a one, like all other Virtues, degenerates into a Vice, by being carried to an Extreme.

But I am most of all concern'd when I hear a Man, having done a gallant Action in the Field, is so far puff'd up with it, that he looks upon himself as a little Deity, and that he may, in Consideration of having been able to fulfil his Duty in one Point, dispense with all other Obligations.

Some Time before the opening of the last Campaign, Amaranthus, a brave young Officer, made his Addresses to Aminta;—his Passion had all the Effect he wish'd it should have on her tender Heart;—she either had too much Confidence in his Honour, or too little Artifice to conceal the Sentiments he had inspired her with.—He was ravish'd at the Discovery;—swore never to be but her's,—and there pass'd between them a solemn Promise of Marriage on his Return from Germany, for which Place it was expected his Regiment would have Orders speedily to embark.

Each Day seem'd to bring with it an Increase of mutual Tenderness, and scarce ever was there a Pair, whose Love in its Beginning promised more lasting Felicity.—Amaranthus, in every Action, testify'd he had no Will but that of his Aminta; and Aminta, by all her Behaviour proved, that whatever she commanded or entreated of her Amaranthus, was only what she knew he wish'd she should do.

At length the fatal Hour of Separation arriv'd, accompanied with all those Agonies, which none but those who love are able to conceive;—Glory, which 'till now had been the darling Idol of Amaranthus's Soul, lost all its Charms, since it tore him from the Society of Aminta; and Aminta, in being about to be deprived of the Presence of Amaranthus, seem'd to have no Life but for Complaints.

The cruel Necessity, however, must be submitted to;—Tears, Sighs, Embraces, and mutual Protestations of everlasting Constancy compleated the tender, but melancholly Farewel;—none that had seen them part could have well distinguish'd which felt the deepest Anguish; but if we consider the Nature of the Circumstance, we shall find the Difference must be wide.—Amaranthus, doubtless, loved with the utmost Passion at that Time, and was going to lose, he knew not for how long, the Sight of her who was the Object of his Flame; but then that Absence was the sole Misfortune he had to struggle with; whereas, Aminta had not only the same in an equal Degree, but attended with others of a more dreadful Kind:—the Dangers to which a Life, far dearer to her than her own, must inevitably be exposed, fill'd her with Apprehensions which she was scarce able to support.—After his Departure, she pass'd the greatest Part of her Time at the Foot of the Altar, offering up her Vows and Prayers for his Protection, nor could the Entreaties of her dearest Friends and Companions prevail on her to partake with them any of those Diversions and Entertainments her Youth had formerly delighted in;—all the Conversation she coveted, was such as inform'd her concerning the Army;—she was continually asking Questions on that Head;—was only pleas'd or sad according as she heard they were near, or at a Distance from the Enemy;—the Arrival of every Courier gave a Palpitation to her Heart, 'till the Receipt of a Letter from Amaranthus convinced her, that her Terrors as yet had been without Foundation.

He wrote to her several times before the Battle of Dettingen,[1] in the last of which he acquainted her, that they were on the Point of leaving Aschaffenburgh, in order to join the Forces at Hanau,[2] from which Place she might expect to hear from him again. Welcome as all his Letters were, this afforded her a double Portion of Satisfaction, because, in case of an Engagement with the French, the Number of the Combin'd Armies would give her less to fear for him who took up all her Care.

But what became of her, when instead of receiving the joyful Intelligence she hop'd, of having made the Enemy fly before them without a Blow, she heard there had been a terrible Rencounter;—that great Numbers of brave Men had fallen on both Sides, and that Amaranthus was among the Number of the Slain!

It would be in vain to go about to describe what 'twas she felt;—her Grief and her Despair were above all Representation, as they were beyond all Bounds, so I shall only say, that both were too violent to endure long Continuance, but must have found a Period with her Life, had she not been relieved by different and more comfortable News.

The Wounds which had occasion'd the Report of his Death, were dangerous indeed, but not mortal; and his Friends had greater Reason to congratulate than condole them, since the Manner in which they were received, purchased him immortal Honour.

'Tis certain he behaved with the utmost Intrepidity, and was so far from being daunted by the Fall of others, that he seem'd rather animated with fresh Courage to revenge their Fate; and tho' the Regiment he was in suffer'd greatly, and he was himself wounded in many Places, yet he would not be prevail'd upon to quit the Field, 'till an unlucky Blow upon the Head quite stunn'd him, and he fell, in all Appearance, dead.

As his Valour had gain'd him Friends, even among those who were 'till now the least acquainted with his Person, he was immediately taken up, but for some Hours discover'd no Symptoms of Breath; so that it was not strange, in the Confusion every one was after the Battle, that in the Accounts transmitted of it, this young Hero's Name should be inserted in the List of those who were kill'd.

Aminta heard of his Recovery, and the Praises which every one gave to his Merit, with a Pleasure conformable to the Love she had for him; but could not help being a little alarm'd when she found he had wrote to others, and she, who flatter'd herself with being the first to whom he would employ his Pen, had received not the least Line from him since the Battle. But it is not without great Difficulty we bring ourselves to have an ill Opinion of those we love;—her Tenderness invented Excuses for him, which, 'tis possible, he would not have had Artifice to invent for himself, and chose to impute his Silence to any Cause, rather than Neglect;—the Distance between them was great;—Couriers might not have Opportunity to wait his writing;—the Post might miscarry, or he might possibly be detach'd to some Place, whence neither Courier nor Post could pass, and what Letters he sent might pass through Hands, which he did not judge proper to entrust with the Secret of his Correspondence with her.

In this manner did she beguile Despair 'till his Return; and tho' she resolved to accuse him, doubted not but he would give such Reasons for his seeming Unkindness, that she would be oblig'd to ask his Pardon for having been unjust enough to suspect him.

Far was she from being truly unhappy, 'till after she was inform'd of his Arrival, and several Days pass'd over without either seeing or receiving any Message from him.—This was, indeed, what all her Love and Tenderness wanted Ingenuity to account for, and she was now compell'd, even in spite of herself, to think him ungrateful and perfidious. Amazement, and some little Share of Pride, which never fails to exert itself in Love abused, prevented her some Time from sending to him; at last she wrote, reproach'd him with the Alteration in his Behaviour, yet mingled her Upraidings with so much Sweetness, as shew'd her ready to forgive whenever he came to entreat it.

To this he return'd an Answer extremely complaisant, but far from any thing that express'd the Ardours of a Lover;—excused himself by the Hurry of his Affairs, for having not yet been able to wait upon her; but assur'd her he would not fail of paying his Respects the first leisure Hour;

concluded with telling her, that nobody could have a greater Regard for her than himself, and that he should be proud of any Opportunity to convince her of it, and subscribed himself, not as he was acccustom'd, her *eternal Adorer,* but her *most humble and obedient Servant.*

She must have been the dullest and most infatuated of her Sex, had she not now seen she had entirely lost a Heart she thought herself so secure of, and had so much gloried in;—Rage and Grief had alternately the Possession of her Soul, yet Love still retain'd a Part, and was so blended with them both, that it would not suffer the one to grow into Disdain, nor the other to destroy some little Remains of Hope, that she should one Day be able to reclaim him.

She was apt to imagine, that if once she saw him, he could not behold those Eyes, which he a thousand times had sworn were the Lights of his Life, now drown'd in Tears, of which he was the Cause, without resuming those Emotions they had formerly inspir'd him with; but having waited his expected Visit longer indeed than is ordinarily consistent with the Impatience of a Lover, and finding he came not, she wrote a second time, conjuring him not to let her languish in this Uncertainty, and told him, that she only begg'd to know, from his own Mouth, her Fate, and after that would never ask to see him more.

This pressing Mandate he comply'd with; the Fashion in which she receiv'd him may easily be guess'd at, by what has been said of the Violence of her Affection; but the excessive Coldness, and distant Air of his Replies to all she said, could not be express'd even by her, who was the Witness of it; but the Sum of what he gave her to understand was, that he was convinc'd a tender Intercourse with the Ladies took up too much of a Soldier's Mind, and that he had made a Resolution to employ all his in the Duties of his Function;—he told her, that were he in any other Situation, or could think it compatible with that Pursuit of Fame he was engaged in, to continue an amorous Correspondence, Aminta should have the Preference of all her Sex; but as he was circumstanc'd, he flatter'd himself her good Sense would induce her to pardon this Change of Temper in him, since his Zeal for the Service of his King and Country was the only Rival which had occasion'd it.

It must be acknowledg'd he deceiv'd her not in this last Article, for in fact, the Promotion he had acquir'd—the Applause of the whole Army—the Praise bestow'd on him by the General, and the Compliments made him by Ladies of the first Quality at his Return, on Account of his Behaviour at Dettingen, have so much elated him, that he is no longer the same Person;—his once soft beseeching Air is now converted into one all reserved and haughty;—a scornful Toss of the Head, a careless Fling of the

Arms;—Eyes that seem intent rather on Things within himself, than any thing he can find without;—in fine, there appears so thorough a Change in his whole Manner, that if the Gestures of the Body may be look'd upon as any Indication of the Affections of the Mind, as questionless they may, his are full of Self-sufficiency; he seems to think what he has done commands, as his Due, the Love and Respect of all who see him, and that it is beneath him even to regard, much less imagine himself oblig'd by it.

Aminta had, therefore, the less to mortify her, as it was not because the superior Beauty of any other had supplanted her in his Affections, but because he in reality now thought no Woman worthy of the serious Passion of a Man like himself.

She was, notwithstanding, utterly unable to support the Shock, and no sooner found his Heart was irrecoverable, than despising all other Conquests, tho' she has Youth, Beauty and Fortune enough to make many, retired to a lone Country House, where she endeavours among rural Pleasures to forget those of the great World, and in the Melody of the sweet Inhabitants of the Woods and Groves, lose the Memory of that Voice by which she was undone.

However some People may approve this Action in Amaranthus, I cannot help thinking there is more of the savage than the true Hero in it; and I am certain we must give the Lye to our Senses, and many modern great Examples, as well as to Numbers in Antiquity, if we should say, that Love and Glory are Things incompatible, or that a wise and prudent Wife, be her Passion never so violent, will not always be too tender of her Husband's Interest and Reputation, to desire, that to prove his Regard to her, he should neglect any Part of what he owes to them.

From Volume I, Book II, 104-17

Explanatory Notes

1 Dettingen: a village near Frankfurt, on the River Main. In 1743 George II's English and Hanoverian troops defeated the French. The battle is notable in that it was the last time a king of England led his army in the field.

2 Aschaffenburgh...Hanau: villages on the River Main, near Frankfurt. English troops were quartered at Aschaffenburgh, the Hanoverians at Hanau. Both forces combined to defeat the French at Dettingen, which lies midway between.

༄༅ 4 ༄༅

On Gaming

Wonderful are the Changes which Difference of Times create! A few Years since, a Gamester was the most despicable Character in Life;—now whose Society more coveted than People of that Profession!—All who had any Reputation to lose, or desired to be thought well of by their Neighbours, took care, whenever they indulged themselves in that Diversion, to do it with as much Privacy as possible.—But *now*, not to love Play is to be unpolite:—Cards were then made use of only as the Amusement of a tedious Winter's Evening:—*Now* all Seasons are alike, they are the Employment of the Year; and at some of our great Chocolate-Houses, many thousand Acres are often swallowed up before Dinner.—Persons, who were observed to have superior Skill in Play, were *then* distinguished by the odious Name of *Sharpers*, and as such avoided by all Men of Sense:—*Now* they are complimented with the Title of great *Connoiseurs*, applauded for their Understanding in all the Niceties of the Game, and that is looked upon as the most useful kind of Learning, which teaches how to circumvent an Adversary at the important Business of *Whist*.

This Vice of Gaming, originally descended from the worst of Passions, is certainly the most pernicious of any to Society.— How great a Misfortune is it therefore that it should become the *Mode*, and by being encouraged by Persons of Figure and Condition, render the lower Class of People (who are always fond of imitating their Superiors) ambitious, as it were, of being undone in such good Company.

To this unhappy Propensity is greatly owing, that so many Shops lately well stock'd and flourishing, are now shut up even in the Heart of the City, and their Owners either Bankrupts or miserable Refugees in foreign Parts: —Nor is it to be wondered at, when the honest Profit that might be made of Trade is neglected, for the precarious Hopes of getting more by *Play*; the Citizen will have but little Share with the Courtier, and, to add to his Mortification, will find that the Misfortunes which attend this going out of his own Sphere, serves only as a Matter of Ridicule to those very Persons who reap the Advantage of his Folly.

We may date this extravagant Itch of Gambling, which, like the Plague, has spread its Contagion through all Degrees of People, from the fatal Year 1720. The alluring Prospect of making a great Fortune at once, and without any Labour or Trouble, so infatuated the Minds of all the Ambitious, the Avaricious, and the Indolent, that for a Time there seemed an entire Stagnation of all Business but what was transacted by the Brokers in Change-Alley.[1]—Then it was that Sharping began to flourish in the Nation, and has ever since continued under various Shapes.—The great Bubble of the South-Sea[2] dissipated, a thousand lesser ones, tho' equally destructive to honest Industry, sprung up:—New Modes of Ruin were every Day invented: Lotteries on Lotteries were continually drawing, in which few beside those who set them up had any thing but Blanks.—These the Wisdom of the Legislature thought fit to put a Stop to, but had not the Power to extirpate the unhappy Influence which a long Inattention to Business had gained.—The People had been too much accustomed to Idleness to return with any Spirit to their former Avocations.—They wanted the golden Fruit to drop into their Laps, and fresh Opportunities of renewing those chimerical Expectations, by which already three Parts in four of the middling Class had been undone.—*Chance* was the Idol of their Souls, and when any of their more sober Friends remonstrated to them the Madness of quitting a certain settled way of getting a *moderate Living*, for the *fleeting visionary* Schemes of a *luxurious* one,—they all returned this common *cant* Answer, that *they were willing to put themselves in Fortune's Way,*—and, *that they might possibly be as lucky as some others, who, being very poor before, had now set up great Equipages, and made a fine Figure in the World.*

This it was that converted Gaming from an Amusement into a Business, it being the only Matter now remaining out of which their so much-beloved Castles in the Air could be formed.—One Night's good Run at Cards, or a lucky Cast of the Dice, would repair all that had been lost in other Ventures, and every one thought it worth his while to stake his last Remains.

There are always a Set of artful People who watch to take Advantage of any public Frenzy.—These soon discovered the general Bent, and to humour it with Novelty, contrived various kinds of Gaming, which never had before been dreamed of; by which every one, if it so happened, might arrive at the End of his Desires. Numbers, by this Stratagem, were taken in, who otherwise perhaps, by a conscious Want of Skill in the old Games, would have been restrained, since it requires neither Thought nor Ingenuity to be successful at these new-invented Tables.

I could name a certain Spot of Ground within the Liberties of Westminster, which contains no less than fourteen public Gaming-Houses in the Compass of two hundred Yards; all which are every Night crowded with a promiscuous Company of the great Vulgar and the Small, as Congreve[3] elegantly and justly calls all such Assemblies.

To hurl the *Tennis-Ball*, or play a Match at *Cricket*, are certainly robust and manly Exercises;—they were originally invented to try and preserve Strength and Activity, and to keep those of our Youth, who were not born to meaner Labours, from Idleness and Effeminacy.—The playing at the latter also, County against County, was designed to inspire a noble Emulation to excel each other in those Feats which might render them more able to serve their King and Country, when the Defence of either required them to take up Arms.—No mercenary Views had any Share in the Institution of these Games:—Honour was the only Excitement,—Applause the only End proposed by each bold Attemptor. These, alas! of later Days, are but Empty Names;—a thousand Pound has more real Charms than any that are to be found in Glory:—Gain, sordid Gain, is all that engrosses the Heart, and adds Transport to Success. Without that, Numbers, who throng to give Proofs of their Activity, would rather chuse to pass the Time away in lolling over a Lady's Toilet[4] while she is dressing, or in his own Easy-Chair at Home, listening to the Music of his Footman's French Horn.

Will any one say that this is true Nature?—No, it is the Vices which deform Nature, and only by being too general and customary, may be called a second Nature.—Would Nature ever direct us to search into the Bosom of the Earth for Gold!—Or when found, to idolise the Ore our Hands had dug!—to pride ourselves more or less according to the Quantity of the shining Pelf we are Masters of, and to place all Honour, Virtue, and Renown in being rich!

However, since the World is so much altered from what it was in the true State of Nature, and there is now no subsisting without some Portion of this Gold, we must not affect to despise it too much. But as we ought not to listen to the Calls of Avarice, in acquiring it by any indiscreet or scandalous Means, so when possessed of it, we ought not to lavish it away in Trifles we have no Occasion for, and perhaps had better be without.—We should reflect, that our Posterity will have need of it as well as ourselves, and look on every Extravagancy we are guilty of as a Robbery of them; that we are no more than Tenants for Life in whatever descends to us from our Parents; and that we should leave it as entire and unembezled as we received it from them.—Nor is the Injustice less when we needlessly, and to gratify any inordinate Appetite, dissipate those Goods of Fortune we may have acquired by our own Industry.—Children being Part of ourselves, are born to share in our Possessions; and nothing is more absurd, in my Opinion, than the Saying of some People, that *their Children may labour for themselves as they have done.*—How are such Parents certain they will be able to do so? A thousand Accidents may happen to render the utmost Efforts they can make of no effect; and when that is the Case, how hardly must a Son think of a Father, who, by a profuse and riotous manner of Living, has reduced to starving those who derive their Being from him!

Not that I would wish any one to deny himself the Necessaries, nor even the Pleasures of Life, for the sake of his Posterity; but in all these Things there is a golden Mean to be observed, which is indeed no other than to follow Nature, enjoy ourselves while we live, and prudently reserve something for those to enjoy who are to live after us.

It is certain that no Age, no Nation ever were equal to us in Luxury of all kinds.—The most private low-bred Man would be a Heliogabalus[5] in his Table; and too many Women there are, who, like Cleopatra, would not scruple to swallow a whole Province at a Draught.

Then as to Dress, they seem to study now not what is most becoming, but what will cost the most:—No Difference made between the young Nobleman and the City-Prentice, except that the latter is sometimes the greater Beau:—Gold-headed Canes, Watches, Rings, Snuff-Boxes, and lac'd Wastcoats, run away with the Fortune that should set him up in Business, and frequently tempt him to defraud his Master, who perhaps also, taken up with his own private Pleasures, examines too little into his Shop-Affairs, and when the Till is drained, borrows a while to support his darling Pride, then sinks at once to Ruin and Contempt.

Our Sex is known to be so fond of appearing fine and gay, that it is no wonder the Tradesmen's Wives should even exceed their Husbands in the Article of Dress; but it is indeed prodigious that so many of them should, merely for the sake of being thought able to afford any thing, destroy the reasonable End of Finery, and render themselves awkward, nay preposterous, instead of genteel and agreeable.—When a Gold and Silver Stuff, enough to weigh a Woman down, shall be loaded yet more with heavy Trimmings, what Opinion can we have either of the Fancy or Judgment of her that wears it?—And is not her Neighbour, whom to out-shine, perhaps, she has strained her Husband's Purse-Strings for this costly Garment, infinitely more to be liked in a plain Du Cape or Almazeen![6]

I am sorry to observe that this false delicacy in Eating, Drinking, Apparel, Furniture and Diversions, so prevalent among us has not only undone half the Nation, but rendered us extremely ridiculous to Foreigners who are Witnesses of it.— Thus Avarice introduced Luxury, Luxury leads us to Contempt, and Beggary comes on apace.

I fear what I have said on these Topics will be but ill relished by a great many of my Readers; but if I have the good fortune to find it has had an Effect on any one of them, so far as to cause them to see the Error they have been guilty of, I shall be the less chagrin'd at the Resentment of the wilfully Blind.—Times like these require Corrosives, not Balsams to amend.—The Sore has already eaten into the very Bowels of public Happiness, and they must tear away the infected Part, or become a Nuisance to themselves and all about them.

From Volume I, Book III, 145-53

Explanatory Notes

1 Change-Alley or Exchange Alley, Cornhill, EC3, near the Royal Exchange, was famous for its coffee houses, such as Jonathan's and Garraway's, which were meeting places for brokers and speculators.

2 Bubble of the South-Sea: The object of the South Sea Company was to buy up the National Debt and to be allowed the sole privilege of trading in the South Seas. The 100 shares soon realised ten times that sum, but the whole 'bubble' burst in 1720 and ruined thousands.

3 Congreve: William Congreve, dramatist (1670-1729). The reference is to his first play, *The Old Bachelor*, Act IV Scene IV, wherein Belinda says: 'Come, Mr Sharper, you and I will take a turn, and laugh at the vulgar; both the great vulgar and the small.'

4 Toilet: originally a piece of cloth thrown about the shoulders during hair-dressing (from the French *toile* for cloth). The word eventually came to mean, *inter alia*, the action or process of dressing.

5 Heliogabalus (or Elagabalus): Roman emperor AD 218-22, so-called because in childhood he was priest of a Syro-Phoenician sun-god. His debauchery and extravagance shocked even the Roman public, and he was slain in AD 222.

6 Du Cape or Almazeen!: Du Cape was a plain-woven stout silk; Almazeen is probably 'armozeen': a similar material, usually black, used for clerical gowns and mourning scarves.

☙ 5 ❧

A Letter from Sarah Oldfashion

In Gratitude and Complaisance to the First Correspondent the *Female Spectator* has yet been favour'd with, it is the Opinion of our Society that the Entertainment prepared for this Month should be postponed, in order to insert her obliging Letter, and pursue the Theme she has been so good to give, which indeed cannot be too often nor too strenuously enforced.

To the FEMALE SPECTATOR.

MADAM,

Tho' you have not thought fit, in those Monthly Lucubrations with which you have hitherto obliged the Publick, to invite any Correspondence, and I am wholly ignorant whether a Hint, communicated to you in this Manner, will be acceptable; yet, as the Intention of your Work is plainly to reform those Errors in Conduct, which, if indulg'd, lead on to Vices, such as must render us unhappy for our whole Lives, I cannot forbear acquainting you with my Sentiments on the Undertaking, and how far I am pleas'd or displeas'd with the Execution.

You are sensible that every Thing which appears in Print passes thro' as many various Censures as there are Opinions in the Readers; but I assure you I am of that Number which Authors call the courteous, and take a much greater Satisfaction in *applauding* than *condemning*.—The Praises you receive from all the Wise and Virtuous, I readily join in, and make as Cause against all the Cavils of conceited Ignorance and open Libertinism; and where I imagine you fall a little short of my Expectations I am entirely silent. This I think is dealing with you as a Friend, and you will not therefore take it ill if I sometimes play the Part of a Monitor, and remind you both now, and as often as I shall find occasion, of any Omissions, which cannot be such as you may not easily attone for in the ensuing Book; or even venture to impart to you a few wandering Notions of my own, since I leave you at full Liberty either to conceal or publish them as you may judge proper.

Nothing certainly can be more just than your Definition of the Passions, or more pathetic than your Representation of the Mischiefs they bring upon Mankind; but I think you have touch'd somewhat too slightly, or at least not been so particular as might have been expected from a *Spectator*, on some of those innumerable Ways that licens'd Luxury has of late invented to *sooth*, or rather to *excite* the most dangerous propensities in Youth.

I am far from being of that austere Nature some are, who make no Allowances for the Difference of Age, and deny to those under their Tuition, the innocent Recreations which the early Years of Life demand.—On the contrary, I am for having them partake, in a reasonable Degree, every Pleasure this great World affords; but then I would not have any of those Pleasures become a *Business*, and engross the Attention so much as to take it off from Subjects of a more profitable Kind, thereby rendering dangerous what is unhurtful in itself, and making *future* Time pay too dearly for the Enjoyment of the *present*.

Some of our modern Diversion-Mongers think it is not enough to be every day contriving new Entertainments for our Evenings Amusement; the Morning too must be taken up in them, as tho' we were born for nothing but Recreation: Vaux-Hall, Cupers, and all those numerous Places of Rendezvous, except Ranelagh[1] Gardens, content themselves indeed with engrossing that Part of our Time, in which Business usually gives way to Pleasure. But this latter is not satisfied without encroaching on those Hours which Reason and Nature require should be otherwise employed.—There is not so great a Space of Time between me and Youth, but I can very well remember, that after having paid my Devotions to Heaven, wash'd, dress'd, and eat my Breakfast, the remaining Hours till Noon were chiefly taken up with those who instructed me in Working, Dancing, Musick, Writing and those other necessary Accomplishments of my Sex; and thought, that if I was allowed to take a little Walk in St. James's Park, or in our own Garden, in order to get a Stomach to my Dinner, it was as much Relaxation as I ought to expect.

I trained up my only Daughter in the same Manner I had been bred up myself, and had no Reason to suspect she was dissatisfied with this Regulation till she arrived at her Fourteenth Year; at which

Time Ranelagh unhappily gave Notice there would be public Breakfasting every morning.—This gave a Turn very vexatious to me, and prejudicial to the Education I intended to bestow on her: I immediately discovered a Remissness in all her former Studies; and, at length, a total Aversion to them.—The French Mistress is now a troublesome Companion; the Needle a most odious Implement; the Spinet is untuned; the Musick Books are thrown aside; nothing seems worthy her Regard but how to appear in the genteelest Deshabille at Ranelagh.—Every Morning my House is crowded with young Ladies to call Miss Biddy to go with them to breakfast at Ranelagh; nothing is talk'd of at their Return but what was said and done at Ranelagh, and in what Dresses they shall repair at Night again to that charming Place; so that the whole Day is entirely taken up with it.

Tell me, dear *Spectator*, is it consistent with the Character of a Woman of Prudence to suffer a young Creature, over whom Heaven and Nature has given me the sole Authority, to conduct herself in this Fashion?—Yet by what means is the growing Mischief to be suppress'd?—When I offer to set any Bounds to this wild Career, I have only Sullenness and Whimpering at Home, and no doubt but Censures Abroad for my great Severity.—In vain are my Remonstrances on mispending Time in those giddy Rambles; all I can say makes not the least Impression; and I dread to drive her to Extremes, by laying those Restrictions on her which are necessary to keep her at Home.— Who knows what Lengths unthinking Youth may run!—We often see People of her Years fatally ingenious in contriving Methods to disappoint the utmost Vigilance of those who have the Care of them; and if, by endeavouring to preserve her from one Danger, I should provoke her to throw herself into others, I should be inexcuseable to myself.—The Dilemma I labour under on this Score is terrible:—I therefore conjure you, as you cannot be insensible of what many afflicted Parents, as well as myself, must feel, in seeing all the Fruit of their long Care and Tenderness so near being blasted, to set forth, in the most moving and pathetick Terms you can, the Folly of gadding eternally to these Publick Places.—Convince our young Ladies of the Loss it is to themselves, how much it disqualifies them for all the social Duties, renders them neglectful of what they owe to Heaven, and to those who gave them Being, and incapable of being either good Wives, good Mothers, good Friends, or good Mistresses; and thereby entails sure Unhappiness on their own future Days, as well as on all those who shall have any Relation to them.

A public Reproof from you may, perhaps, be more effectual than all the private Admonitions of their Friends, which they are too apt to look upon as Words of course.—The Advice of a Person who can have no other Interest in giving it, than the generous Part she takes in the Happiness of her Fellow-Creatures will certainly sink into the Soul of every one, not wholly lost to all Sense of her own Good, and complete the Wishes of a great Number of your Readers, as well as of

Your real Admirer,
And most humble Servant.

Hanover Square.
August 2, 1744   SARAH OLDFASHION.

P.S. If the Hopes I have in the *Spectator* should fail me, I am resolved to send Biddy to a Relation I have in Cornwall, whose nearest Neighbour is twelve Miles distant; and whence if she continues her rambling Humour, huge craggy Rocks on one Side, and no less dread Mines on the other, will be her only Prospect.

The Case of this Lady I must confess is greatly to be commiserated, and must be felt by all who either are, or have been Mothers.—Could Children be sensible of the endless Cares, the Watchings, the Anxieties which attend Parental Tenderness, and how impossible it is for them to return in Kind those Obligations, they would certainly avoid doing any Thing that might render fruitless the Pains and Labour employed for their Interest:—Gratitude as well as Self-Love would make them use their utmost Efforts to improve the Education bestowed on them; but how hard it is to bring young People to a just Way of thinking, I have already taken Notice of in a former *Spectator*, as I have somewhere read.

> *Experience Vainly in our Youth is sought,*
> *And with Age purchas'd is too dearly bought.*[2]

Too many there are who know not how to live in the World till they are ready to go out of it; but, as Dryden says,

> *Let Life pass thro' them like a leaky Sieve.*[3]

Much therefore is it to be lamented that such Encouragements are given to the natural Giddiness of Youth, and that the Prevalence of Example in those of riper Years should afford a Sanction to those in whom the Love of Pleasure is less inexcusable.

Yet after all, what are the mighty Pleasures which these Walks afford?—Have not most of our Nobility who frequent them much more delightful Recesses of their own!—Can either Ranelagh, or any of these Places where they pay for Entrance, equal in Elegance or Magnificence many of those Gardens, which they need but step out of their own Apartments to enjoy the Pleasures of!—Nobody sure will pretend to say the contrary; but then indeed it may be alledg'd, that to such Persons, who by their high Offices in the State, or Attendance at Court, are obliged to keep much in Town, such Places of Relaxation are both necessary and agreeable. It must be acknowledg'd that they are so, and it would be the highest Injustice as well as Arrogance in a *Spectator*, to pass any Censure on the great World for Amusements, which seem calculated chiefly for them; and which are indeed prejudicial to the People of an inferior Condition, only by being indulged to an Excess.

But the Misfortune is, that whatever is done by Persons of Quality presently becomes the Mode, which every one is ambitious of apeing let it suit ever so ill with their Circumstances. It is not the fine Prospect that Ranelagh is happy in, the pleasant Walks, the magnificent Amphitheatre, nor the melodious Sounds that issue from the Orchestre, that makes the Assembly there so numerous; but the Vanity every one has of joining Company, as it were, with their Superiors.—Of having it in their Power to boast, when they come Home, of the Notice taken of them by such a Lord, or such a great Lady; to descant upon their Dresses, their Behaviour, and pretend to discover who likes who; what fine new-married Lady coquets it with her Husband's Intimate; what Duke regards his Wife with no more than an enforced Complaisance; and whether the Fortune, or Person, of the young Heiress is the Object of her obsequious Follower's Flame.

This ridiculous Desire of being thought to have a Knowledge of Things, no less out of their Sphere to attain than unprofitable if acquired, is extremely prevalent in many People, especially among the little Gentry; and is one of the chief Motives which draw them in such Crowds to all Places where their Superiors resort.

An Affectation of this Sort is not confined to any Age.—We see it from Sixteen to Sixty; but when it happens to gain Entrance in the Mind of a Lady so very young as Miss Biddy, and is joined with that Vanity of attracting Admiration, and a Train of Lovers, which naturally arises on the Entrance into their Teens, it is not to [be] wondered at, that it is so difficult to restrain them from going to any Place which flatters them with the

Gratification of their Pride in both these Points.

I am afraid, therefore, that Mrs. Oldfashion will find all her Endeavours for this Purpose unavailing, unless she has Recourse to Force, which she seems little inclined to put in Practice, and I can by no Means approve, as the Remedy might prove to be of worse Consequence than the Disease:— Much less would I advise her to send her into Cornwall.—A young Lady of her Vivacity, and who seems to have so high a Relish for the Pleasures of the Town, finding herself snatch'd away from every thing she thinks a Joy in Life, and plung'd into so frightful a Solitude, would certainly be able to preserve no Degree of Moderation.—If of a mild and gentle Nature, inward Repinings and a wasting Melancholly would prey upon her Vitals, impair her Health and Understanding, and by degrees, render her both stupid and diseased.—If, on the contrary, there be the Seeds of Obstinacy and Perverseness in her Soul, she will resent the Cruelty she imagines herself treated with; and, as Consideration is not to be expected at those Years, perhaps throw herself into much greater Misfortunes than she was sent thither to avoid, merely to prevent the too great Caution of those who have the Power over her.— Either of these Consequences must be terrible to a Parent; so that I am wholly against running such a Hazard by exerting Authority in this Manner.

From Volume I, Book V, 261-71

Explanatory Notes

1 **Vaux-Hall, Cupers,…Ranelagh** were all eighteenth-century pleasure gardens.

2 **Experience…bought:** Source unknown.

3 **Let…Sieve:** Dryden (1631-1700). Nearest identification is from the Translation of the latter part of the Third Book of *Lucretius*, line 129. Actual text:

If all the blessings I cou'd give
Thou hast enjoy'd, if thou hast known to live,
And pleasure not leak'd thro' thee like a Seive [sic]....

N.B. The story of Christabella which follows is partly a response to the letter from Sarah Oldfashion, and should be read as such. [Ed.]

✿✿ 6 ✿✿

Christabella: A Disobedient Daughter

Alvario, a Gentleman of Fortune and Figure in the World, was left a
Widower with two Daughters, who, in Right of their Mother, were Co-
heiresses of an Estate of upwards of a thousand Pounds a Year; the Eldest,
whom I shall call Christabella, was extremely beautiful and full of Spirit,
but Lucilla, her younger Sister, was of a sickly Constitution, and consequently more dull, and less qualified or inclined to Conversation. She never
cared for stirring out or entertaining any Company at home; but Christabella's airy Disposition would scarce suffer her to be ever at home.—The
Park, the Play, the Opera, the Drawing-Room, were the Idols of her
Heart:—Dress, Equipage, and Admiration took up all her Thoughts:—
Youth, Beauty, and Fortune are rarely possest without an adequate
Proportion of Vanity; and it must be owned, this Lady was not without
it.—She plumed herself on the daily Conquests her Charms gain'd her; and
tho' she had too much Wit to believe all the flattering Declarations made to
her, by some Persons who were not in a Condition to fulfil their Pretences,
yet she had not enough to defend her from taking Pleasure in them.

In fine, tho' perfectly innocent, even in Thought, of every Thing to
which Virtue was repugnant, the Gaiety of her Behaviour rendered her
liable to the Censures of some, who take a malicious Pleasure in blasting
the Characters of those more amiable than themselves.—Her Father, who
was a Man of Gallantry himself, and consequently too ready to misinter-
pret any little Freedoms taken by our Sex as the Effect of an amorous
Inclination, opened his Ears to all the Insinuations made him by those of
their Kindred, who had no good Will to Christabella, on account of her not
being able to restrain herself from frequently throwing out bitter Jests on
some of their too rigid Rules; among whom, or rather at their Head, was an
old Maiden Aunt, who lived in the same House, and was, as it were, a kind
of Governante over the two young Ladies. This ill-natured Creature pick'd
up all the Stories she could from the Envyers of her Niece's Perfections,

and reported them, with the most aggravating Additions, to Alvario, conjuring him to lay his Command on her to be more circumspect in her Conduct.

Christabella started at finding herself accused of Crimes which she never had the least Notion of, and would have dyed rather than been guilty of; but neither the Displeasure she found it gave her Father, nor the Regard she had of her own Reputation, was powerful enough to make her retrench any of those Liberties she had accustomed herself to take and as she knew them to be only such as she could answer to her own Honour, seem'd altogether indolent how they might appear in the Eyes of the World.

In vain Alvario remonstrated, menac'd, forbad her, on pain of forfeiting all Pretensions to his Favour, ever to come any more into some Company, or be seen in some Places she had been used to frequent. No Considerations of the Duty she owed to him as a Parent were sufficient to restrain her from following her Inclinations; and [she] thought herself more injured by his believing the Aspersions thrown on her, than she cou'd injure him by her Disobedience.

'Tis highly probable, that the Knowledge she was born to a Fortune independent on him, went a great Way towards emboldening her to act in this Manner.—Certain it is that her Conduct was such as plainly testified she had but a small Share either of Love or Fear of him, which so enrag'd him, as indeed he had just Cause to be, that he made her be lock'd up in her Chamber, and suffered her to see nobody but her Aunt, whose Society she would have been glad to have dispensed with, and a Maid Servant, who came in to bring her Food and other Necessaries.

But this Confinement, was so far from humbling the Haughtiness of her Spirit, that on the contrary it rendered her more obstinate; and looking on the Treatment she received as the effect of Tyranny rather than Parental Care, she no longer considered Alvario as her Father, but a cruel Goaler, to whom she would not condescend to make the least Submission. And when her Aunt told her, that if she would promise to make a better Use of her Liberty than she had done, she would endeavour to prevail with her Brother to pardon what was past; she answer'd, that she knew herself guilty of nothing that requir'd Amendment, and therefore would not pretend to make any Alteration in her Conduct.

In fine, she behaved with so little natural Affection or Duty, that Alvario was soon convinced that he had taken a wrong Method to bring her to a better Way of thinking, and repented he had not made Tryal of more gentle Means; but tho' he extremely loved her, he thought it would be unbecoming his Character to be the first that should recede; therefore continued her Confinement, flattering himself that she would in Time petition him at least for a Release.

But while he was vainly expecting to bend a Spirit so untameable, she was contriving Means to make her Escape at once from his House and Authority, resolving, if she could once get loose, to take Lodgings, and oblige her Father to put into her Hands, or those of some Person she would nominate as her Guardian, that Part of the Estate, which she was too sensible he could not with-hold from her.

The first Attempt she made for this Purpose was to get the Maid that waited on her into her Interest; but all the Promises she made being ineffectual to corrupt the Integrity of this faithful Creature, she had Recourse to a Stratagem, which one would be surprized to think should ever enter into the Head of one who was not yet arrived at her Sixteenth Year.

Pen, Ink, and Paper unhappily being not refus'd her, she wrote a great Number of little Billets, complaining of the Injustice she receiv'd from an inhuman Father, who had lock'd her up on purpose to make her pine herself to Death, that the whole of the Estate might descend to his other more favour'd Daughter.—These she folded up and directed

To any charitable Person who shall pass this Way and has Compassion enough to assist an abused Daughter in her Escape from the most barbarous of all Fathers.

Several of these Letters she threw out of the Window as soon as it was dark, but they were either not seen and trod under Foot, or fell into the Hands of such, as either knew not what to make of them, or did not care to interfere in the Affair.—At length, when she grew half distracted at the Stupidity and Insensibility of the World, and began to despair of the Success she aimed at by this Means; as she was throwing out the last she intended to make Tryal of, Fate directed it to light on the Shoulder of a Gentleman, who happened to be Knight-Errant enough to attempt the Relief of this distress'd Damsel.

He saw from whence it fell by the Light of a Lamp which was opposite to the House, and heard the Window shut just as he took it up.—The Moment he came home he examined the Contents, and found something so whimsical in the Adventure that he resolv'd to fathom the Bottom of it.—He was a Man of no Fortune, and had supported the Appearance of a Gentleman meerly by Gaming; so thought, that if the confined Lady was really such as her Letter signified, he ought not to neglect what his good Genius had thrown in his Way, but make use of the Opportunity which gave him such fair Hopes of establishing himself in the World.

Early the next Morning he made it his Business to enquire among the

Neighbourhood into the Circumstances of Alvario, and was soon inform'd of the Truth of every Thing.—To be assur'd that the young Lady, who implor'd Assistance, had an Estate independent either of her Father, or any one else, flatter'd his most sanguine Views, but which Way he should let her know how ready he was to obey any Injunctions she should lay upon him for the Recovery of her Liberty, was the great Difficulty.—To write he perceived would be in vain, he supposed by the Method she took, that she had no Person whom she could confide in, either for sending or receiving any Letters, or if she had, was wholly ignorant who that Person was.—At last, after various Turns of Invention, he bethought himself of one, dangerous enough indeed, but somewhat he thought was to be ventured.

The Window, from whence he found the Letter came, was but one Story from the Ground; and being a Back-Room look'd into a little Court, which, tho' a Thoroughfare, was not much frequented in the Night. He therefore resolved to climb it, which he did, by the help of a Step-Ladder he procured, and brought himself to the Place about the· same Hour he had received the Letter. As he made not the least Noise in mounting, he look'd through the Glass, and by the Curtains not being entirely clos'd saw the fair Authoress of the Summons sitting in a melancholly Posture, leaning her Head upon her Hand.—He found she was alone, and ventur'd to knock softly against the Window.—She startled at the Noise, but being of a Disposition far from timid, stepp'd toward the Window, which he immediately drew up on the Outside, and making as low a Bow in the Posture he was in would admit, *Be not alarmed, Fair Creature*, said he, *I come to offer you that Assistance, which this Mandate tells me your Condition requires.*—In speaking these Words, he presented her with the Billet she had thrown.—The Sight of which dissipating all the Apprehensions she might have on his being there, on some less agreeable Design; she thank'd him for the Trouble he took, and the Danger to which he expos'd himself in the most grateful and obliging Terms; after this, as Time would not permit much Ceremony on either Side, she informed him that the Service she entreated of him, was first to provide a Lodging for her in some House of Reputation, and that he would come again the next Night, and help her to descend from that Window, there being no other Way of her getting out of the House.—This he assur'd her of performing, and she promis'd him that she would return the Obligation with every Mark of Gratitude a virtuous Woman had to bestow, or a Man of Honour could expect.—After which he descended, and she made fast her Window, both of them highly satisfied with this Interview, tho' for different Reasons; *she* full of Hopes of regaining her dear Liberty; and *he*, of having it in his Power to oblige her to enter into a Second, and more lasting Confinement.

The Gamester was not remiss in any Thing that might contribute to the gaining so rich a Prize as Christabella; he prepared a Lodging for her furnished in a very compleat Manner, but it was at the House of a Person to whom he communicated the whole of this Affair, and who had Reasons to act in such a manner as should forward his Designs.

When the appointed Hour arrived, he repair'd to the Window, where Christabella stood in full Expectation of his coming, and no sooner saw the Ladder fix'd than she descended, without exacting any other Promise from her Deliverer than what she had receiv'd from him the Night before.

Some Hours before her Departure, she wrote a Letter to her Father, and laid it in a Place where she was certain it would be found as soon as her Flight should be discover'd. The Terms in which she express'd herself to him were as follows.

SIR,
The cruel Usage I have received from you makes me imagine you forgot you gave me Being, and absolves me from the Duty I otherwise should owe you as a Father:—I go for ever from you, and expect you will not force me to take any Measures unbecoming the Character of a Daughter in order to gain Possession of my Birth-Right, which you have long enjoyed the Use of, and is high Time should now devolve on,
    SIR,
        Your much injured Daughter,
        CHRISTABELLA.

A Coach that waited at the End of the Court conveyed her to her new Lodging, and the Person who attended her thither omitted nothing that might inspire her with a high Idea of his Honour, and also make her think he was not her Inferior either in Birth or Fortune. Late as it was, he oblig'd her to sit down to a very elegant Collation he had caused to be provided.

At first she was highly delighted with her Reception; but Supper was no sooner over than he began to speak his Mind more freely, and let her know he had not taken all this Pains but with a View of becoming the Master both of her Person and Estate. He made this Declaration however, in the most submissive terms, and accompanied with a Shew of the utmost Passion and Adoration of her Charms; and as she had been accustomed to hear Professions of this Nature, she was not greatly displeased with those he utter'd, and affected to railly what he said with the same Gaiety she had treated her former Admirers; but alas! She soon found he was not to be put off in that Manner, he press'd her for an immediate Promise of marrying him the next Morning, told her that he was extremely serious in the Affair, and expected she should be so too, and that he was determined not to quit her Presence till he had an Assurance of being her Husband.

She now began to tremble, and as she has confess'd, wish'd herself again under Alvario's Roof.—She was in the Power of a Man utterly a Stranger to her, and who seemed resolute enough to attempt any Thing he had a Mind to:—No visible Way of escaping the Danger with which her Honour was threatened, unless she comply'd with his Desires, offered itself to her:—The more she reflected on her Condition, the more dreadful it appear'd; and she at last in spite of all the Greatness of her Spirit, burst into a Flood of Tears.

As he did not want Wit, and exerted it all on this Occasion, he said the most endearing Things to her, laying the Blame of the Compulsion he was obliged to make use of, on the Excess of his Love, and the Apprehensions he was in, that if he let slip this Opportunity, she would not hereafter listen to his Vows.—He added also, that if the Place of her Abode should be discover'd by Alvario, the Authority of a Father might force her back into that Confinement, from which she had, but with the utmost Difficulty, got out of.—Whereas when she was once a Wife, all former Duties and Obligations would be dissolv'd, and she would be only under the Power of a Husband, to whom her Will should ever be a Law.

During this Discourse a strange Vicissitude of different Passions rose in her troubled Mind.—Sometimes softened by the flattering Expressions of his Love and Admiration: Enflam'd with Rage at others, when she consider'd that he had the Boldness to think of forcing her Inclinations.—The Indiscretion of trusting herself in the Hands of a Man so wholly a Stranger, now shewed itself to her in its true Colours; one Moment she argued mildly with him how incompatible the laying her under Constraint was, with the Respect he pretended for her, the next she reproach'd him, and testified the utmost Scorn at his Proceeding. By turns descended to sooth and to revile, both which were equally ineffectual; he reply'd to every Thing she said with all the Humility of the most beseeching and obsequious Lover, yet the Purport of his Words convinced her the Resolution he had taken was unalterable, that she had no Means of avoiding being his, and that all in her own Choice, was to be his Mistress or his Wife.

Great Part of the Night being now elaps'd, and no Possibility of prevailing with him; she at length yielded to Necessity, and consented to marry him; on which, he left her to take what Repose so unexpected a Change of Fortune would permit; but that no Chance or Contrivance might deprive him of his Hopes, obliged her to make the Woman of the House the Partner of her Bed.

When at Liberty to ruminate on the Accident that had befallen her, the

Compulsion she was under seem'd to her the most vexatious Part of it.— The Person and Conversation of her intended Bridegroom had nothing in them disagreeable to her, he had the Appearance of a Man of Fashion and had sworn a thousand Oaths that his Birth and Fortune were such, as none of her Kindred would have Cause to blame her Choice of him.—He had told her his Name, which happening to be the same of a very great Family, (tho', in reality, he was not at all related to them) she imagin'd it would be no demeaning of herself to be called by it; therefore easily flatter'd herself that it was, as he pretended, only Violence of the Passion she had inspired him with, which made him take the Methods he did for the Gratification of it.— This Vanity contributed greatly to her Ease, and made her, with less Reluctance, perform the Promise he had extorted from her.

In fine, they were married, after which he carried her into the Country under the Pretence of diverting her, but in reality to elude any Prosecution which might be made against him for stealing an Heiress.

Alvario, indeed, no sooner found the Letter she had left for him, than he search'd for her at every House where it was known she had the least Acquaintance; and not being able to hear the least Tidings of her, doubted not but she was gone away with some Person for whom she had a secret Affection.

Christabella, in the mean time, grew perfectly reconcil'd to her Lot and not in the least doubting but her Husband was in reality of the Family and Fortune he had told her, was continually importuning him to demand the Writings of the Estate out of her Father's Hands; but he had too much Cunning to comply, and seeming not to regard her Wealth since he got Possession of her Person, won so far upon her as to create in her a most perfect Affection; and it was not till after he found himself assured that she would not join in any thing against him, by being the Master of her Heart, and that she was pregnant, that he brought her to Town, and suffered their Marriage to be declared; but it no sooner was so, than the whole Truth of his Circumstances was also divulg'd.—Alvario was like a Man deprived of Reason; all her Kindred and Friends were inconsolable; every one that wish'd her well, amazed and shock'd, and the whole Town full of no other Subject of Discourse.

Christabella herself at the first Discovery of the Deception had been put upon her, felt a Resentment, which nothing but her own Behaviour can describe.—She threaten'd to abandon this unworthy Husband, and leave him to that Punishment the Law inflicts on the Crime he had been guilty of.—She had even pack'd up her Cloaths and Jewels for that Purpose; yet did his Entreaties, and pretended Passion for her, added to the Condition she was in, and the Reflection how dreadful a Reproach it would be to the

Child she was to bring into the World, should the Father of it be brought to so infamous a Fate, prevail on her to continue with him, and content herself with venting her Indignation in the most bitter Terms she could invent. All which he bore with a Shew of Patience, as he knew it was not yet Time to exert any Authority, but kept in Mind every reviling Word, resolving to revenge it hereafter.

But not to spin this little Narrative to a too tedious Length, he had Artifice, and she had good Nature enough, to bring about an entire Forgiveness on her Part.—She did every Thing he requested of her.—She assured whoever spoke to her of the Affair, that no Imposition had been practised on her,—that she knew before-hand the true Circumstances of the Person who was now her Husband, and that the Love she had for him made her overlook the Disparity between them.—She employed a Lawyer to go to her Father on the Account of her Estate, and before the Affair was wholly determined, the Death of her Sister gave her a Right to the Whole; which Alvario, seeing there was no Remedy, was obliged to resign.

The Possession of this Estate discovered to Christabella how miserable she was, the seeming Tenderness and submissive Temper of her Husband, had made her not doubt but she always would be the sole Mistress both of her Actions and Fortune; but all being now compleated, and he having nothing more to fear from her Displeasure, he presently made her feel the Effects of the Power he had over her, and that he had not forgot the Disdain with which she had treated him during the Continuance of her Rage.

A Spirit like hers was not easy to be broke, yet did he accomplish the Task in a very few Months.—It is now her Turn to sue, and often sue in vain for a small Share of her own Wealth, which he profusely lavishes Abroad among his former Companions, leaving her at Home to lament alone her wretched State.

Never was a greater Tyrant, he denies her even the Privilege of visiting, or being visited by those who would wish to continue a Correspondence with her; as for her Father and Kindred, not one among them would ever see her since her Elopement and the Discovery of her Marriage.—No Words can paint the Misery of her Condition, and to render it worse, there is not the least Appearance of any Relief but by Death.

It is certain that the Fate of so disobedient a Daughter, cannot excite much Commiseration in the World; but it ought to be a Warning to all Parents who wish to see their Children happy, to study carefully their Dispositions before they go about to treat them with ungentle Means, and rather condescend to *sooth* an obstinate Temper than *compel* it to a Change.—Where there is Vanity and Self-sufficiency, it must be only Time and Reflection that can convince them what they ought to do; and if, by laying some Pleasures in their Way less prejudicial than those to which they are addicted, one could divide the Inclination so as to render the former less strong, it might be easy, by Degrees, to bring them to an Indifference for all.—This is a Method which might at least be made Tryal of, and, I fancy, would more often answer the End than fail.

If Mrs. Oldfashion would, therefore, wean Miss Biddy from the immoderate Delight she has taken at present in Ranelagh Gardens, and the Company who frequent that Place, it might be right to vary the Scene; but in my Opinion altogether the Reverse, to change it to one where only dismal Objects offering to the View, should render the past more pleasing in Idea than they were even in Enjoyment.

From Volume I, Book V, 271-87

ഇൗ 7 ജ

The Reclamation of Dorimon

Dorimon and Alithea were married almost too young to know the Duties of the State they enter'd into; yet both being extremely good-natur'd, a mutual Desire of obliging each other appear'd in all their Words and Actions; and tho' this Complaisance was not owing to those tender Emotions which attract the Heart with a resistless Force, and bear the Name of Love, yet were the Effects so much the same as not to be distinguish'd.

The first Year of their Marriage made them the happy Parents of an Heir to a plentiful Estate.—The Kindred on both Sides seem'd to vye with each other, which should give the greatest Testimonies of their Satisfaction.— All their Friends congratulated this Addition to their Felicity; and for a Time, the most perfect Joy and Tranquility reigned, not only in their own Family, but in all those who had any Relation to them.

Alithea after she became a Mother began to feel, by Degrees, a greater Warmth of Affection for him that made her so; and having no Reason to doubt an equal Regard from him, thought herself as happy as Woman could be, and that there were Joys in Love greater than before she had any Notion of.

Quite otherwise was it with Dorimon; the Time was now indeed arrived, which taught him what it was to love.—The Hopes, the Fears, the Anxieties, the Impatiences, all the unnumber'd Cares which are attributed to that Passion, now took Possession of his Heart.—He pin'd, he languish'd, but alas, not for his Wife.— He had unhappily seen a young Lady at the Opera, who had Charms for him, which he had never found in the whole Sex before.—As he happen'd to sit in the same Box with her, he had an Opportunity of speaking to her, which tho' only on ordinary Subjects, every Answer she made, to what he said, seem'd to him to discover a Profusion of Wit, and gave him the most longing Desire to be acquainted with her.

Fortune, favourable to his Wishes, presented her to him the next Day in the Park, accompany'd with a Lady and a Gentleman, the latter of whom he had a slight Knowledge of;—he only bow'd to them the first Turn, but gather'd Courage to join Company with them on the second; and perceiving that it was to the other Lady that the Gentleman seem'd most attach'd, he was at the greater Liberty to say a thousand gallant Things to her, who was the Object of his new Flame.

Melissa, for so I shall call her, was vain, gay, and in every respect one of those modish Ladies, of which a former *Spectator* has given a Description: she receiv'd the Compliments he made her in a Manner, that made him see his Conversation was not disagreeable to her; and some mention happening to be made of a Masquerade that Night, she told him, as if by Chance, that she was to be there, and that her fair Companion and herself were going to bespeak Habits at a Warehouse she mention'd, as soon as they left the Park.

The Hint was not lost upon him, and thinking that it would seem too presuming to ask leave to wait on her at her House, the first Time of being in her Company, he resolved to make it his Business to find out, if possible, what Habit she made choice of, to go to the Masquerade, where the Freedom of the Place might give him a better Opportunity of testifying the Desire he had of improving an Acquaintance with her.

Accordingly, after their quitting him at the Park-Gate, he followed at a Distance the two Chairs that waited for them, and placing himself near enough to the Habit-Shop, to see whoever went in or out, found his Adorable had not deceiv'd him in what she said.—The Ladies having dispatch'd what they came about, went again into their Chairs.—They were no sooner gone than he went into the Shop, and on a pretence of ordering a *Domine* for himself, fell into Discourse with the Woman behind the Counter, whom he easily prevail'd on to let him know, not only what Habits the Ladies who had just left her had bespoke, but also of what Condition and Character they were.—She inform'd him that Melissa had a large Fortune, and her Parents being dead was under the Care of Guardians, whom, notwithstanding, she did not live with, but had Lodgings to herself near Grosvenor Square. That she kept a great deal of Company, was what the World call'd a Coquet, but had hitherto preserv'd her Reputation. That the Lady who was with her was the Daughter of a Country Gentleman somewhat related to her, how nearly she could not tell, but heard she was on the point of Marriage with a Person of Rank.

Dorimon was transported at this Intelligence, as it seem'd to promise him an easy Access to her Acquaintance, and the Privilege of visiting her; which, probably, in these early Days of his Passion was all he aim'd at. Or if he thought on any thing further, the Difficulties in accomplishing his Desire seem'd less formidable than they would have done, had she been of a more reserv'd Temper, were already married, or under the Direction of Parents.

Never did Time appear so tedious as that before the Hour of going to the Masquerade. His Impatience brought him there the very first, and by that means he had the Opportunity of observing every one as they came in.— Melissa, he was told, would be in the Habit of a Nun; and tho' there were several drest in that manner, yet he distinguish'd her from the others by her Tallness the Moment she appear'd.

He accosted her with the usual Phrases of—*Do you know me?*—and—*I know you!*—but was not long before he made her sensible of his more particular Attachment; and told her, that having lost his Heart that Morning in the Park, it now directed him how to discover the lovely Thief, tho' disguised, and amidst so numerous an Assembly.

This, and some other Expressions of the same nature, convincing her that he was the Gentleman who had made her so many Compliments in the Morning, immediately flatter'd her Vanity with a new Conquest; and as she found him a Man of Wit, and doubted not of his being a Person of Condition by his Appearance, resolv'd to omit nothing that might secure him. Accordingly, as all true Coquets do at first, she affected to listen with a pleas'd Attention to the Assurances he gave her of his Passion, and frequently let fall some Words, as if they escaped her inadvertently, that might make him think she would not be ungrateful if he persisted in giving her Testimonies of a constant Flame. Ladies of her Character have always this Maxim at heart,

> *Kindness has resistless Charms,*
> *All Things else but faintly warms:*
> *It gilds the Lover's servile Chain,*
> *And makes the Slave grow pleas'd and vain.*[1]

But the Misfortune is, that such a Behaviour for the most part proves fatal to themselves in the End.—They toy so long with the Darts of Love, that their own Bosoms are frequently pierced when they little think of it; and the deluding She, who has made Numbers languish, becomes a Prey perhaps to one who least merits or regards the Victory he gains.

Dorimon, however, was transported to find the Offer he had made of his Heart so well received, and made so good Use of the Opportunity she gave him of entertaining her the whole Time of the Masquerade, that he obtained her Permission to attend her home, and as it was then too late for them to continue their Conversation, to visit her the next Day in the Afternoon.

This quite established an Acquaintance between them; he went every Day to see her; she admitted him when all other Company were denied; he had always the Preference of waiting on her to the Park, the Opera, the Play, and, in fine, wherever she went; and when some of her more prudent Friends took notice of their being so frequently together, and had heard that he was a married Man, she only laughed at their Remonstrances, and replied, that as she had no farther Concern with him than merely to gallant her about to public Places, she had no Business to enquire into his private Circumstances;—that if he were married, his *Wife* only had to do with it; and as for her own Part, she thought him a very pretty Fellow, and quite fit for the Use she had made of him; adding, that if she were Mistress of his Heart, it was indifferent to her who had his *Hand*.

Melissa, 'tis probable, had indeed no other View in entertaining Dorimon, and receiving his Addresses, than the same she had in treating with a like Behaviour Numbers before him, merely for the sake of hearing herself praised, and giving Pain, as she imagined, to others of her Admirers, who were less frequently admitted.

But how dangerous a Thing it is to have too great an Intimacy with a Person of a different Sex, many of a greater Share of Discretion than Melissa have experienced.—This unwary Lady, in meditating new Arts, the more to captivate her Lover, became ensnared herself;—in fine, she liked, she loved as much as any Woman of that airy and volatile Disposition can be said to love.—What she felt for him, however, had all the Effects which the most serious Passion in one of a different Temper could have produced, and Dorimon had as ample a Gratification of his Desires, as his most sanguine Hopes could have presented him an Idea of.

Alithea all this while lost Ground in his Affection;—she every Day seemed less fair, and whatever she said or did had in it a kind of Aukwardness, which before he was far from discovering in her;—every thing was now displeasing in her;—if endearing, her Fondness was childish and silly; and if she was more reserved, sullen and ill-natured.—One Moment he was out of Humour if she spoke, the next offended at her Silence.—He was continually seeking some Pretence to find Fault with the most justifiable Conduct that ever was, and even vexed that he had nothing in reality to condemn.—Unhappy, but certain Consequence of a new Attachment, which not content with the Injury it does, also adds to it by Ill-Humour, and a Wish of some Occasion to hate the Object we no longer love.

The poor Lady could not but observe this Alteration in his Behaviour; but as she was far from guessing the real Motive, imputed it to some unlucky Turn in his Affairs, tho' of what Nature she could not imagine, he having a large Fortune settled on him at their Marriage, beside the Reversion of what his Father should die possessed of, and was in the Power of nobody to deprive him of.

On the first notice she took of his Discontent, she asked him, as became a tender and affectionate Wife, if any thing had happen'd either from her Family or his own to give him Subject of Complaint? But he answering with Peevishness, she desisted from any further Enquiry, judging, as he did not think proper to trust her with the Secret, it would but add to his Disquiets to testify a Desire of knowing it.

For more than a whole Year did she combat his Ill-Humour with Sweetness, Gentleness, and the most obliging Behaviour; and tho' she began to think herself lost to his Affection, bore even that afflicting Reflection with the most submissive Patience, still flattering herself that, if it were even so, he would one Day consider she deserved not her ill Fortune.

Jealousy was, however, a Passion she was wholly unacquainted with. Many very beautiful Ladies often visited at her House, and she had never seen the least Propensity in him to Gallantry with any of them;—he rather behaved to them with a greater Reserve than was consistent with the good Breeding and Complaisance which might have been expected from a Man of his Years. So that she imagined rather a Disgust to the whole Sex was growing on him, than any particular Attachment to one.

Thus did her Innocence and unsuspecting Nature deceive her, till one Day a Female Friend, more busy than wise, open'd her Eyes to the true Reason of her Husband's Coldness.

This Lady, by means of a Servant Maid she had lately entertained, and who had lived with Melissa long enough to know the whole Secret of her Amour with Dorimon, and was dismissed on some Dislike, was made acquainted with all that passed between that guilty Pair.—She learned from this unfaithful Creature, that Melissa had been made a Mother by Dorimon, and that the Child was disposed of to a Person, who, for a Present of fifty Guineas, had taken the sole Charge of it, so as it should never appear to the Disgrace of the unnatural Parents.—Not the most minute Circumstance relating to the Affair but was betrayed by this Wretch, partly in Revenge for her having been discarded by her former Lady, and partly to gain Favour with the present, who, she easily pereceived, loved to hear News of this kind.

Alithea would fain have treated this Account as fabulous, and have perswaded her Friend to regard it only as a Piece of Malice in the Reporter; but the other was positive in her Assertion, and told her, that it was utterly impossible for such a Creature to dress up a Fiction with so many Particulars, and such a Shew of Truth;—*besides*, added she, *if there were nothing in it, we might easily disprove all she has said, by going to the Woman who* has the Care of the Child, and whose Name and Place of Abode she has told me.

Compelled at last to believe her Misfortune but too certain, a-while she gave a loose to Tears, and to Complainings, but her good Sense, as well as good Nature, soon got the better of this Burst of Passion; and when her Friend asked her in what Manner she would proceed in order to do herself Justice?—*What can I do*, reply'd this charming Wife, *but endeavour to render myself more obliging, more pleasant, more engaging if possible than my Rival, and make Dorimon see, he can find nothing in Melissa that is wanting in me.*

O Heaven! cried the Lady, *can you forgive such an Injury?*—*Yes*, resumed Alithea, stifling her Sighs as much as she was able, *Love is an involuntary Passion.*— *And will you not upbraid him with his Ingratitude, and expose Melissa?* said she.—*Neither the One, nor the other*, answered Alithea coldly; *either of these Methods would indeed render me unworthy of a Return of his Affection; and I conjure and beseech you*, added she, *by all the Friendship I flatter myself you have for me, that you will never make the least Mention of this Affair to any one in the World.*

This Moderation was astonishing to the Person who was Witness of it; however, she promised to be entirely silent, since it was requested with so much Earnestness. But how little she was capable of keeping her Word, most of her Acquaintance could testify, to whom not only the Fault of Dorimon, but the Manner in which his Wife received the Account of it, was not three Days a Secret.

Alithea was no sooner left alone, and at Liberty to meditate more deeply on the shocking Intelligence she had received, than she again began to fancy there was a Possibility of its being false:—The Suspence, however, seeming more uneasy to her than the Confirmation could be, she resolved to be more fully convinced of the Truth, if there was any means of being so.

Accordingly she made an old Woman, who had been her Nurse in her Infancy, and whose Fidelity and Discretion she could depend upon, her Confidante in this Affair; and it was concluded between them, that a Spy should be employed to follow Dorimon at a Distance wherever he went, and also to make a private Enquiry into the Behaviour and Character of Melissa among the Neighbours which lived near her.

A very little Search served to unravel the Mystery, and corroborate all that had been said to her concerning it.—The Emissary soon learned that Dorimon failed not one Day in his Visits to this Engrosser of his Heart;— that they were often seen to go out together in a Hackney-Coach in the beginning of the Evening, and that the Lady returned not till near Morning;— that she had been observed some Months past to be more gross than usual, and had affected to wear a loose Dress;—that she had been absent from her Lodgings three to four Days, came home very much indisposed, and kept her Bed for more than a Week, yet had neither Physician nor Apothecary to attend her; and on the whole it was believed by every body, that she had been in that Time delivered of a Child.

The unhappy Wife of Dorimon, now as much assured of his Perfidy as she could be without ocular Demonstation, set herself to bear it with as much Patience as she was able; which was indeed sufficient to render her Behaviour such as made him certain in his own Mind, that she had not the least Suspicion of the wrong he did her, and also compelled him very often to accuse himself for being guilty of what he could not answer to his Reason, yet had not Strength enough of Resolution to refrain, even tho' the Conduct of Melissa, who could not help coquetting with others even before his Face, occasioned him to have many Quarrels with her, and made him see, in spite of the Passion he still continued to have for her, the Difference between a Mistress and a Wife.

Whenever Alithea reflected on this Change in her Husband, as she had little else in her Mind, there was no Part in the Adventure appeared more strange to her, than that a Lady born and educated in the Manner she knew Melissa was, and who had so far yielded to the Temptations of her Passion, as to throw off all Modesty and Honour for the Gratification of it, should have so little Regard for the innocent Babe, the Produce of her guilty Flame, as to abandon it to the Miseries of she knew not what kind.—This was a Barbarity she thought exceeded the Crime to which it owed its Birth, and she more readily forgave the Injury done to herself, than that to the helpless Infant.

The more she reflected she more was astonished, that Womankind could act so contrary to Nature; and by often picturing to herself the Woes to which this poor deserted Child might probably be exposed, became at length so dissolved in soft Compassion, as to form a Resolution which, I believe, few beside herself was ever capable of.

She had been inform'd, by her officious Friend, both of the Name and Habitation of the Woman with whom this poor little Creature had been left; and without making any one Person privy to her Design, muffled herself up in her Capuchin,[2] and went in a Hackney-Chair to her House. The other received her with a great deal of Respect and Kindness, imagining she was come on the same Business Melissa, and many besides her, who love the Crime, but hate the Shame of being detected in it, had done.—She was immediately conducted into a Private Room, and told, that she might be free in communicating any thing to her, for she was a Person who had been entrusted by those who would not be thought guilty of a false Step for the World.

The virtuous Alithea blushed, even at being suspected by this Woman to be guilty of an Act her Soul shuddered at the Thoughts another could commit, and soon put an end to the Harangues she was making on her own Care, Skill, and Fidelity:—*I come not*, said the Wife of Dorimon, *on the Business you seem to think, yet which no less requires your Secresy:—I have no unhappy Infant to leave with you; but to ease you of one whom you have lately taken charge of.*

The Midwife looked very much surprized to hear her speak in this Manner, and knew not well what Answer to make; but Alithea soon put an End to her Suspence, by telling her that she was in the Secret of the Lady who was delivered of a Child at her House such a Time, which she mentioned exactly to her, and who had given fifty Guineas to be eased for ever of the Trouble of it.—*I am*, said Alithea, *a near Relation of that Gentleman to whom the little Wretch owes its Being, and who cannot consent that any thing which does so, tho' begot in an unwarrantable Way, should be deserted and exposed in the Fashion such Children often are;—I therefore desire that, if alive, you will let me see it, that I may provide for it in a different Way than it can be expected you should do for the poor Pittance left with you by the Mother.*

The Woman then began to expatiate on the Impossibility of her taking the Care she could wish to do of Children left with her on those Terms; but that Heaven knew she did all she could, and often laid out more than she received.—She assured her that the Child she enquired after was alive, and a fine Boy; and that he was with a Person who indeed nursed for the Parish, but was a very good Woman, and did her Duty.—

That may be, said Alithea, *but I must have him removed; and if you can provide another who can be depended on, I have Orders from the Father to satisfy you for your Trouble, in a more ample Manner than you can desire. In the mean time*, continued she, putting five Guineas into her Hand, *take this as an Earnest, and let the Child be brought here To-morrow about this Time, and a new Nurse whom you can recommend, and I will give them a Meeting.*

A great deal of farther Discourse past between them on this Affair, on the Conclusion of which the Woman agreed to do whatever was required of her; and was doubtless no less rejoiced at the Offer made by this unknown Lady, than she was that by accepting of it she should preserve from Misery an innocent Creature, who tho' she had not seen she felt a kind of natural Affection for, as being Dorimon's.

This excelling Pattern of Good-Nature and Conjugal Love, took with her the next Day every Thing befitting a Child to wear whom she was determined to make her own by Adoption; and no sooner saw him in his new Nurse's Arms, than she took him, embraced and kiss'd him with a Tenderness little less than maternal; and having agreed upon Terms for him, made him be dress'd in her Presence in the Things she had brought, which were very rich and had belonged to her own Son at his Age; and every thing being settled highly to the Satisfaction of all Parties concerned, returned home with a secret Contentment in her Mind which no Words are able to express.

Nor was this a sudden Start of Goodness and Generosity, which I have known some People who have manifested for a Time and afterward repented of. The more she reflected on what she had done, the more Pleasure she felt in it.—She never let a Week pass over without going to see her Charge, and how the Person entrusted with him behaved.—Had he been in reality her own, and Heir of the greatest Possessions, her Diligence in looking over the Management of him could not have been more.

Dorimon all this while persisted in his Attachment to Melissa, tho' her ill Conduct gave him such frequent Occasions of quarrelling with her, that they were several times on the point of seeing each other no more.—The long Intimacy between them, however, gave sufficient room for Censure.—Those least inclined to judge the worst of things could not help saying, that it looked ill for a married Man to appear in all publick Places without his Wife, and in Company with a Lady whom she was not even acquainted with; but others there were who were informed of their more guilty Meetings in private, and talked with so little reserve on the Occasion, that what was said reached the Ears of the Kindred of them both.—Those of Alithea's were extremely troubled and incensed at the Indignity offered to a Woman, whose Behaviour not Envy itself could traduce;—but desirous of being better informed of the Truth than by common Fame, they asked her many Questions concerning the Conduct of her Husband towards her; and gave some Hints, plain enough to be understood, that the World had but an ill Opinion of him on that Head.

To all which this excellent Wife replied, with an Air that shewed how little she was pleased with any Discourses of that nature,— telling them, that the idle Scandal of Persons, who made it their Business to pick Meanings out of nothing, ought to be despised, not listen'd to;—that she herself, who must be allowed the best Judge, found nothing in Dorimon's manner of living with her to complain of; and that she should never believe that Person wished her well, who endeavoured to fill her Mind with any Suspicions on that Score.

These Answers at length silenced all who took an Interest in her Happiness;

her Friends wisely reflecting, that tho' all they had heard of Dorimon was true, the greatest Addition that could be to her Misfortune, was to be convinced of it.

But the Father of Dorimon, who was a Person of great Sobriety, and to whom the Virtues of Alithea had rendered her extremely dear, was less easily put off than those of her own Blood.—He chid his Son in the severest Manner; and on his denying what he was accused of, and throwing out some Insinuations as if he imagined his Wife had uttered some Complaints against him.— *No*, said the old Gentleman, *she bears the Wrong you do her but with too much Patience; and either not sees, or pretends not to see, what is obvious to the whole Town beside.* He then ran into many Encomiums on the Sweetness of her Disposition; said, that whether her Complaisance toward him were owing either to an unsuspecting Nature, or to her Prudence in aiming to regain his Love by such ways as were most likely to succeed; either of these Qualities ought not to lose their Merit with a Man of Understanding; *and methinks*, added he, *should make you ashamed, as often as you reflect that you have acted so as to oblige her to exert all her Love and Virtue to forgive.*

These kind of Discourses lost not all their Effect on Dorimon:— He had often been astonished that all the Rumours which had been spread concerning his Amour with Melissa, and which seemed to him next to an Impossibility not to have reached the Ears of his Wife, had never occasioned her to let fall some Hints at least, as if she feared a Rival in his Heart.—He very well knew she wanted not a great Share of Discernment in other things, and to be blind to that alone, wherein she had the most Concern, he never could account for.—He had often heard from his Acquaintance, and sometimes been a Witness of the Behaviour of Women to their Husbands on the Subject of Jealousy, and found that of Alithea so widely different from all he had been told of others, that he could not help being extremely puzzled what Motive to ascribe to it; but was obliged to acquiesce in his own Mind with the Remonstrance made by his Father, that whether it were owing to her own Innocence, which would not suffer her to think another could be guilty, or to the Strength of Resolution and Discretion which enabled her to bear the Injury done to her; he was however either way more fortunate than any Husband he knew of in the like Circumstance, and in spite of his faulty Inclination for Melissa, presented her to his cooler Thoughts in the most amiable Light.

'Tis highly probable, that in maturely balancing the solid Merits of the *Wife*, against the light and trifling Allurements of the *Mistress*, he would in Time have brought himself to do Justice to the *one*, and entirely ceased to have any Regard for the *other*; but the Virtues of Alithea had already sustained a sufficient Trial, and Heaven thought fit to reward them, when she, so long inured to Suffering, least expected a Relief.

By accustoming herself to perform the Duties of a Mother to the Child of Melissa, she grew really to love him as such; and what at first was only Pity, converted by degrees into a tender Affection.—When Dorimon was abroad she would often order him to be brought to her, and sending for her own at the same time, diverted herself with observing the little Grimaces which the two Infants would make at each other.—She was one Day employed in this manner when Dorimon unexpectedly returned, and came directly into the Room where they were.—Whatever Indifference he had for his Wife, he had always shewn the greatest Tenderness to her Son; and he now took him in his Arms and kiss'd him, as was his Custom to do.—*Here is another little One*, said Alithea smiling, *who claims some Portion of your Kindness too*, and at the same time presented Melissa's Child to him. *By what Right, Madam?* replied Dorimon, in the same gay Tone. *As he is mine*, resumed his Wife. *Yours!* cried he. *Yes*, answered she, *he is mine by Adoption; and I must have you look upon him as your's also.—My Complaisance for you may carry me great Lengths*, said he: *but as I know you do nothing without being able to give a Reason, should be glad to learn the Motive of so extraordinary a Request.*

One of the Children beginning to whimper a little, Alithea ordered the Nurses take them both into another Room; and finding Dorimon in an exceeding good Humour was pushed on by an irresistable Impulse, to speak to him in the following Manner.

The Infant you saw, said she, in a more serious Tone than before, *and whom I have in Reality taken under my Care, owes its Being to two Persons of Condition; but being illegally begot, the Care of Reputation prevailed above Nature; and this innocent Produce of an inconsiderate Passion I found abandoned, a wretched Cast-away, either to perish, or, surviving, survive but to Miseries much worse than Death.—The Thought was shocking to me, and I resolved to snatch him from the threatened Woes, and provide for him out of my private Purse, in such a Manner as may not make Life hateful to him.*

An Action truly charitable, said Dorimon, a little perplexed; *but this is not the Reason I expected, since by the same Rule your Pity might be extended to Hundreds, whom doubtless you may find exposed in the like Manner.—It must therefore be some Plea more forcible than mere Compassion that attaches you particularly to this Child.*

Alithea, who had foreseen what Answer her Husband would make, was all the Time he was speaking debating within herself, whether it would be best for her to evade or to confess the Truth of this Affair; and not being able to determine as yet, appeared no less confused and disordered than she would have done, if about to make an Acknowledgement for some great Offence.—At last, *A Plea there is indeed*, said she, *but*—here her Voice and Courage failed her, and she was utterly unable to [give] him the Satisfaction he had asked.

Dorimon was confounded beyond Measure, and not knowing what to think of a Behaviour so new, and which seemed to denote she laboured with some Secret of great Importance, he looked steadfastly on her for some Minutes, and perceiving that she changed Colour, and had her Eyes fixed on the Earth, grew quite impatient for the Certainty of what, as he has since confessed, he then began to conceive, cried out, *What Plea?— What Mystery?*

A Mystery, replied she, *which I had much rather you would guess at than oblige me to unravel.—Oh Dorimon!* continued she, after a Pause, *is there no Instinct in Nature that can inform you; my Affection for the Father makes his Offspring, of whomsoever born, dear to me? I cannot hate Melissa so much as I love Dorimon; and while I am performing the Offices of a Mother to this Child, forget the Share she has in him, to remember what I owe to him as yours.*

The Reader's own Imagination must here supply the Place of Description.—Impossible it is for any Words to give a just Idea of what a Husband, circumstanced like Dorimon, must feel!—To have his Fault thus palpably made known to her, whom he most desired should be ignorant of it;—to receive the highest Obligations, where he could have expected only Resentment;—and to hear the Detection of what he had done discovered to him by the injured Person, in such a manner as if herself, not he, had been the Criminal, so hurried his Thoughts, between Remorse, Astonishment, and Shame, as left him not the Power of making the least Reply to what she said.—He walked several Turns about the Room in a disordered Motion, endeavouring to recover a Presence of Mind, which seemed so necessary on this Occasion, but in vain; and at last, throwing himself into an easy Chair, just opposite to that in which his Wife was sitting, *Good God!* cried he, *am I awake!—Can it be possible there is such a Woman in the World!*

The sweet tempered Alithea could not see him in these Agitations without a Concern, which made her almost repent her having occasioned them.—She ran hastily to him, and throwing her Arms about his Neck, *My dear, dear Dorimon*, said she, *let it not trouble you that I am in Possession of a Secret which I neither sought after, nor, when in a manner forced upon me, ever divulged to any Person in the World.—Consider me as I am— your Wife—Part of yourself,—and you will then be assured you can be guilty of no Errors, which I shall not readily excuse, and carefully con-*

ceal.—*Judge of my Sincerity*, continued she, renewing her Embraces, *by my Behaviour, which you are sensible has not the least been changed by my Knowledge of this Affair.*

O Alithea, cried he, pressing her tenderly to his Bosom, *I am indeed sensible how little I have deserved such Proofs of your amazing Goodness;—my Soul overflows with Gratitude and Love.—Yet how can I attone for my past Crime?—By mentioning it no more*, interrupted she, *and to let me share in that Heart my Want of Charms denies me the Hope of filling wholly.*

To these endearing Words he answered only in broken Sentences, but such as more testified what she wished to find in him towards her than the most eloquent Speeches could have done.— She now was convinced that the Victory she had gained over him was perfect and sincere, and would have known a Transport without Alloy, but for the tender Pain it gave her to find so much Difficulty in perswading him to forgive himself.

He held her sitting on his Knee, with his Arms round her Waist, while she related to him the means by which she was made acquainted with his Crime; concealing no Part either of what she heard, the Steps she took after the Knowledge of her Misfortune, and the various Emotions which passed in her Soul, during the long Series of his Indifference to her. In all which he found something to admire, and the more he saw into the Greatness, as well as Sweetness of her Mind, the more his Love and Astonishment increased.

The first Proof he gave her, that she should have nothing for the future to apprehend on the Score of Melissa, was to write a Letter to that Lady; wherein he acquainted her, that, sensible of the Injury he had done the best of Wives and Women, he was determined to pursue no Pleasures in which she did not participate.—He represented to her the Shame and Folly of carrying on an Intrigue of the Nature theirs had been in the most pathetick Terms, and advised her to think of living so as to regain that Reputation in the World which, he was obliged to confess, he had contributed to make her lose;—assured her that the Resolution he had now made, of seeing her no more, was not to be shaken by any Arguments in her Power to make use of, therefore begged she would endeavour to follow his Example, and forget all that had passed between them.

This, he shewing to Alithea, gave her a new Opportunity of exerting her Good-Nature.—She made him write it over again, in order to soften some Expressions in it, which she would have it were more harsh than was becoming in him, to a Woman he had once loved; and perhaps would have rendered it at last too gentle for the Purpose it was intended, could she have prevailed on him to alter it according to the Dictates of her own compassionate and forgiving Soul. But he best knew the Temper of the Person he had to deal with, and would not bid her Adieu in such a Manner as should give her the least room to flatter herself it would not be his last.

Tho' he desired no Answer he received one, filled with the most virulent Reproaches on himself, and mingled with many contemptuous Reflections on his Wife.—The first he was unmoved at, but the other totally destroyed all the Remains of Regard and Consideration he had for her.—He tore the Letter into a thousand Pieces, and, to shew this injurious Lady the Contempt and Resentment with which he had treated what she said, gathered up the scattered Fragments, and sent them back to her under a sealed Cover, but without writing a Word.

After this he was entirely easy, Melissa made no Efforts to regain him, but contented herself with railing against him and the innocent Alithea wherever she went; but, most People knowing the Motive, her Malice had no other Effect than to make herself laughed at.—She soon, however, entered into a new Amour, and in the Noise that made, all Talk of her former Engagement was laid aside; while the happy Alithea enjoyed the Recompence of her Virtue in the continued Tenderness of a Husband, who never could have loved her half so well had he not loved elsewhere, because he never could have had an Opportunity of being so well acquainted with those Virtues in her, which were the Ground of his Affection.

The Compassion she had shewn for the Child of Melissa was not a temporary Start of Goodness,—she persisted in the most tender Care of him,—had him educated in the same manner with her own,—and to alleviate the Misfortune of his Birth, engaged Dorimon to set apart a considerable Sum of Money, in order to put him into a Business, which, when he grows of Years to undertake, it will, according to all human Probability, be his own Fault if he does not succeed in.

I have been the more tedious in this Narrative, because I think there is no Particular in the Conduct of the amiable Alithea that ought to be omitted, or may not serve to shew how much a perfect Good-Nature may enable us to sustain, and to forgive.

I would have no Husband, however, depend on this Example, and become a Dorimon in Expectation of finding an Alithea in his Wife.—It is putting the Love and Virtue of a Woman to too severe a Test, and the more he thinks her capable of forgiving the less ought he to offend.

From Volume I, Book VI, 356-83

Explanatory Notes

1 Kindness...vain: source unknown.

2 Capuchin: a garment consisting of a cloak and hood, in imitation of the dress of Capuchin friars: hence its name.

🎜 8 🎝

A Musick Master's Ingratitude

Celemena was the Daughter and sole Heiress of a Gentleman of a very large Estate, perfectly agreeable in her Person without being a Beauty; she had a good Capacity and an excellent Disposition.—Being such, it is not to be wonder'd at that her Parents were extremely tender of her, nor that they made her be instructed in all the Accomplishments befitting a Person of her Sex and Fortune.

But that to which she most apply'd herself was Musick and Singing; she would sit the whole Day, if not call'd from it, at her Harpsicord, practising those Lessons which had been given her in the Morning, and by degrees became so attach'd to it, that in Effect she regarded nothing else.—Her Governess often chid her for devoting herself so much to one thing, and reminded her, that tho' Musick was very agreeable, yet there were other Studies more worthy her Attention, and ought at least to have their Share.—This she seem'd sensible of, but could not be brought to lay aside her Books without Reluctance, and whatever she employ'd herself in, the last new Song ran always in her Head.—When the Hour in which her Master in this Science accustom'd to visit her approach'd, she was continually looking on her Watch, and if he came not at the Moment she expected, discovered an Impatience which was never seen in her on any other Score.

This, with some Glances she was ignorant of herself, yet observ'd by the Governess, made that careful Creature tremble, lest her young Charge should be no less pleas'd with the Person of her Master than with his Art.—She kept those Suspicions however for some time to herself, but imagining that every Day gave her fresh Reasons to believe they had not deceiv'd her, she thought it her Duty to acquaint the Mother of Celemena with them.

The old Lady imparted what she had heard to her Husband, and on reasoning on the Subject, when they considered their Daughter's Youth, her excessive Fondness for Musick, and the handsome Person of the Man in question, they began to fear the Governess had not been mistaken.

After debating what was best to be done in so vexatious an Affair, it seem'd most proper to them both, to discharge Mr. Quaver, for so I shall call him, from his Attendance, without giving any other Reason for it than that they thought Celemena had made sufficient Progress, and had no occasion for further Instructions.

The putting this Resolution into Execution convinced them, that what they fear'd was too sure a Truth.—The Melancholly which Celemena fell into on the Loss of this Master, shewed not only that she loved, but also loved him to an uncommon Degree.—All that could be done for her Amusement or Diversion, had not the least Effect, and the Disorders of her Mind had so great an Influence over her Body, that she fell in a short Time into a violent Fever.—Her Life for some Days was despair'd of, but her Youth, Strength, and Constitution, joined with the Skill of the Physicians, at length repell'd that Enemy to Nature.—The Fever left her, but the Cause still remaining, threw her into another Distemper, which threaten'd no less fatal, tho' less sudden Consequences.—In fine, she had all the Symptoms of a Consumption, and those who had the Care of her, both in her late and present Illness, easily perceiving that she labour'd under some inward Grief, told her Parents, that without that were remov'd, it would be in vain for thcm to hope they should preserve their Daughter.

A second Consultation was held on this afflicting News, between the Father, Mother, and Governess of the young Lady; the Result of which was, that the latter should, by all the Stratagems she could invent, draw her into a Confession of the Truth.—They flatter'd themselves, that if the Secret was once reveal'd, the Arguments they might make use of to her would enable her to overcome a Passion so unworthy of her; but if all fail'd, they resolved rather to gratify it than see her perish in the hopeless Flame.

It was no difficult Matter for a Person, who by her Age doubtless had some time or other in her Life experienc'd the Passion she was about to speak of, to talk of it in such a Manner as should discover the Progress of it in another. Celemena betray'd herself without knowing she did so; and when she found her Secret was reveal'd, scrupled not to confess, that she took a strange Liking of Mr. Quaver's Person and Conversation from the first Time he was introduced to her;—that the more she saw him, the more her Inclination increased, till it entirely engrossed her whole Heart; and that by what she had endured since she had been deprived of seeing him, she was very well convinced she could not live without him; but added, that she believed he was ignorant of the Love she bore him. *At least*, says she, *I hope he is; for I should dye with Shame, if I thought he suspected me guilty of a Weakness which I cannot forgive in myself.*

The Governess comforted her the best she could, and perceiving that the Hurry of Spirits this Discourse had put her in made her ready to faint away, exceeded her Commission so far as to give her Hopes that if she really loved to that Excess she appear'd to do, and thought him worthy of being her Husband, her Parents might be brought to consent.

This seemed too great a Happiness for the enamour'd Maid to give much Credit to; yet the Transport she was in at the bare mention of it, and the Agonies she fell into, as Reason abated the pleasing Idea, assured the Person who was Witness of them, that there was no other Means of saving her Life than such a Confirmation.

She went directly from her to the old Lady's Apartment, and related to her the whole of what had pass'd between them.—How great was her Affliction any one may guess. But flattering herself that Shame might work some Effect on her, she bid the Governess let her know she had acquainted both her and her Father with the Secret, *and you may tell her,* added she, *that you have endeavour'd to prevail on us to comply with her Inclinations; but that the Surprize and Grief we are in at hearing she had so much demean'd herself, as to entertain a Thought of such a Fellow, made us give no Answer to what you said.*

The Governess went immediately about making this Essay, tho' certain in her Mind of the little Success it would have.—The Passion Celemena was inspired with, was indeed too strong to be overcome this way; and tho' dutiful, and wanting in none of those Respects owing from Children to their Parents, not all the Sorrows she occasioned them in this Point, had Power to turn the Current of her Affections.

Finding her Mother came not into her Chamber the next Day as usual, she doubted not but her Indignation against her Passion was at least equal to the Grief for her Condition; and despairing of any Effect of her Governess's Promises, her Heart, over-press'd beneath a Weight of Anguish, refused its accustomed Motion, and she fell into Faintings, out of which she was not without great Difficulty recover'd.

Her Mother distracted at the Danger of so darling a Child, cry'd out to her, that her Inclinations should no longer be opposed;— that since Quaver was so necessary to her Life, he should immediately be made acquainted with his good Fortune, and that the Moment of her Recovery should join their Hands.

The Father, no less anxious, made the same Promise, which Celemena still doubting the Performance of, they both confirmed with the most solemn Oath.

As it could not be supposed but that the Musician would receive an Offer of this Nature with an Excess of Humility and Joy, he was sent for, and told by the Parents of Celemena, that as notwithstanding the Disparity between them the young Lady had thought him worthy, they too dearly prized her to thwart her Inclinations, and would bestow her on him in case he had no previous Engagement.

The Astonishment he was in at the Beginning of this Discourse was very visible in his Countenance, but being Master of a good Share of Cunning it abated, and he not only recover'd himself entirely before they had finish'd what they had to say, but also resolved what Answer he should make.

He had heard the young Lady had been dangerously ill some Time, and that she still kept her Bed, and so sudden and unexpected a Proposal made to him by her Parents left no room to doubt the Motive of it; so without any Consideration of what he owed either to her Love, or this Condescension in them, he meditated only how to make the best Bargain he could for his pretty Person, which he now thought he could not set too high a Value on.

After having assured them that he was under no Engagement, and slightly thanking them for the Honour they did him in making choice of him for a Son in Law, he begg'd leave to know what Portion they intended to give their Daughter.

Such a Question from a Man, whom they expected would have rather thrown himself at their Feet all in Extacy and Transport, might very well astonish them.—They look'd one upon another for some Minutes without being able to reply; but the Father first regaining presence of Mind,—*Mr. Quaver*, said he, *since I am willing to give my Daughter to you, there is little room for you to suppose I should bestow a Beggar on you; but since you seem to doubt it, I will put Five Thousand Pounds into your Hands for the Present, and according as I find you behave will add to it.*

Five Thousand Pounds! cry'd the Musician: *Sir, I live very well as I am on my Business, and will not sell my Liberty for twice the Sum.*

Nothing could have been a greater Proof of the Consideration this tender Father had of his Child, than that he did not resent this Arrogance in the Object of her Affection, by ordering his Footmen to turn him out of Doors; but his Fears for her over-rul'd all he owed to himself, and he only reply'd, *Well, Mr. Quaver, I will think of your Demand, and if you call Tomorrow will acquaint you with the Result.*

'Twould be needless to repeat the Shock such a Behaviour must be to Persons of their Rank and Figure in the World; or how great an Aggravation it was to their Affliction, that Celemena should have bestowed her Heart on a Man whose Mind was as sordid as his Birth was mean.—They were fearful of acquainting her with the little Regard he seem'd to have for her, but on her being extremely urgent to know what had pass'd at an Interview her Peace was so deeply interested in, they at last ventured to repeat not only the Demand that Quaver had made, but also describ'd the insolent Manner in which he spoke and look'd; but withall assured her, that for her Sake they would both forgive and comply with it.

Celemena listen'd attentively to the Narrative, but seem'd much less troubled than their Apprehensions had suggested.—She fainted not, she even wept not, but after a little Pause thank'd her Father for the unexampled Tenderness he express'd for her, and beseech'd him, that since he was so good to grant every thing desir'd by a Man, who, she confess'd, was worthy of little either from him or herself, that she might be placed the next Day in some Room, where she might hear, unseen by him, how he received the Condescension would be made him.

This Request was easily granted, and when they were told he was below, a Servant was order'd to conduct him into a Room divided only by a thin Wainscot from Celemena's Chamber. She had quitted her Bed that Day, which for a long Time she had not been able to do, and sat with her Governess as close as she could to the Partition, so that she could hear all that pass'd with the same Ease as if she had been in the Room with them.

Well, Mr. Quaver, said the old Gentleman, *I think you told me Yesterday that the Price at which you set your Liberty was Ten Thousand Pounds.—It is certainly a great Sum for a Person of your Vocation, who have no other Jointure to make my Daughter than a few Music Books; but as she has set her Heart upon you, I will not refuse you, and the Money shall be paid on the Day of Marriage.*

Alass, Sir, reply'd the other, *I am sorry I was so unhappy to be mistaken; I told you that I would not marry for twice the Sum you offer'd at first, which you may remember was Five Thousand Pounds;—and I think you cannot give me less than fifteen Thousand, and five Thousand more at the Birth of the first Child; besides, I expect you should settle your whole Estate on me after your Decease, that your Daughter, who I know is Heiress, may not assume too much, as many Wives do, when they have the Power of receiving Rents lodg'd in their own Hands.*

At these Words the Father was oblig'd to summon all his Moderation, yet could not restrain himself from crying out, *Heavens! What have I done to merit a Punishment so severe?—Unhappy Celemena, to love where there is nothing but what ought to create Contempt!*

Whatever Opinion you may have of me, Sir, returned Quaver with a most audacious Air, *I know myself, and shall not abate an Ace of my Demand. If you think fit to comply with it I will make a good Husband to your Daughter;—If not, I am your humble Servant.—She must die.*

Celemena no sooner heard this, than she sent her Governess to beg her Father to come into her Chamber before he made any farther Reply to what was said; and on his entering threw herself at his Feet, and embracing his Knees with a Vehemence which surpiz'd him,—*O Sir*, said she, *by all the Love and Tenderness you have ever used me with, by this last, the greatest Proof sure that ever Child receiv'd, I conjure you, suffer not yourself nor me to be a Moment longer affronted and insulted by that unworthy Fellow, whom I almost hate myself for ever having had a favourable Thought on:—Spurn him, I beseech you, from your Presence;—let him seek a Wife more befitting him than Celemena, who now hates and scorns him.*

But are you certain, my Dear, said this fond Father, *that you can persist in these Sentiments?*

Forever, Sir, answered she, *and your Commands to unite me to such a Wretch would now render me more miserable, than two Days past your Refusal would have done.*

It is not to be doubted but that the old Gentleman was transported at this unlook'd for Change, and returning to Quaver, whom he found looking in the Glass, and humming over a Tune of his own composing, he told him, *That the Farce was entirely over, Celemena had only a Mind to divert herself with his Vanity, which having done, he might go about his Business, for there was no Danger of her dying, unless it were with laughter at his so easily believing that to be serious which was only a Jest.*

The Musician, so lately blown up with Self-Conceit, was now quite crush'd at once; and as those too soon elated with the Appearance of any prosperous Event are, with the same Ease dejected with the Reverse, he look'd like one transfix'd with Thunder; but when he was about to say something in a stammering Voice, by way of Reply,—the old Gentleman cut him short, by telling him in the most contemptuous Manner, *That as neither himself nor his Daughter had any Disposition to continue the Frolick, he had no more Business there, but might go Home and dream of a fine Lady with fifteen thousand Pounds, and a great Estate.*

To prove how much he was in earnest, he rang his Bell, and ordered his Servants to shew him out; on which he muttered somewhat between his Teeth, and went away justly mortified, and ready to hang himself for what he had lost by his egregious Folly.

Celemena, perfectly cured of her Passion, and no otherwise troubled than ashamed of having ever entertained one for a Person such as he had now proved himself, soon resumed her former Health and Vivacity; and was some time after married to a Person of Condition, who knew how to esteem her as he ought.

From Volume II, Book VII, 55-67

₪₪ 9 ₪₪

A Letter from Distrario concerning the State of the Theatre

Correspondents beginning to thicken upon us, and every one being desirous of somewhat by way of Comment or Reply, due Order must be observed as to inserting and answering the Letters as they come to Hand; we therefore hope those of a later Date will not take it ill that we give the first Place to that of Distrario, as having been first received.

To the FEMALE SPECTATOR.

MADAM,

The Justice you have done in recommending Dramatick Performances, before any other of the present more encourag'd Diversions of the Town, renders your Monthly Essays a proper Vehicle to convey the Groans of the Stage to the Ears of the Publick; nor can those Gentlemen who unhappily have devoted themselves to the Muses, find any Means of making their Complaint with so much probability of Success, as through your nervous and pathetick Strains.

Be not startled, I beseech you, at the Sight of this long Epistle, nor imagine it is my Intention to trouble you with any Animadversion on the late or present Contests between the Patentees and Players; the Town is already sufficiently pester'd with Cases and Replies, and I am afraid these idle Quarrels among themselves will rather contribute to bring Acting in general into Contempt, than be of any Service to the Persons concern'd in them.

No, Madam, my Aim is to obviate the more real Misfortunes of the Theatres, and shew how the Drama is wounded through the Sides of those by whom alone it can exist with any Honour or Reputation.

There are two Reasons commonly assign'd why the Nobility and better Sort of People have of late Years very much withdrawn that Encouragement they used to vouchsafe to the Stage.—The first is, that the Parts in which Wilkes, Booth, Cibber senior, Oldfield, Porter, and some others appear'd in with great Propriety, are but ill supplied by their Successors; but I cannot look on this as any real Objection, because it would be both cruel and unjust: Actors cannot always retain the same Faculties any more than other People, much less can they be immortal. Besides, there are at this Time several whose Merit ought not be be absorbed in the Regard we pay to the Memory of those who went before them. And if even they are less excellent, I do not perceive but [that] the Audiences are satisfied with their Endeavours to please us, by imitating them as far as it lies in their Power.—The second, were it founded on Truth, would be of Weight indeed, and that is, that there are now no Gentlemen of any Abilities that will write for the Stage, and that the Town is obliged to be content with seeing the same Things over and over again for several Seasons together, without any one new Subject of Entertainment being exhibited. The latter Part of this Objection is founded on too known a Fact not to give some Credit to the former, especially when propagated by those whose Interest one would imagine it was to inculcate a contrary Opinion; but this it is I take upon me to confute, by displaying those latent Motives which have occasioned a Report so injurious to the present Age, that I wonder no-body has yet taken the Pains to examine into it.

First, let us ask the Question whether there are, or are not, any surviving Genius's truly qualified to write for the Stage?—I believe no-body will answer in the Negative, because nothing could be more easy than to prove the contrary.—This being granted, let us ask farther, whence it comes to pass that every one should now despise an Avocation which was once attended with considerable Profit, and so much Reputation, that some of our greatest Men have valued themselves more on their Talents this way, than on their Coronets.—Strange it seems, that the Name of a Dramatick Poet should at present be so contemptible, that no Person of real Abilities will chuse to be distinguished by it!

Yet it is easily accounted for, if the tedious Delays, the shocking Rebuffs, the numberless Difficulties an Author is almost sure to meet with in his Attempt to introduce any new Thing on the Stage, were laid open and consider'd as they ought.

A Person of Condition would make but an odd Figure, if, after having taken Pains to oblige the Town, and do Honour to the Stage, he should be made to dance Attendance at the Levee of an imperious Patentee for Days, Weeks, nay Months together, and receive no other Answers than that *he had not had Time to look over his Play;—that he had mislaid it;*—or perhaps affects to forget he ever saw it.—At last the Actors must be consulted, and it often happens that those among them who are least capable of judging, are called into the Cabinet Council.—If any one of these happens to dislike the Character he imagines will be allotted for him, then the whole Piece is condemned; and at the Conclusion of the Season, or it is possible at that of two or three succeeding ones, the Author has it return'd, and is told, *It is not Theatrical enough,* a Term invented by this august Assembly, to conceal their Inability of pointing out any real Faults, and the Meaning of which can neither be defined by themselves nor any body else.

But you will say, *Why should they behave in this manner?—Is it not the Interest of both Manager and Actors to receive a good Play, which will be certain of putting Money in the Pocket of the one, and securing the Payment of the Salaries of the other.*

To which I answer, That it is doubtless their true Interest; but Avarice and Indolence render many People blind to what is so.— The Manager flatters himself, that if the Town cannot have new Plays they will come to old ones, and he shall thereby save the Profits of the third Nights;[1] and the Actors (those I mean of them who are at what they call the Top of the Business, for the others have no Influence) having their Salaries fixed, think they have no Occasion to take the Trouble of studying new Parts, since they know they must be paid equally the same without it.

These, Madam, are the false ill-judg'd Maxims by which both Patentee and Company are swayed to reject the most excellent Pieces submitted to their Censure, and are the Motives which deter, as far as it relates to them, an Author from offering any thing to the Stage.

Yet while I condemn the little Inclination those Gentlemen for the most Part testify to oblige the Town, or give Encouragement to the Poets, I must do them Justice to say that it has not been always owing to them that so many improving and delightful Entertainments have been deprived of seeing the Light. There is another more terrifick Cloud from a superior Quarter hangs over the Author's Hopes, and threatens the Destruction of his most sanguine Expectations.

I believe neither yourself, nor any of your Readers will be at a Loss to understand I mean the Licence-Office,[2] at the Head of which a great Person is placed who cannot be supposed to have Leisure to inspect every one, nor indeed any of the Pieces brought before him; and there is much more than a bare Possibility that his Deputies may either through Weakness or Partiality err in their Judgment, and give an unfair Report; nay, some go so far as to imagine they are under a secret Compact with the Managers of both Houses to reject indiscriminately every Thing that comes, except recommended by the higher Powers; but this I am far from being able to lay to their Charge, nor do indeed think either the one or the other capable of entring into any such Combination.

But to what, unless one of the foregoing Reasons, can we impute forbidding the Tragedies of *Edward and Eleonora*,[3] *Gustavus Vasa*,[4] and some other excellent Performances, founded on the most interesting Parts of History, supported by various Turns and surprizing Incidents, and illustrated with all the Strength and Beauty of Language, especially the former, which for every thing that can render a Piece improving and entertaining, finds itself not excelled (I had almost said equall'd) by any Thing either of the antient or modern Writers.—Yet it was this admirable Play, when just ready to make its Appearance, forbad to be acted, the longing Expectations of the Publick were disappointed, and we had been totally deprived of so elegant an Entertainment, did not, thank Heaven, the Liberty of the Press still continue in some measure with us.

Tho' stript of all the Ornaments of Dress and Action, it gives in the Reading a lasting and undeniable Proof that it is neither Want of Abilities, or an Indolence in exerting those Abilities, but Permission to exhibit them in a proper manner, that the Stage at present affords so little Matter of Attraction.

But I will now come to the Point which chiefly induced me to trouble the *Female Spectator* with this Letter; and having enumerated the many Hardships Authors in general go through in attempting to get their Plays acted, I will proceed as briefly as the Circumstance will admit, to lay before you those which myself in particular have labour'd under.

I must inform you, Madam, that I have wrote several Things which have not only been well received by the Publick, but have also been favoured with the Approbation of some of our best Judges; and that it was no less owing to their Encouragement than my own Ambition, that I resolv'd to try the Force of my Genius in the Dramatick Way, which, according to one of the greatest of our English Poets,

Is a bold Pretence
To Learning, Breeding, Wit and Eloquence.[5]

I ventured at it, notwithstanding; and, undeter'd by Example, launch'd into that Sea, on whose Rocks and Quicksands so many much more skilful Pilots than myself had been wrecked before my Eyes.

To confess the Truth, I was greatly embolden'd by the Favour and Friendship of a Person of Condition, a Courtier, and who I imagin'd had Interest enough both with the Licenser and Players to introduce whatever he should recommend. But to return:—

As my Genius inclin'd me chiefly to the Sublime, my first Attempt was Tragedy.—The Part of History I made Choice on, was the famous Combat between Edward, surnamed Ironside, King of England, and the great Canute of Denmark.—There appear'd to me so true a Magnanimity and paternal Affection for his People in that heroick Prince, when, to save the Effusion of their Blood, he set all his own, as well as Kingdom at Stake, and fought Hand to Hand with one who had no Equal but himself in Strength and Courage, while both Armies stood admiring Spectators only of his wondrous Valour, that I thought a more proper Subject could not have employed my Pen.—I am not apt to be vain of my own Performances, but the Friend abovemention'd assured me I had done my Part as a Poet; but withal said, he was sorry I had not pitched upon some other Story;—that this would never do; that it would be look'd upon as too romantick;—that Customs were entirely chang'd since the Days of Ironside;—that Kings were now too sacred to hazard their Persons in that manner; and concluded with advising me not to expose it, as it would never pass the Office, and might render me obnoxious.

This was a very great Mortification to me, however I submitted to his Judgment, and chang'd the Scene to the last Part of that glorious Monarch's Life, where himself and Kingdom were betrayed and given up to Ruin, by the Treachery and Avarice of his first Minister and Favourite, Edrick Duke of Mercia; but alas! my Patron disapproved of this more than the former, and told me, *A first Minister*, especially an ill one, ought never to be represented on the Stage; because seditious People might take upon them to draw Parallels, thereby lessening the Reverence due to those in Power.

I then took the Liberty of intreating he would recommend some Part of History for me to write upon; but he told me, as to that, he had not Leisure to think of such Things; all he could do was to advise me either to find out or invent some agreeable Fable, where no King or Prime Minister of any sort had any Business to be introduced; and above all Things not to lay the Scene in any of the independant Common-Wealths, *because*, said he, *it may naturally draw you into some Expressions that may favour of Republicanism.*

Some Months I pass'd in considering what he had said, and searching History in order to find out, if possible, some Event, the Representation of which might be liable to none of these Objections; but the Thing was in itself an utter Impossibility, and all my Endeavours served only to convince me it was so.

My Ambition of acquiring the Name of a Dramatick Author not being quelled by the Disappointments I receiv'd, still flatter'd me with better Success in the Comick Vein.—A Whim, which I thought would be entertaining enough, came into my Head, and I threw it immediately into Scenes, which I afterwards divided into five Acts, and gave the Piece the Title of *The Blunderers,* from two odd Fellows I had introduced, who were continually labouring to do and undo, and made whatever was bad still worse.

But, good Madam *Spectator,* how shall I describe the Passion my Friend was in at seeing this Title! *If I did not know,* said he, *that you were an honest Man, I should take you for the most arrant Rascal in the World:—What is it you mean by calling your Comedy* The Blunderers? *Are you insensible that the* Jacobites, *and Enemies to the Government, aspers'd the late Ministry with the Name of* Blunderers, *and are they not beginning to load the present with the same odious Appellation?—I am surpriz'd a Poet can have so thick a Head.*

Tho' what he accused me of had never before come in my Thoughts, I was now sensible I had committed an Error, and having confessed as much, told him, That the Title need be no Objection to the Play itself, which might with the same Propriety be called *The Bubbles,* there being several Characters in it which might well deserve that Name.

This, instead of appeasing, as I expected it would have done, his Rage, more enflam'd it.—*How,* cried he, *then I perceive you are aiming at Popularity:—You cannot be so ignorant as not to know, by* The Bubbles *will be understood the common People:—I will have no more to say to you or your Productions.*

He left me in speaking these Words, nor could I prevail on him to renew our former Familiarity for a long Time; and I was so much disquieted at the Thoughts of having so foolishly forfeited the

Interest I before had with him, that I had no Capacity for writing any thing.—At length, however, he was reconcil'd; I recover'd his Esteem, and with it my Inclination for the Drama, but told him, That the Mistakes I had been guilty of had determin'd me not to go upon my own Bottom till I had more Experience, but would build on the Plan of some old Author, whose Fable could no way be brought into Comparison with the present Transactions.

This he seeming to approve of, I mention'd a Comedy wrote near a Century and a half ago, by one Drawbridge Court Belchier, a Gentleman it seems much applauded for his poetic Works in the Age he lived: The Title of it is, *Hans Beer Pot*, or *the Invisible Comedy of see me and see me not*; which I had no sooner repeated than he cried out,—*You must not think of it;—it will be taken for a Reflection on the Dutch, who, you know, tho' they have of late played a little the Will o' the Wisp with us, are, notwithstanding, our good Friends and Allies, and must not be affronted.*

I knock'd under, in token of yielding myself in the wrong; and having read over a great many old Comedies in order to find one for my Purpose, I asked what he thought of a Play of Middleton's, called, *A Mad World my Masters.*—On which he shook his Head and answer'd, *That may affect some Princes of Germany;—I would not have you meddle with it.*

I then told him, that *the Knight of the burning Pestle*, wrote by Beaumont and Fletcher, could not give Offence to any Party. *You are deceived*, said he, *who knows but it may with some ignorant People bring the noblest Orders of Knighthood into Contempt.*

Well then, resumed I, *the Isle of Gulls, wrote by Mr. Day in the Reign of our Elizabeth of immortal Memory, may surely be moderniz'd, without incurring the Censure of any Party.*

Fye, fye, replied he peevishly, *you are as ill a Judge of other Men's Productions as of your own:—Such a Play would be look'd upon as a most scandalous Libel.*

Quite impatient to hit on something out of the Reach of Cavil, I proposed the Revival of *Breneralt*, or *the Discontented Colonel*, a Play of Sir John Suckling's; but that it seems border'd too near on some late military Disgusts.—*The Glass of Government*, by Gascoigne, might also be construed into an arrogant Attempt to point out Defects which ought to be concealed.—*The Supposes*, by the same Author, might affront a certain great Man who is thought to build all his Schemes on Supposition. By *the Hog has lost his Pearl*, tho' wrote by Taylor in the Year 1611, I should infallibly be understood to insinuate a present Loss of British Liberty.—Mr. Broom's Play of the *Court Beggar* would be a glaring Insult on some of the chief Nobility round Whitehall, and some other Places;—and the *Court Secret*, by Shirley, was a Thing too delicate to be pry'd into.—*The Doubtful Heir*, by the same Gentleman, and *the Fall of Tarquin* by Hunt, were equally rejected by this State Critic, tho' without explaining his Reasons for doing so on these two last.

Judge, Madam, how much I was vexed and confounded at hearing Inuendoes, which one could not have imagin'd should ever enter into the Heart of Man; but as I was resolv'd to try this pretended Friend to the utmost, I told him, that since it was so impossible a Thing either to write a new Tragedy or Comedy, or to revive what had been wrote so many Ages past without giving Offence, I would content myself with modernizing an Interlude of more than two hundred Years old, compos'd by John Heywood, and intitled *The four P's*. On this he paused a little, but at last reply'd gravely, *That he could by no Means encourage me in any such Attempt; for*, said he, *by the* four P's *may be implied Prince, Power, Parliament and Pension,— or perhaps, People, Poverty, Prison, and Petition:— No Sir, no*, continued he, *avoid all such seditious Allegories I beseech you, or we must be no longer acquainted.*

This put me beyond all Patience, and I could not forbear answering with some Warmth, that I found he endeavour'd to pick Meanings where they were never intended. *If the four P's*, said I, *contain any Allegory, why must it needs be a seditious one?*—*Why may they not as well be understood to mean Penitence, Pardon, Peace, and Plenty;—or if that should seem a little strain'd, in the present Age, may it not with greater Propriety be turned on the coquet Part of the fair Sex, and stand for Proud, Pretty, Prating, and Playful?*

This Argument, tho' certainly reasonable, had no manner of Weight with him, any more than some others I made use of for the same Purpose; and only serv'd to convince myself that there was no Possibility of writing any thing but what might be liable to Censure from those who made it their Business to find Matter for it.

Thus, Madam, I have pointed out the Obstacles which lye in the Way of a Dramatic Author, and you will easily conceive the little Probability there is that a Person of Fortune will descend to that servile Dependance and Sollicitation now requir'd for the Admission of his Play; and a Poet, whose sole Support is his Muse, is deterred from risquing on so precarious a Hope that Time, which he is sure to be largely paid for, if employed in the Service of some Persons, not altogether convenient to name.

Without some better Regulation therefore on the Part of the Theatres, and some Abatement of the present Severity on that of the Licenser, the Town must despair of seeing any new Thing exhibited, the Drama be entirely neglected, and the Stage in a short Time become a Desart.

Nothing can be more worthy the Pen of a *Female Spectator* than to set this Affair in a proper Light;—that good Nature you have so amiably described, requires it of you in behalf of distress'd Authors:—Justice demands you should stand up in the Defence of an Institution calculated for public Service;—and Reason will, I doubt not, engage you to exert yourself on so laudable an Occasion.

        I am, MADAM,

Oct.21,   Very much your Admirer and
1744.   Most obedient humble Servant,
               DISTRARIO.

We were pretty much divided in our Opinions on the first Perusal of this Letter, but at last agreed, that tho' the Complaints contained in it might be, and it is highly probable are perfectly just, yet Distrario may perhaps have taken the Latitude allowed to Poets, and represented Things somewhat higher than the Life.—We know not how to think that either of the Patentees, who are both of them Gentlemen of Families, and doubtless have had an Education conformable to their Birth, should be able to bring themselves to treat, even the least meritorious of those who endeavour to serve them and oblige the Town, with that Haughtiness and Contempt he seems to accuse them of. Good Manners is a Debt we owe to ourselves as well as to others, and whoever neglects to pay it forfeits all the Pretensions he might otherwise have both to the Love and Respect of the World. A civil Refusal takes off the Asperity of the Disappointment, and is given with the same Ease as a more rough and poignant one. Sure therefore those who are at the Head of an eternal Scene of Politeness, cannot so far vary from what they have continually before their Eyes. But as this is a Punctilio which regards only the Persons of the Poets, who are very well able to return in kind any slights they may imagine put upon them, and is of much less Consequence to the Public than those their Productions meet with, it were to be wish'd that some of the great World would vouchsafe to interest themselves in this Affair, and not leave it at the Option of those who live by the Good Humour of the Town, to deprive the Town of any Entertainment

94 C 12

THE

Female Spectator.

VOL. I.

Ill Customs, by Degrees, to Habits rise,
Ill Habits soon become exalted Vice.
DRYDEN.

LONDON:

Printed and published by T. GARDNER, at
Cowley's Head, opposite St. *Clement's* Church,
in the *Strand,* MDCCXLV.

A, a Sacrifice to Priapus. B, a pair of Lecheromoders shewing ye Company. Introduction as they appear'd to 'em. Invented for the use of Kings & Gentlemen Gc. by ye Ingenious Mr. Ac———r. price one shilling.

Masquerade Ticket

The Inside View of the Rotunda in Ranelagh Gardens *Vüe de la Compagnie a Déjeuner dans la Rotonde au*
with the Company at Breakfast. *Milieux des Jardins de Ranelagh.*

Published according to Act of Parliament 1751.

27

A general Prospect of Vaux Hall Gardens, Shewing at one view the disposition of the whole Gardens.

Vüe Détaillée des Jardins de Vaux Hall.

Printed for John Bowles, at the Black Horse in Cornhill.

it has a Right to expect from them.

As therefore there is an Office to forbid the Exhibition of such new Plays as by it are judg'd to have any thing in them offensive or indecent, it would not, methinks, be unbecoming the Wisdom of the Legislature to erect one for the commanding and enforcing such to be acted as on Perusal are found proper to entertain a polite and virtuous Audience.

Such an Office, under the Direction of Gentlemen qualified to judge of Dramatic Performances, would take away all Occasion of Complaint from the Poets, and be a Motive to induce many Gentlemen to write for the Stage, who, if it be as Distrario says, are now deterred from it.

Besides, to prevent the Shock an Author feels in having his Piece rejected, as well as all Jealousies of Partiality in the Affair, every one might send his Play without ever being known from what Hand it came, till it had been approved and was ordered to be acted.

'Tis certain, that according to the Opinion we have of the Man, we are greatly prejudic'd in Favour or Dislike of his Work; yet this is in truth a Piece of Injustice which we ought not to indulge ourselves in.—It is possible to excel in one kind of Writing, yet be very bad in another.—Few there are, if any, whose Talents are universal.—Mr. Pope, whose poetical Works will always be read with an equal Share of Pleasure and Admiration, had, notwithstanding, no Genius to Dramatic Writing; and Mr. Rymer, that awful Critic on the Productions of his Contemporaries, that great Pretender to a Reformation of the Stage, by attempting to give a Proof what Plays ought to be, has only shewn how little he was qualified to write one. This, I believe, will be allowed by every one who has read his *Edgar*,[6] a Piece which, after all his long Labour, can but at best be called correctly dull, since the two chief Beauties of Tragedy, Pity and Surprize, are entirely wanting in it. Yet doubtless the Town were in high Expectations of something wonderful from a Pen which had been so severe on the Performances of others.

I therefore cannot help smiling within myself, when on the first Talk of a new Play being in Rehearsal, the Name of the Author is presently enquir'd into, and a strict Scrutiny made into the Merit of his former Works; and if he has wrote any thing, tho' never so foreign to the Stage, that has had the good Fortune to succeed, People cry out,—*Oh, if it is his, it must be good!* and following this Conclusion, run [to] the first Night to give an Applause to that which perhaps, after they have seen and well considered, they are ashamed of having ever countenanc'd.

Nor am I less concern'd, and even shock'd, when I hear with what Contempt the Performance of a young Author, who is in a manner but clambering up the Hill of Fame, is treated by some who speak of it;—how they throw aside his Tickets, and cry,—*What obscure Fellow is this?— What Stuff does he invite us to?*—and either not go to his Play at all, or go with a Prepossession which will not suffer them to give it a fair Hearing.

This is a Piece of Cruelty in some who would be thought good Judges, yet are entirely governed by Prejudice; and I have known has been practised long before those new Hardships which Distrario complains of were ever heard of.

Such an Office, therefore, as I have mentioned, where Plays should be candidly examined, without any Regard to the Merits of their Authors in other Respects, or even knowing who they were, would remedy all these Inconveniences to the Poets, and also be a Means of obliging the Town with three or four at least new Pieces every Season at each Theatre.

As to the Power of forbidding Plays to be acted, now lodg'd in the Licenser, it must be granted, that in an Age so dissolute as this, there ought to be some Restraint on the Latitude Poets might otherwise take, and some whom I could name have taken, in Expectation of crowded Audiences of the looser Part of both Sexes; but then methinks this Restriction should have its Bounds.—Whatever is offensive to the Majesty of Heaven, or of its Viceregents on Earth, would be indeed very unfit Subjects to be exhibited on a Stage; but to reject a valuable Play for the sake of such strain'd Inuendoes as the Friend of Distrario suggested, seems to overthrow that decent Liberty which in all Ages, and in all free Nations, has ever been allowed.

The Stage by its Institution is the School of Virtue, and the Scourge of Vice; and when either of these noble Purposes is defeated, it is no wonder that Persons of true Sense and Honour chuse to absent themselves, and oblige their Families to do so.

From Volume II, Book VIII, 69-89

Explanatory Notes

1 third Nights: by custom, the receipts from the third night of a new play, after deduction of expenses, went to the author, who often got no other payment from the theatre.

2 Licence-Office: the Licensing Act of 1737 required all theatres either to hold a royal patent or receive a special licence form the Lord Chamberlain, and all new plays had to be submitted to the Chamberlain's Office two weeks in advance of performance, so that the text could be censored as thought necessary. Theatrical performances were thus regulated until 1968.

3 *Edward and Eleonora*, a play by James Thomson (1700-48), poet and dramatist. Published in 1739, it was not performed.

4 *Gustavus Vasa*, a tragedy by Henry Brooke (1703-83), was printed in 1739, and was actually in rehearsal when it became the first play to be banned under the Licensing Act of 1737 (the two main characters apparently bore too great a similarity to King George II and Sir Robert Walpole).

5 *Is Bold Pretence...Eloquence.*: not identified.

6 *Edgar*: an unsuccessful tragedy by Thomas Rymer (1641-1713), the critic and historiographer, who gained some notoriety for attacking Shakespeare in *A Short View of Tragedy* (1693).

🕮 10 🕮

A Letter On the Immoderate Use of Tea

To the FEMALE SPECTATOR.

MADAM,

As I look upon you to be a Person who knows the World perfectly well, and has the Happiness of your own Sex very much at Heart, I wonder you have never yet thought fit to throw out some Admonitions concerning the immoderate Use of Tea; which however innocent it may seem to those that practise it, is a kind of Debauchery no less expensive, and perhaps even more pernicious in its Consequences, than those which the Men, who are not professed Rakes, are generally accused of.

This, at first Sight, may be looked upon as too bold an Assertion, but, on a nearer Examination, I am perswaded will be found no more than reasonable, and will undertake to prove that the Tea-Table, as manag'd in some Families, costs more to support than would maintain two Children at Nurse.—Yet is this by much the least Part of the Evil;—it is the utter Destruction of all Oeconomy,—the Bane of good Housewifry,—and the Source of Idleness, by engrossing those Hours which ought to be employed in an honest and prudent Endeavour to add to, or preserve what Fortune, or former Industry has bestowed.—Were the Folly of wasting Time and Money in this manner confined only to the Great, who have enough of both to spare, it would not so much call for public Reproof; but all Degrees of Women are infested with it, and a Wife now looks upon her Tea-Chest, Table, and its Implements, to be as much her Right by Marriage as her Wedding Ring.

Tho' you cannot, Madam, be insensible that the trading Part of the Nation must suffer greatly on this score, especially those who keep

Shops, I beg you will give me Leave to mention some few Particulars of the Hardships we Husbands of that Class are obliged to bear.

The first Thing the too genteel Wife does after opening her Eyes in the Morning, is to ring the Bell for her Maid, and ask if the Tea-Kettle boils.—If any Accident has happened to delay this important Affair, the House is sure to eccho with Reproaches; but if there is no Disappointment in the Case, the Petticoats and Bed-Gown are hastily thrown over the Shoulders, Madam repairs to her easy Chair, sits down before her Table in Querpo[1] with all her Equipage about her, and sips, and pauses, and then sips again, while the Maid attends assiduous to replenish, as often as call'd for, the drain'd Vehicle of that precious Liquor.

An Hour is the least can be allowed to Breakfast, after which the Maid carries all the Utensils down to the Kitchen, and sits down to the Remains of the Tea (or it is probable some fresh she has found Opportunity to purloin) with the same State as her Mistress, takes as much Time, and would think herself highly injur'd should any one call her away, or attempt to interrupt her in it. So that, between both, the whole Morning is elapsed, and it is as much as the poor Husband can do to get a Bit of Dinner ready by two or three o'Clock.

Dinner above and below is no sooner over, than the Tea-Table must be again set forth.—Some friendly Neighbour comes in to chat away an Hour.—Two are no Company, and the Maid being very busy in cutting Bread and Butter, one 'Prentice is called out of the Shop to run this Way and fetch Mrs. Such-a-one, and another that Way to fetch Mrs. Such-a-one, so that the Husband must be his own Man, and if two Customers chance to come at the same Time, he frequently loses one for want of Hands to serve them.

It often happens, that when the Tea-drinking Company have almost finished their Regale, and the Table is going to be removed, a fresh Visitor arrives, who must have fresh Tea made for her; after her another, who is always treated with the same Compliment; a third, perhaps a fourth, or more, till the Room is quite full, and the Entertainment prolonged a considerable Time after the Candles are lighted, when the Days are of a moderate Length.

This is sufficient to shew the Loss of Time both as to the Mistress and Servants, and how much the Regularity of the Tea-Table occasions a Want of Regularity in every Thing beside; but, Madam, there is yet another, and more mischievous Effect attends the Drinking too much of this Indian Herb.

What I mean is too notorious a Fact not to be easily guessed at;

but lest it should be misconstrued by any of your Readers, I shall venture to explain it.

Tea, whether of the Green or Bohea[2] kind, when taken to Excess, occasions a Dejection of Spirits and Flatulency, which lays the Drinkers of it under a kind of Necessity of having recourse to more animating Liquors.—The most temperate and sober of the Sex find themselves obliged to drink Wine pretty freely after it. None of them now-a-days pretend to entertain with the one without the other; and the Bottle and Glass are as sure an Appendix to the Tea-Table as the Slop-Bason.

Happy are those who can content themselves with a Refreshment, which, tho' not to be had in any Perfection in England, is yet infinitely less destructive to the human System than some others too frequently substituted in its Place, when it is found too weak to answer the End proposed by taking it.

Brandy, Rum, and other Spirituous Liquors, being of a more exhillerating Nature, at least for the present, are become a usual Supplement to Tea, and, I am sorry to say, by their frequent Use grow so familiar to the Palate, that their intoxicating Qualities are no longer formidable, and the Vapours, Cholic, a bad Digestion, or some other Complaint, serves as an Excuse for drinking them in a more plentiful degree, than the best Constitution can for any length of Time support.

Hence ensue innumerable Maladies, Doctor's Fees, Apothecary's Bills, Bath, Tonbridge, the Spa, and all that can destroy the wretched Husband's Peace, or impoverish him in his Fortune.

The more is his Affection for a Wife who takes so little Care of his Interest and Happiness, and of her own Health and Reputation, the more will his Affliction be; and the less will she be able to forgive herself, when brought by a too late and sad Experience to a right way of Thinking.

That you will therefore use your Endeavours that so great an Enemy to the Felicity of the meaner sort of People may be banished from their Houses, is the unanimous Desire of all Husbands, and most humbly petition'd for by him who is,

With the greatest Admiration of your Writings,

    MADAM,

             Your most humble, and Most obedient Servant,

Fryday Street.   JOHN CAREFUL.

Nov. 2, 1744.

A Letter on the Immoderate use of Tea

I dare say one Half of my Readers will expect me to be very angry at this Declamation against an Amusement my Sex are generally so fond of; but it is the firm Resolution of our Club to maintain strict Impartiality in these Lucubrations; and were any of us ever so deeply affected by the Satire, (which thank Heaven we are not) we should, notwithstanding, allow it to be just.

There cannot certainly be a Subject more tickling to the Spleen of the Ill-natur'd, or afford more Matter of Concern to the Gentle and Compassionate, than the Affectation of some Tradesmen's Wives in the Article Mr. Careful complains of; and, it must be own'd, he has done it in so Picturesque a manner, that it is impossible to read him without imagining one sees the ridiculous Behaviour he describes.

No Woman, who is conscious of being guilty of it, can, in my Opinion, behold herself thus delineated without a Confusion, which must occasion a thorough Reformation.

Tea is, however, in itself a very harmless Herb, and an Infusion of it in boiling Water agrees with most Constitutions, when taken moderately; but then, it must be confess'd, we have Plants of our own Growth no less pleasing to the Palate, and more effectual for all the Purposes which furnish an Excuse for the Afternoon's Regale.

This is a Truth allowed by all, even by those from whom we purchase Tea at so dear a Rate; but alas! the Passion we have for Exotics discovers itself but in too many Instances, and we neglect the Use of what we have within ourselves for the same Reason as some Men do their Wives, only because they are their own.

The three Objections which Mr. Careful makes, or indeed that any body can make against the Tea-Table, are, First, The Loss of Time and Hindrance to Business;—Secondly, The Expence;—and, Lastly, The Consequences, often arising from it, *Dram-drinking* and *Ill-health.*

To the first it may be answered, that were Tea to be entirely banished, and Baum, Sage, Mint, or any other English Herb substituted in its Place, and used in the same manner, the Effect would be the same as to that Point, because the one would engross the Hours as well as the other.—Nor does the second carry any great Weight, the Expence of Tea itself, exclusive of those other Apurtenances, which would be equally necessary with any other Herb is an Indulgence, which, where there is any thing of a Competency, might be allowed the Wife without Prejudice to the Circumstances of her Husband.—But the third is not so easily got over: This is what indeed renders the Use of Indian Tea, above all other, pernicious. None, I believe, that drink it constantly twice a Day, but have experienced the ill Effects it has on the Constitution.—They feel a sinking of the Heart, a kind of inward Horror, which is no ways to be removed but by that dangerous Remedy Mr. Careful mentions, and which, in Time, proves worse than the Disease itself.

It is therefore to be wished, that People of all Ranks would endeavour to wean themselves from it; and I have the more room to hope it will be so, because Persons of Quality, whose Example made it first the Mode, begin every Day to take less and less Pleasure in the Tea-Table.—As it gain'd not, however, Estimation all at once, we cannot expect it should entirely lose its Credit all at once; and those who suffer by the Use of it, may comfort themselves in the Assurance my spectatorial Observation gives them, that it is already very much declined.

I cannot conclude this Subject without repeating what was said to me some Years ago by a certain Lady with whom I was intimately acquainted:—She was one of the greatest Devotees to the Tea-Table I ever knew:—Bohea and Bread and Butter was her chief Sustenance, and the Society of those who loved it as well as she did, her only Amusement.—An Accident, not material to mention, separated us for a considerable Time; but on the first Visit I made her afterward, was very much surpriz'd to find she had left off Bohea, and would drink only Green, which I thought more prejudicial to her Constitution than the other, she being extremely lean, and inclining to a Consumption.—Having expressed my Sentiments to her on this Head, *I am sensible,* replied she, *that it is very bad for me:—I have had continual Pains in my Stomach ever since I drank it, and cannot enjoy one Hour's sound Sleep in a whole Night:—Yet what can I do?—I had rather endure all this than have my Brain disordered, and, I assure you, if I had continued the Use of Bohea but a very little longer, I should have been mad.*

These words, delivered in the most grave and solemn Accents, made me not only then, but ever since, as often as I think on them, smile within myself at the Infatuation of making the drinking Tea of some kind or other of such Importance, that there is no such thing as quitting it, and to chuse that sort which will do us the least Mischief, is all we have to consider.

From Volume II, Book VIII, 95-104

Explanatory Notes

1 in Querpo: usually 'cuerpo' that is, in a state of undress.

2 Green or Bohea: 'Green' tea is produced by allowing the leaves of the tea plant to wilt and dry rapidly. Bohea, or 'black' tea (in which the tissues are bruised before the leaves are dried) produces tea of lower quality from the last crop of the season.

☙ 11 ❧

A Reprimand from Curioso Politico

...I am now called upon to discuss Topics of a higher and more public nature, and it is likely that, by this Time, a certain Gentleman, who has lately sent me a very angry Letter, may be laughing in his Sleeve at me, as wanting either *Courage* to insert, or *Ability* to answer it.—The first, however, he shall find himself mistaken in; and as for the other, he may be sure of an Attempt, at least on all those Heads which are proper for me to touch upon; those which are not so, the Public will easily see into the Motives which oblige me to Silence, and on that Account excuse it.

He shall, however, have no Pretence to accuse me of stifling or suppressing any Reproaches made me: I shall present the Public with his Letter entire as I received it, without omitting or changing any one Word, Syllable, or even Period or Comma.

To the FEMALE SPECTATOR

Was the Superscription on the Cover of this doughty Epistle; but on the Top of the Enclosure he salutes me in these Terms:

Vain Pretender to Things above thy Reach!

Then begins at the very Bottom of the Paper, thinking, perhaps, by that Piece of good Breeding, to soften the Asperity of the Invectives he had brewed against me; or else to shew that, however unworthy I might seem in his Eyes as an *Author*, he would not forego the Decorum owing to me as a *Woman.*

'Tho' I never had any very great Opinion of your Sex as Authors, yet I thought, whenever you set up for such, you had Cunning enough to confine yourselves within your own Sphere, or at least not to raise the Expectations of the Public by such *mountainous* Promises

95

as you have done, when you could not be insensible they must in a short time discover themselves to be but of the *Mole-hill* kind.

Whatever Design you had in this it was a very shallow one, and betrays a Want of Judgment, which, to do you Justice, by your manner of handling some Subjects, I should not have suspected you guilty of.

For God's sake, what could move you to make use of all those pompous Flourishes in the sixth Page of the first Book of the *Female Spectator*?—Did the Spies you boasted of in every Corner of Europe, deceive the Trust you reposed in them? Or did you only dream you had established such an Intelligence?—The latter, I am afraid, is the most likely.—But did you never reflect that People would grow uneasy at the Disappointment, when, instead of that full and perfect Account of the most momentous Actions you made them hope, they find themselves for several Months together entertained only with Home-Amours, Reflections on Human Nature, the Passions, Morals, Inferences, and Warnings to your own Sex;—the most proper Province for you, I must own, but widely inconsistent with the Proposals of your first setting out.

Every body imagin'd you had a Key to unlock the Cabinet of Princes,—a Clue to guide you through the most intricate Labyrinths of State,—and that the secret Springs of Ambition, Avarice and Revenge, which make such dreadful Havock, would have been all laid open to our View.—Yet the eternal Fund of Intelligence you vaunted of, has given us not a Word of all this.—Not the least Tittle from Flanders, Italy, Germany, France, or Spain.—Great Armies have been continually in Motion, and the first Monarchs in Europe at the Head of them.—The Rhine has been passed and repassed.—The Elb, Moldau and Neckar crossed.—Cities have been depopulated.—Towns laid Waste. —*Ravage! burn! and destroy all before you.—Spare neither Sex nor Age*, have been the Words of Command!—Sieges, Battles, Rencounters and Escapes have filled the World with Clamour, but not been able to move the peaceful Bosom of the *Female Spectator*.—Contributions, Loans, Subsidies, Military and Ministerial Arts have drain'd the Sustenance from the wretched Subjects of almost all the Kingdoms round us, even to Starving, yet the *Female Spectator* seems ignorant or insensible of their Calamities.—Excursions, Incursions, Invasions, and Insurrections have been talked of by every body but the *Female Spectator*.—Huge Fleets cover the Ocean with their spreading Sails, but not all the Wind that fills them wafts to the *Female Spectator* any Account to what intent equipped, where directed, or what great Feats they yet have done, or are about to do.

A Reprimand from Curioso Politico

Do you not blush at all this?—Are you not under most terrible Apprehensions that, instead of the Woman of Experience, Observation, fine Understanding, and extensive Genius you would pass for, you should be taken for an idle, prating, gossiping old Woman, fit only to tell long Stories by the Fire-side for the Entertainment of little Children or Matrons, more antiquated than yourself?

I do assure you, I am truly ashamed for you.—It is not my Nature to be severe on the Failings or Mistakes of any one; and had your Boastings been less glaring, or your Execution of what you pretended to undertake, any way answered the Expectation of the Public, I would have been the last that should have condemned you, but had overlooked small Deficiencies in Consideration of your Sex, and the Desire you shewed of performing your Promises, which, at the Time of making, I should have been charitable enough to have judg'd you thought less difficult to accomplish than you afterwards found them.

Yet were it so, some modest Apology methinks would have become you.—The least you could have done was to have confessed your Inability, entreated Pardon of the Town for having imposed on their Credulity, and as you now perceived you had overshot your Mark, and had it not really in your Power to entertain them with Matters of any very great Importance, at least to the Generality of your Readers, beseeched them to accept of such as fell within your Compass.

To deal plainly with you, the best that can be said of the Lucubrations you have hitherto published, is, that they are fit Presents for Country Parsons to make to their young Parishioners; —to be read in Boarding Schools, and recommended as Maxims for the well regulating private Life; but are no way fit for the polite Coffee-Houses, or to satisfy Persons of an inquisitive Taste.

Whether you have received any Remonstrances of the Nature I now send you, and have thought it prudent to take no Notice of them, I will not pretend to say, nor do I accuse you with it; but of this you may be certain, that I have alledg'd no more against you than is the Sense of most of the Wits, as well as Men of Fashion I converse with, as it is probable you may hereafter have further Reason to be convinced of from others beside

Curioso Politico.

White's Chocolate House
Nov. 9, 1744

P.S. To shew you that Malice had no Share in dictating the above

Lines, if there is any Possibility of your mending your Hand, you are at your own Liberty to insert them or not.—My Intention, in sending them, being not so much to *expose* as to *reprove*, I shall be very glad to find that, by holding to you this faithful Mirror, you are enabled to wipe off whatever is a Blemish in your Writings, and for the future supply those Deficiencies which you seem to me to have hitherto been wholly insensible of.————————*Farewel.*

I heartily thank Mr. Politico for the Permission he is so good to vouchsafe me as to keeping his Reprimand a Secret; but it would be abusing so extraordinary a Favour to accept it.—The Pains he has been at must not be totally thrown away, and whether I am able or not to improve by what he has wrote, it would be [a] great Pity he should not have the Satisfaction of seeing it in Print.

The Public will be the best Judges how far I deserve the Severity he has treated me with, and to them I readily submit my Cause.

I do not pretend to deny but that, in the Introduction to this Work, I said that I had found Means to extend my Speculations as far as France, Rome, Germany, and other foreign Parts, and that I then flattered myself with being able to penetrate into the Mysteries of the Alcove, the Cabinet, or Field, and to have such of the Secrets of Europe, as were proper for the Purpose of a *Female Spectator*, laid open to my View; but I never proposed, nor, I believe, did any body but this Letter-Writer expect that these Lucubrations should be devoted merely to the Use of News-Mongers.—A Change-Broker might, I think, have as much Cause to resent my taking no Notice of the Rise or Fall of Stocks.

Several of the Topics he reproaches me for not having touch'd upon, come not within the Province of a *Female Spectator*;—such as Armies marching,—Battles fought,—Towns destroyed,—Rivers cross'd, and the like:—I should think it ill became me to take up my own, or Reader's Time, with such Accounts as are every Day to be found in the public Papers.

Oh but the Meaning of all this he calls upon me to unravel.—I must unfold the Mystery, lay open the secret Springs which set these great Machines in Motion.—Why he has done it for me, Ambition, Avarice, and Revenge have set the mighty Men of the Earth a madding, and there is indeed no other Mystery in it than what all the World may, and do easily see into.

I grant some Turns and Counter-Turns in Politics have been too abstruse to be accounted for by the Rules of common Reason, and no way to be fathom'd but by that Intelligence he wants me to receive from the Cabinets where they were hatch'd;—and yet perhaps, if once revealed, there would appear so little in them, that one might justly enough compare them to the Knots Children tye at School in Packthread, only to puzzle one another to undo again.

Be that as it may;—how far soever the *Female Spectator*, or any one else, may be able to penetrate into these dark Paths of State, the Attempt of making them a common Road might be imprudent, and perhaps unsafe.

There is an old Adage in the Mouth of every one, *viz.—All Things that are lawful are not expedient*: To which one may add, that *many Things are expedient, or necessary, which may not be deemed lawful*: If either of these should happen to be the Case, the Silence of the *Female Spectator* may very well be pardoned.

If Princes have a Mind to play at Bo-peep with each other, or with their respective Subjects, who shall dare to draw the Curtain, and call the Rabble in to be Witness of what they do!—We little People may hear and see, but must say nothing.—There are some sort of Secrets which prove fatal if explored, and like massive Buildings erected by Enchantment, will not endure too near Approach, but fall at once, and crush the bold Inspector with their Weight.

But I will not pretend to measure what Extent of Power the Guardian Angel entitled the Liberty of the Press may yet retain. Of this I am certain, that the better we regulate our Actions in *private* Life, the more we may hope of *public Blessings*, and the more we shall be enabled to sustain *public Calamities*.

To check the enormous Growth of Luxury, to reform the Morals, and improve the Manners of an Age, by all confess'd degenerate and sunk, are the great Ends for which these Essays were chiefly intended; and the Authors flatter themselves that nothing has been advanced, but may contribute in a more or less Degree to the accomplishing so glorious a Point.—Many little Histories, it is true, are interspers'd, but then they are only such as serve to enforce Precept by Example, and make the Beauty of Virtue, and the Deformity of Vice sink deeper into the Reader's Mind.— When we would strike at any favourite Passion, it requires the utmost Delicacy to do it in such a manner as shall make the Person guilty of it ashamed of being so, without being angry at the Detection; and no way so likely to succeed, as to shew him the Resemblance of himself in the Character of another.

Thus much I thought proper to say in Defence of myself and Partners in this Undertaking, which I doubt not but will be look'd upon as a sufficient Answer to all the Objections Mr. Politico has started for the present, and hereafter perhaps we may be better Friends.

From Volume II, Book VIII, 117-26

ᚱᚱᚯ 12 ᚯᚱᚱ

A Letter from Cleora

To the FEMALE SPECTATOR.

LADIES,

Permit me to thank you for the kind and generous Task you have undertaken in endeavouring to improve the Minds and Manners of our unthinking Sex.—It is the noblest Act of Charity you could exercise in an Age like ours, where the Sense of Good and Evil is almost extinguish'd, and People desire to appear more vicious than they really are, that so they may be less unfashionable. This Humour, which is too prevalent in the Female Sex, is the true Occasion of the many Evils and Dangers to which they are daily exposed.—No wonder the Men of Sense disregard us! and the Dissolute triumph over that Virtue they ought to protect!

Yet, I think, it would be cruel to charge the Ladies with all the Errors they commit; it is most commonly the Fault of a wrong Education, which makes them frequently do amiss, while they think they not only act innocently but uprightly;—it is therefore only the Men, and the Men of Understanding too, who, in effect, merit the Blame of this, and are answerable for all the Misconduct we are guilty of.—Why do they call us *silly Women*, and not endeavour to make us otherwise?—God and Nature has endued them with Means, and Custom has established them in the Power of rendering our Minds such as they ought to be;—how highly ungenerous is it then to give us a wrong turn, and then despise us for it!

The Mahometans, indeed, enslave their Women, but then they teach them to believe their Inferiority will extend to Eternity; but our Case is even worse than this, for while we live in a free Country, and are assured from our excellent Christian Principles that we are capable of those refined Pleasures which last to Immortality, our

Minds, our better Parts, are wholly left uncultivated, and, like a rich Soil neglected, bring forth nothing but noxious Weeds.

There is, undoubtedly, no Sexes in Souls, and we are as able to receive and practise the Impressions, not only of Virtue and Religion, but also of those Sciences which the Men engross to themselves, as they can be.—Surely our Bodies were not form'd by the great Creator out of the finest Mould, that our Souls might be neglected like the coarsest of the Clay!

O! would too imperious, and too tenacious Man, be so just to the World as to be more careful of the Education of those Females to whom they are Parents or Guardians!—Would they convince them in their Infancy that Dress and Shew are not the Essentials of a fine Lady, and that true Beauty is seated in the Mind; how soon should we see our Sex retrieve the many Virtues which false Taste has bury'd in Oblivion!—Strange Infatuation! to refuse us what would so much contribute to their own Felicity!—Would not themselves reap the Benefit of our Amendment? Should we not be more obedient Daughters, more faithful Wives, more tender Mothers, more sincere Friends, and more valuable in every other Station of Life?

But, I find, I have let my Pen run a much greater Length than I at first intended.—If I have said any thing worthy your Notice, or what you think the Truth of the Case, I hope you will mention this Subject in some of your future Essays; or if you find I have any way err'd in my Judgment, to set me right will be the greatest Favour you can confer on,

LADIES,

Your constant Reader,
And humble servant,

Hampton Court,   CLEORA.
Jan 12, 1744-5.

After thanking this Lady for the Favour of her obliging Letter, we think it our Duty to congratulate her on being one of those happy Few who have been blest with that Sort of Education which she so pathetically laments the Want of in the greatest Part of our Sex.

Those Men are certainly guilty of a great deal of Injustice who think, that all the Learning becoming in a Woman is confined to the Management of her Family; that is, to give Orders concerning the Table, take care of her Children in their Infancy, and observe that her Servants do not neglect their Business.—All this no doubt is very necessary, but would it not be better if she performs those Duties more through Principle than Custom? and will she be less punctual in her Observance of them, after she becomes a Wife, for being perfectly convinced, before she is so, of the Reasonableness of them, and why they are expected from her?

Many Women have not been inspired with the least Notion of even those Requisites in a Wife, and when they become so, continue the same loitering, lolloping, idle Creatures they were before; and then the Men are ready enough to condemn those who had the Care of their Education.

Terrible is it, indeed, for the Husband, especially if he be a Tradesman, or Gentleman of small Estate, who marries with a Woman of this Stamp, whatever Fortune she brings will immediately run out, and 'tis well if all his own does not follow.—Even Persons of the highest Rank in Life will suffer greatly both in their Circumstances and Peace of Mind, when she, who ought to be the Mistress of the Family, lives in it like a Stranger, and perhaps knows no more of what those about her do than an Alien.

But supposing her an excellent Oeconomist, in every Respect what the World calls a notable Woman, methinks the Husband would be yet infinitely happier were she endued with other good Qualities as well as a perfect Understanding in Houshold [sic] Affairs.—The Governess of a Family, or what is commonly call'd Houskeeper, provided she be honest and careful, might discharge this Trust as well as a Wife; but there is, doubtless, somewhat more to be expected by a Man from that Woman whom the Ceremony of Marriage has made Part of himself.—She is, or ought to be, if qualified for it, the Repository of his dearest Secrets, the Moderator of his fiercer Passions, the Softner of his most anxious Cares, and the constantly chearful and entertaining Companion of his more unbended Moments.

To be all this she must be endued with a consummate Prudence, a perfect Eveness of Temper, an unshaken Fortitude, a gentle affable Behaviour, and a sprightly Wit.—The Foundation of these Virtues must be indeed in Nature, but Nature may be perverted by ill Customs, or, if not so, still want many Embellishments from Education; without which, however valuable in itself, it would appear rude and barbarous to others, and lose more than half the Effect it ought to have.

...Our Sex, from their very Infancy, are encourag'd to dress and fondle their Babies; a Custom not improper, because it gives an early Idea of that Care and Tenderness we ought to shew those real Babes to whom we may happen to be Mothers. But I am apt to think, that without this Prepossession, Nature would inform us what was owing from us to those whom we have given Being.—The very Look, and innocent Crys of those little Images of ourselves would be more prevailing than any Rules could be.—

This the meerest Savages who live without Precept, and are utterly ignorant of all moral Virtues, may inform us;—nay, for Conviction in this Point, we may descend yet lower, and only observe the tender Care which the Beasts of the Field and the Fowls of the Air take of their young ones.

To be good Mothers, therefore, tho' a Duty incumbent on all who are so, requires fewer Lessons than to be good Wives.—We all groan under the Curse entail'd upon us for the Transgression of Eve.

'Thy Desire shall be to thy Husband, and he shall rule over thee.'

But we are not taught enough how to lighten this Burthen, and render ourselves such as would make him asham'd to exert that Authority, he thinks he has a Right to, over us.

Were that Time which is taken up in instructing us in Accomplishments, which, however taking at first Sight, conduce little to our essential Happiness, employ'd in studying the Rules of Wisdom, in well informing us what we are, and what we ought to be, it would doubtless inspire those, to whom we should happen to be united, with a Reverence which would not permit them to treat us with that Lightness and Contempt, which, tho' some of us may justly enough incur, often drives not only such, but the most innocent of us, to Extravagancies that render ourselves, and those concern'd with us equally miserable.

Why then, as Cleora says, do the Men, who are and will be the sole Arbitrators in this Case, refuse us all Opportunities of enlarging our Minds, and improving those Talents we have received from God and Nature; and which, if put in our Power to exert in a proper Manner, would make no less their own Happiness than our Glory?

They cry, of what use can Learning be to us, when Custom, and the Modesty of our Sex, forbids us to speak in public Places?—'Tis true that it would not befit us to go into the Pulpit, nor harangue at the Bar; but this is a weak and trifling Argument against our being qualify'd for either, since all Men who are so were never intended for the Service of the Church, nor put on the long Robe; and by the same Rule therefore the Sons as well as Daughters of good Families should be bred up in Ignorance.

Knowledge is a light Burthen, and, I believe, no one was ever the worse for being skilled in a great many Things, tho' he might never have occasion for any of them.

From Volume II, Book X, 230-7

✐ 13 ✐

A Letter concerning French ladies, and how easily they improve themselves

To the FEMALE SPECTATOR.

MADAM,

A former Essay of Yours, I think it was Book the Fourth, wherein you so agreeably discant on the Mis-use of Time, charm'd me to a very great Degree, and also has given me Courage to add some crude Notions of my own concerning it.—You seem to think, that it is to this all our Misfortunes, all our Irregularities are owing; and to me it is plain, that if we were well instructed in our Youth, of the true Value of Time, we could not possibly do amiss.

But on whom shall the Blame of this be laid, if not on our Governors?—Those who have the Care of us in our most early Years, should inform us, that, of all our Jewels, none are so inestimable as Time;—that a Moment lost is never to be retrieved; and that if we husband well the present, it will produce a Crop hereafter, that may not only serve us for our whole Lives, but entail eternal Blessings on our Names, by rendering our Virtues immortal in a late Posterity.

A letter subscribed Cleora, which you have favoured the Public with inserting in your tenth Book, has very pathetically set forth the Remissness of the Men in this Point; and your Remarks upon it have been very convincing to me, and many other of your Readers, that there are Women capable of attaining a thorough Knowledge in the most abstruse Sciences; yet, as I am also convinced by an Examination into myself, that every one is not so, or, at least, that we cannot all have Patience to go through the Drudgery of School-Learning, methinks it would not be unbecoming the Politeness of our

English Wits, to take the same Methods of instructing us as they do in France.

I had the Pleasure of being in that elegant Country for three Years, and but for the unhappy Eruption between the two Nations, had not so soon left it.—I was highly satisfied at my first coming among them, to see the Respect paid in general to our Sex, but infinitely more to find they so well deserved it, by their most agreeable Manner of Conversation. Besides, that easy Freedom, which is the Essence of good Breeding, I discovered, even among very young Ladies, a Skill in Philosophy, Geography, and other Sciences, which surprized me, as not being able to comprehend how, at an Age when we in England know little beyond our Music-Books and Dancing, they should attain such a Compass of Learning, as I imagined, would require a long and continued Application; but my Wonder ceased, when I perceived, that, to speak justly of things, was rendered as easy to them as to speak at all, and by a way which I doubt not but you are as well acquainted with as myself; but least [sic] any of your Readers should be ignorant of it, permit me to inform them, that all Men of Learning, Wit, and Genius, have not only a free Access to the Ladies, but are received by them with particular Marks of Distinction.—They have them with them at their Toilets, in all their Parties of Pleasure, and never think a Company compleat, in which there are not mingled one or more who is celebrated for his Capacity and fine Sense. The Time which we allow to Milliners, Mantua-makers, and Tire-women, is with them taken up in the Conversation of Men of Letters; for tho' the French Ladies are certainly the genteelest Creatures upon Earth, they take the least Pains to be so of any.—They leave the whole Care of their Dress to their Women, and never think of what they are to wear, till it is brought to them, and put on.

Not that the Discourses with which they are entertained by these great Men, have any thing in them that favour of Pedantry, or that can make a Lady consider herself as with her Tutor.—On the contrary, all they say is a continual round of Gaiety and sprightly Wit; yet is their very Raillery on such Subjects, as mingle Information with Delight; and I protest to you, Madam, I have been sometimes more edified by a single Sentence laugh'd out, than by a formal, stiff, pedantick Harangue of an Hour long.

But this is the least Advantage a French Lady reaps from her Regard for Men of Learning.—Has she an Inclination to Philosophy, Theology, History, Astronomy, or in fine, any particular Study, she has only to make Mention of it, and is certain of receiving a Letter the next Day, in which is contained the whole Pith and Marrow of the Science, and at one View takes in the Substance of I know not how many Volumes.

The Men are the industrious Bees, which suck the Sweets of many Author's Works, and having collected whatever they find worthy, present it in the most concise and briefest Manner possible to the Lady who expects this Tribute from them, and honours it with her Acceptance.

By this Means they are enabled to make a Part in Conversation on all sorts of Subjects,—and those among them who are least inclin'd to think intensely, have yet so general a Knowledge of every thing, as may make them pass for very learned with those who do not enter into any deep Arguments.

Why, dear *Female Spectator*, is it not so with us? I am sure we have Men whose Capacities are at least equal to any that France produces.—Is it then owing to their Indolence and Disregard for our Sex, or to our own Remissness and Neglect of those who perhaps have not the Advantage of Title and Estate, to render their Abilities conspicuous?—I sincerely wish, for the Honour of my Country-Women, that this latter is not the true Motive. I am apt to believe, did a Woman of Quality express a Desire of being instructed in this agreeable Way, in any thing she is ignorant of, no Man of Letters but would rejoice in the Opportunity of obliging her, and at the same Time of testifying his own Abilities.

In France a little Copy of Verses, or a well-turn'd Epigram, is sufficient to recommend the Author to the first of the Nobility, and frequently to the King himself.—*There* such-a-one is not only taken Notice of, but always provided for in a handsome Manner; whereas, I am sorry to observe, that *here* nothing is more contemptible than a Needy Wit. They are excluded the Conversation of the great World, and seldom permitted even to see the Faces of those who cannot but allow the Merit of their Works.

The Ladies however, methinks, should have more Softness; and if they could bring themselves off from these darling Foibles, which at present engross too much of their Time and Attention, I dare answer they would find so much Pleasure in improving their Genius's [sic] by the Means I have been describing, that they would look on a Man of Wit, as not only an agreeable, but a necessary Appendix.

But, as you have in several of your instructive Lucubrations taken Notice, this must be despaired of, till Recollection shall once more take Place, and the present absurd and preposterous Inventions for *killing Time* (as they justly term it) be expelled this Island, and driven back to their native Climes, where Talents for more elegant and polite Entertainments have been seldom known.

If you should think what I have said too severe, I submit to your Correction; but if not, shall look on your testifying an Approbation, by giving it a Place in your next Book, as the greatest Honour can be confer'd on,

MADAM,

Your Constant Reader,

And Humble Servant,

PHILENIA.

Whitehall,
Feb. 14th, 1744-5

Nothing certainly can be more just than what Philenia has advanced, and it were greatly to be wished her Proposal could be brought into Execution; but I am afraid it will be attended with more Difficulty than she at present may be aware of.—She seems not to have sufficiently consider'd the different Tempers of the two Nations, and that what in France is looked upon as no more than, what it indeed is, innocent Gallantry, might here be censur'd as an unbecoming Familiarity. Our Fathers, our Brothers, our Husbands are, perhaps, more tenacious of the Honour of their Family than they need to be. The phlegmatic Disposition of the English can ill endure any Galliardisms in the Females belonging to them; they would be apt, some of them at least, to think the Admiration we profest for Learning, was only a Veil to cover our Admiration of the Person who possessed it; and though it must be own'd, that our Sex at present indulge very great Liberties, yet, as the Number of Men of Wit is but small, an Intimacy with one of those is look'd upon as infinitely more dangerous than that with a thousand Beaus.

It is evident enough, that the Men in general imagine they find their Account in permitting us to trifle away our Time in Follies, which renders us ridiculous Abroad, and insignificant at Home.—A Piece of Cruelty indeed, which but ill agrees with their Professions, but is what we must resolve to bear, till we can pluck up Spirit to assert the Dignity of our Natures, and of ourselves, throw off those senseless Avocations, that make the finest among us of no more Account than a pretty Play-thing.

Yet let it not be said we are the only thoughtless, gawdy Flutterers of the human World:—There are Men-Butterflies as well as Women:—Things that are above the Trouble of Reflection, and suffer themselves to be blown

107

about by every Wind of Folly.—Whatever has the Name of Novelty will carry them through thick and thin;—led by that resistless Charm, no matter if the Chair be overturned, the gilded Chariot broke, and the Coachman's Neck into the Bargain, still they press on a mingled motley Crowd; as witness the Audiences at the Little Theatre in the Hay-market,[1] to see the Entertainment of the Dutch Children, as they were called, though most of whom were bred up to the Tumbling Art in Broad St. Giles and White-Chapel,[2] and hack'd about at all the petty Wells near London, while Shakespear and Otway warbled their pathetic Strains to empty Boxes at Covent Garden and Drury-Lane.[3]

From Volume II, Book XII, 341-8

Explanatory Notes:

1 Little Theatre in the Hay-market,: Mrs Haywood was not unacquainted with the Little Theatre in the Haymarket, having herself, some ten years previously, acted there in some of Henry Fielding's anti-Government satires which led to the censorship imposed by the Licensing Act of 1737.

2 Broad St. Giles and White-Chapel,: both very insalubrious areas of London.

3 Covent Garden and Drury-Lane.: Covent Garden Theatre and the Theatre Royal, Drury Lane, were the two most popular and fashionable playhouses in London at that time.

ॐ 14 ॐ

Two Tales of Exemplary Wives

To the FEMALE SPECTATOR.

MADAM,

The Story of Dorimon and Alithea at the latter end of your first
Volume, gave me a great deal of Pleasure:—I look on the Character
of Alithea to be of the highest Value;—so exemplary a Patience
under a Provocation the most irritating to our Sex, has a just Claim to
our Admiration; but even that is yet less difficult to be imitated than
the Sweetness, the amazing Gentleness [with] which she conceal'd
the Knowledge of her Wrongs, not only from the World, but from the
Man who offered them.

Nothing can be so terrible a Misfortune to a Woman who loves
her Husband tenderly, as to be conscious she has lost his Affections,
and that another triumphs in those Endearments which are alone her
Right; but when Insults are added to Injuries, and the neglected Wife
is obliged to bear them from the very Wretch who has supplanted
her; to behave, I say, in such a Circumstance with Decency and
Complaisance, requires not only an elevated Virtue, but a Discretion
more consummate than is ordinarily found in our Sex;—not that we
want Capacities to attain it, but because a due Care is wanting to
form our Minds in Youth.

The great Number of Separations and Divorces, which we see of
late, is a Testimony that few Ladies are educated in such a Manner as
to have good Qualities sufficient to enable them to bear so great a
Disregard of themselves.—*Miss* is sent, indeed, to the best School
can be heard of to be brought up; but then *Mamma* tells her at
parting, *My Dear, if every thing does not please you there, or if you
are cross'd, let me know, and I will take you away.* Fine Education to
be expected after such a Promise! How can those Mothers think that

their Children will make good Wives, when they are taught to be their own Mistresses from the Cradle, and must learn nothing but what they have a Mind to for fear they should fret.—This false Indulgence, and the Want of being a little accustomed to Contradiction in the early Years of Life, it is, that chiefly occasions that wild Impatience we often see in Maturity.

But tho' ill Habits contracted in our Youth are difficult to be worn off, Reason and Reflection may enable us to accomplish so glorious a Work, if we set about it with a firm Resolution.

How great a Pleasure must that Woman feel, who is conscious of having reclaim'd her Husband meerly by her own Sweetness of Behaviour;—how justifiable, nay, how laudable will be her Pride whose Merit is forcible enough to conquer all the Follies of an ungovernable Man, and make him own he has been to blame!—Affections thus obtain'd are generally more tender, more fond than ever, and cease not but with Life.—Whatever Conflicts, therefore, a Wife may endure within herself in the Endeavour, and how long soever she may suffer, the Reward at last will more than compensate for all the Pains.

I wish this Point were more considered, and that Ladies would take Example by your Alithea, or that amiable Princess mentioned in the same Book, but as too many Instances cannot be given of Patience and Forbearance in such a Circumstance, I beg leave to present your Readers with a little succinct Account of two of my particular Acquaintance, who have reclaim'd their Husbands, and recovered the Love they once thought wholly lost, with Interest.

The first, whom I shall call Eudosia, had been the most unfortunate Woman upon Earth, had she not been endu'd with an equal Share of Patience as good Sense.—She was married very young to Severus, a Man of a most haughty austere Disposition, and one, who like too many of his Sex, had got it into his Head, that Women were created only to be the Slaves of Men.—Her Beauty, however, and the submissive Mildness of her Disposition, made him very fond of her, and they lived in a great deal of Harmony together; 'till Severus happening to see Laconia at a public Place, became enamour'd of her, and his Pride making him above attempting to put any Restraint on his Inclinations, he from that Moment resolv'd to know her more intimately, if there was a Possibility of doing so. By a strict Enquiry he found who she was, and that she had no Fortune to support her Extravagancies.—This he so well improved that he soon accomplished his Wishes; and tho' after he was familiar with her, he discovered he had not been the first who had receiv'd her Favours, yet he continued attach'd to her by an invincible Fatality.

So careless was he of what either his Wife or the World might think of him, that both were soon apprized of his Amour.—Those of his own Kindred took the Liberty to reprove him sharply for it; but Eudosia prevailed on those of her own to be silent in the Affair, as she herself resolved to be, well judging, that to a Person of his Disposition, all Opposition would but add Fewel to the Fire, and that he would rather persist in what he knew was wrong, than confess himself convinced by the Arguments of others.

He very well knew she could not be ignorant of what he took so little Pains to conceal; but where there is a Dislike, as during his Intrigue with Laconia he certainly had for his Wife, nothing can oblige,—nothing can be acknowledged as a Virtue;—instead of esteeming her, as he ought to have done, for the Regard she shewed for his Peace in never murmuring, nor upbraiding him with his Fault, he imputed it all to a mean Timidity of Nature in her, and only glory'd in himself for knowing so well how to keep a Woman within what Bounds he pleased, and render even her very Wishes subservient to his Will.

Confident that he might now act as he pleased, he brought Laconia into his House, commanded Eudosia to treat her as a Lady, whom he infinitely esteemed, and having laid this Injunction on her, whom he look'd upon as only his Upper Servant, gave adequate Orders to the others.

This Creature now became the entire Mistress of the Family, and tho' Eudosia kept her Place at the Head of the Table, yet nothing was served up to it but what was ordered by Laconia.

Some Women will look on this tame enduring in Eudosia as wholly unworthy of a Wife, and too great an Encouragement for other guilty Husbands to treat their Wives in the same Manner; but this Pattern of Prudence and Good-nature knew very well the Temper of the Person she had to deal with, and that nothing was to be gain'd by the Pursuit of any rough Measures.—She seemed, therefore, to think herself happy in the Company of Laconia, carry'd her into all Company she went into as her particular Friend, and was so perfectly obliging to her in every Respect, that the other, even in spite of their Rivalship, could not help having a Regard for her, which she testify'd in downright quarrelling with Severus, whenever he refused her any thing she asked; and in truth, this injured Wife would frequently have gone without many Things which her Rank in

Life demanded, had it not been for the Intercession of Laconia.

Severe Tryal, however, for a Woman of Virtue, and who in spite of his Injustice and Ingratitude, still retained the most tender Affection for her Husband, yet she bore all with a seeming Tranquility, but while the guilty Pair imagined her easy and resign'd to her Fate, she was continually laying Schemes to change it. Long she was about it, being loth to venture at any thing which, in case of failure, might render her Condition worse; but at last her good Genius inspired her a little Plot, which threaten'd nothing if the Event should not answer Expectation, and promised much if it succeeded.

She feign'd herself seized with a sudden Indisposition, took [to] her Bed, and so well acted her Part, that the Physician who attended her was deceived by it, and reported her Condition as dangerous.—It cannot be supposed Severus felt any great Anxiety at hearing it, yet order'd she should be carefully look'd to, and nothing spared that would contribute to her Recovery.—Laconia appear'd very assiduous about her, but whether out of a real or counterfeited Tenderness I will not pretend to say.

It served, however, to forward Eudosia's Design; and one Day, seeming to come out of a fainting Fit while the other was sitting by her Bed-side, she called to her Maid, and bad her bring her a Sheet of Paper, and Pen and Ink, which being done she wrote a few Lines, and ordered a small India Cabinet, in which she was accustomed to keep her Jewels, and other little Trinkets, to be held to her, in which she put the Paper, and turned the Key with a great deal of seeming Care to make it fast; but in truth, to prevent it from being lock'd, so that it might easily be opened.

Now, cry'd she, *I shall die in Peace, since my dear Severus will know, when I am gone, every thing I wish him to be sensible of:—I beg you, Madam*, continued she to Laconia who was very attentive to all she did, to *let my Husband know my last Will is contained in that Cabinet.*

With these Words she sunk down into the Bed, as fatigued with what she had been doing, and the other doubted not but her last Moment was near at Hand.

A Woman circumstanced as Laconia was, might very well be curious to discover what Eudosia had wrote; but not knowing how to come at it without the help of Severus, she acquainted him with the whole Behaviour of his Wife on this Occasion, on which he grew little less impatient than herself; and at a Time when she seem'd to be asleep, took the Cabinet out of the Room, and carry'd it into his own Closet, resolving to examine the Contents without any Witnesses.

Eudosia, who was very watchful for the Success of her Project, saw well enough what he had done; but looking on the Reception he should give the Paper as the Crisis of her Fate, past the Remainder of the Night in such disturb'd Emotions, as rendered her almost as ill in reality as she had pretended.

Severus was little less disordered after having read the Letter, which was directed to himself, with the Title of her Ever dear Severus, and contained these Lines.

Had I Millions to bequeath, you alone should be my Heir; but all I have, all I am, is already yours, all but my Advice, which living I durst not presume to give you; but as this will not reach your Ears till I am no more, it may be better received.—It is this, my Dear, that as soon as Decency permits you will marry Laconia;—neither of you ought to make any other Choice.—The World, you know, has been loud in its Censures on that Lady's Score, I alone have been silent.—What the Duty of a Wife bound me to while living, I persevere to observe in Death; my only Consolation under inconceivable Agonies of Mind and Body, being a Consciousness of having well and truly discharged all the Obligations of my Station.—I beg Heaven your second Nuptials may be more agreeable than your first;—that she who has so long enjoy'd your Heart may continue to deserve it, by loving you as I have done, and you be more happy with her than you could possibly be with

The unfortunate EUDOSIA.

He afterwards confess'd, that he read this above an hundred Times over, and that every Word sunk into his Soul the deeper as he examined it the more; till quite melted into Tenderness, he look'd back with Horror on his past Behaviour.—All the Charms he had formerly found in the Mind and Person of Eudosia returned with added Force, and those of Laconia grew dim and faded in his Eyes.

But when he reflected that he was about to lose forever so inestimable a Treasure as he now own'd his Wife to be, and that there was the strongest Probability that his Unkindness had shortened her Date of Life, he fell into the bitterest Rage against himself, and the Object of that unlawful Flame which had occasion'd it.

Laconia, who wondered he did not come to Bed, for he had promis'd to sleep with her that Night, ran to his Closet, where she found him in very great Agitations; on her enquiring into the Cause, he sullenly told her *she was*, and bid her *leave him*. As this was Treatment she had not been accustomed to, she had not Presence enough of Mind to conceal her Resentment at it, but immediately flew into a Rage, which his Temper was little able to endure, and served as a Foil to set Eudosia's Virtues in a still fairer Light; he contented himself, however, with making her go out of the Room, after which he returned to his former Meditations.

In fine, he thought so long, 'till Thought made him as perfect a Convert as Eudosia could wish; and the Imagination that he was about to lose her, made him lose all that haughty Tenaciousness of Humour he was wont to use her with.—He went several Times to her Chamber-Door, but being told she seem'd in a Slumber returned softly back, and would not enter till he heard she was awake, then enquired in the tenderest Manner how she did; to which she answered, that his Presence had given her more Spirits than she could have hoped ever to have enjoyed in this World.

O, cry'd he, quite charmed with her Softness, *if the Sight of me can afford you Comfort, never will I quit your Chamber.—Believe me,* continued he, taking her Hand and pressing it, *My Dear Eudosia, that how much soever I have been to blame, there is nothing so terrible as the Thoughts of losing you:—O that my recovered Love, and all the Tenderness that Man can feel, could but restore your Health.—What would I not give!—What would I not do to preserve you!*

These Words were accompanied with some Tears of Passion that bedew'd her Hand, and left her no room to doubt of their Sincerity. How much she was transported any one may guess.—*Now,* said she, raising herself in the Bed and clasping him round the Neck, *in Life or Death I have nothing more to wish.*

It would be endless to repeat the fond obliging Things they said to each other; the Reader will easily conceive by the Beginning that nothing could be more tender on both Sides. But what added most to Eudosia's Satisfaction, was the Assurance he gave her that Laconia should quit his House that Day, and that he never would see her more.

On this, she insisted on his making some Provision for her, telling him it was Punishment sufficient for her Fault to lose the Affection she had so long enjoy'd; and that for her Part, if she should live to possess the Happiness his Behaviour now seem'd to promise, it would be damp'd if she knew any thing he had once loved was miserable.

This Generosity engag'd new Caresses on the Part of Severus, but he desired she would not mention that Woman any more, but leave it to himself to act as he thought proper.

He kept his Word; Laconia was put out of the House that Day. In what Manner they parted is uncertain, but it is not so that the Amour between them was ever renewed. Eudosia having gained her Point, pretended to recover by Degrees, and at length to be fully establish'd in her former Health; to which now, a Vivacity flowing from a contented Mind being added, she became more agreeable than ever; never was there a happier Wife, or more endearing Husband.

All their Acquaintance beheld the Change with Astonishment, but none were entrusted with the innocent Stratagem which brought it about: Eudosia had the Prudence to conceal it not only from Severus himself, but from all others; nor till after his Death, which happened not in several Years, was any Person made privy to it.

The other whom I mentioned, as a happy Instance of recovering a decayed Affection, I shall call Constantia; she was a young Gentlewoman of strict Virtue but no Fortune.—She had been courted above a Year by Tubesco, a substantial Tradesman, before she married him, but had not been a Wife above half the time, when she perceived there was another much more dear to him than herself.—She bore it, however, with a consummate Patience, and even after she heard that he had a Child by her Rival, who was a wealthy Tradesman's Daughter, did she ever reproach him with it, or attempt to expose it.

He had even the Folly, as well as Impudence, to own his intrigue before her Face; yet all this did not move her to any unbecoming Passion. She was not, however, insensible to such Usage, nor without the most ardent Wishes to reclaim him both for his and her own Sake. Many Projects she contrived, but all without Success, 'till a Person, who was a Friend to them both, perswaded him to leave England, and go to settle at Dundee, of which Place they were Natives. Absence from his Mistress she hop'd would make a Change in his Temper in her Favour; but in this she was deceived, at least for a long while.—For two long Years did he repine, and all that time used his Wife so very ill that she almost repented she had engaged him to quit the Presence of one who she now began to think he could

[not] live without.—To add to her Afflictions, she was extremely ill treated by his Relations on the Score of having brought no Portion; but when she thought herself the most abandoned by good Fortune, she was nearest the Attainment of it. Heaven was pleased that she should prove with Child, which, together with her continued Sweetness of Behaviour, turn'd his Heart; he became from the worst, one of the best of Husbands, detests his former Life, and all Women who endeavour by their Artifices to alienate Men from their Wives.

Constantia is now very happy, and the more so, as she knows the Recovery of her Husband's Affections is chiefly owing to her own good Conduct, and Sweetness of Behaviour.

But I have troubled you too long.—If these Examples may serve to enforce the good Advice you have given our Sex, it will be an infinite Satisfaction to,

MADAM,

Your most humble Servant,

March 26, 1745.   DORINDA.

This amiable Lady's Letter stands in no need of a Comment; but we think ourselves obliged to thank her for the Zeal she testifies for the Happiness of Society.—Could the generality of Womankind be brought to think like her, Marriage would no longer be a Bugbear to the Wife, and a Laughing-stock to Fools.—Would they, instead of reporting the Follies of their Sex, set forth, as she has done, the bright Examples some of them have given of Virtue and Discretion, Men would venerate instead of despising; we should recover that Respect we have too much lost through our own Mismanagement greatly, but more by our Bitterness and railing against each other.

From Volume III, Book XIII, 28-42

✇ 15 ✇

A Letter from Claribella concerning the Misfortunes of Aliena

To the Authors of the FEMALE SPECTATOR.

LADIES,

You cannot be insensible how little Compassion the Woes, occasioned by Love, find from this Iron-hearted Age; nor how ready every one is, on the least Breach of Decorum, to censure and condemn, without considering either the Force of that Passion, which those who are most upon their Guard against, have not always the Power of restraining, or what particular Circumstances may have concurred to ensnare a young Creature into a Forgetfulness of what she owes herself.—Her Fault alone engrosses the Discourse and Attention of the Town, and few there are will take the Pains to enquire if any Excuses may be made for it.—All the Misfortunes her Inadvertency brings upon her are unpity'd, and look'd upon as a just Punishment; all her former Merit is no more remember'd; and People no longer allow her to be possess'd of any Virtues, if once detected in transgressing one.

I am sure you are too just not to condemn such a Proceeding as highly cruel, and also too generous, not to make some Allowances for heedless Youth, when hurry'd on by an Excess of Passion to Things which cooler Reason disapproves.

In this Confidence I take the Liberty to give you the Narrative of an Adventure, which, tho' exactly true in every Circumstance, has in it something equally surprizing with any that the most celebrated Romance has presented to us.

The Heroine of it, whom I shall distinguish by the Name of

117

Aliena, is the Daughter of a Gentleman descended of a very antient Family, who, from Father to Son, had, for a long Succession of Ages, enjoyed an Estate, not inferior to some of the Nobility; but by an unhappy Attachment, in his immediate Predecessor, to the Race of the Stewarts, was depriv'd of the greatest Part of it; and as he had several Children besides this Aliena, none of them, excepting the eldest Son, could expect any other Fortunes than their Education, which he indeed took care should be very liberal.

But tho' his paternal Tenderness seemed equally divided among them all, and Aliena had no more Opportunities of Improvement than her other Sisters, yet did she make a much greater Progress in every thing she was instructed in than any of them; and as Nature had bestowed on her a much larger Share of Beauty, so was also her Genius more extensive than that which either one who was elder, and another a Year younger than herself, had to boast of.

In fine, dear Ladies, she was at Fourteen one of the most charming Creatures in the World.—As her Father lived in London, she went frequently to public Places, and those Diversions which were too expensive for the Narrowness of her Circumstances were, however, not deny'd her.—She was never without Tickets for the Masquerades, Ridotto's, Operas, Concerts, and Plays presented to her by her Friends; none of whom but thought themselves happy in her accompanying them to these Entertainments.

I was intimately acquainted with her, and have often thought her one of the happiest of our Sex, because, whether it was owing to her good Conduct or good Fortune, she lived without making any Enemies.—The Sweetness of her Behaviour charm'd all who were Witnesses of it; and tho' there are many equally innocent with herself, yet some have a certain Sourness or Haughtiness in their Deportment, which renders People industrious to find out something to condemn them; and those who think themselves insulted by any Airs of that Kind are apt enough to construe to themselves, or at least represent to others, the most harmless Actions as highly criminal.

But Aliena was the Darling of all that knew her;—wherever she came a general and unfeign'd Pleasure diffused itself in every Face through the whole Company. 'Tis scarce possible to say whether she was more admir'd by the Men, or loved by the Women.—A Thing wonderful you will own, and what some People take upon them to say is incompatible, yet so in reality it was.—Dear, sweet, agreeable, entertaining Aliena, how I lament the sad Reverse of thy Condition!

But, Ladies, I detain you too long from the promised Narrative;

compelled by the resistless Impulse of my Commiseration for this unfortunate Creature, I have, perhaps, too much encroach'd upon your Patience and that of your Readers, for which I ask Pardon of both, and will now come to the Point.

Among the Number of Aliena's Admirers, there was a Commander of one of his Majesty's Ships, a Gentleman of good Family, agreeable Person, and handsome Fortune, exclusive of his Commission.—Whether he had more the Art of Perswasion than any of his Rivals, I will not pretend to say; but it is certain, that either his Merit or good Fortune rendered every thing he said to her more acceptable than the most courtly Addresses of any other Person.

To be brief, she loved him.—His Manner, whatever it was, ensnared her young Heart, and the Society of her dear Captain was preferable to her to any other Joy the World could give.

I am very well assured his Pretensions were on an honourable Foot, otherwise they had been rejected at the first; all her Acquaintance expected every Day to hear of the Completion of their Wishes by a happy Marriage; when contrary to her, and it may be to his Expectations, he was order'd to sail for the West-Indies, and to be station'd there for three Years.

How terrible a Rebuff this was to her dearest Hopes any one may judge, and the more so as he did not press her to complete the Marriage before his Departure.—She thought with Reason, that if his Passion had been equal to his Pretensions he would have rejoiced to have secured her to himself; but instead of that, he seemed rather less assiduous than he had been, and seem'd more taken up with the Vexation of being obliged to be so long absent from his Native Country, than from that Person, whom he had a thousand times sworn was infinitely more valuable to him than any thing beside, either in that or the whole World.

I will not pretend to be so well acquainted with her Thoughts, as to say positively he had never loved her; but, I believe you will be of Opinion with me, that this Behaviour was far from being the Indication of a sincere and ardent Passion.

She had too much Wit not to perceive this Slight, but too much Tenderness to resent it as she ought to have done; and when he told her, as he sometimes vouchsafed to do, that he depended on her Constancy, and that he should find her at his Return with the same Inclinations he had left her possess'd of in his Favour, she always answer'd, that it was impossible for Time, Absence, or any other Sollicitations, ever to prevail on her to call back that Heart she had given him; and confirm'd the Promise of preserving herself entirely for him with all the Imprecations the most violent and faithful Passion could suggest.

Had there been no Possibility for him to have implor'd, nor she to have granted stronger Assurances for his future Happiness, he doubtless might, and ought to have been content with these; but as there was Consent of Friends, Licenses, and Wedding Rings easy to be had, and Churches, Chapels, and Clergymen plenty, no Impediment to prevent their being join'd forever, how could the dull Insensible entertain one Thought of going away without having first settled so material a Point!

But in all the tender Interviews that pass'd between them after the Arrival of those Orders, which were to separate them for so long a Time, he never once ask'd her to marry him; and as he made no Offers that way, her Modesty would not suffer her to be the first Proposer.

At length the cruel Day of taking leave was come.—Never parting had more the Shew of mournful: I say the *Shew*, because I cannot think the Captain had any real Grief at Heart; but on the Side of Aliena it was truly so. Yet did not all she express'd in his Presence come in any Competition with what she suffered after he was gone.—No Description can any way equal the Distraction she was in; I shall therefore not attempt it, but leave you to judge of the Cause by the Consequence.

For some Days she shut herself up, gave a loose to Tears and to Complainings, and scarce could be prevailed upon to take needful Nourishment.—Her Father's Commands, however, and Remonstrances, how much this Conduct would incur the Ridicule of the World, at last made her assume a more chearful Countenance, and she consented to see Company, and appear Abroad as usual; but while we all thought her Grief was abated, it preyed with greater Violence by being restrain'd, and inspir'd her with a Resolution to sacrifice every thing she had once valued herself upon, rather than continue in the Condition she was.

In fine, one Day when she was thought to be gone on a Visit to one of her Acquaintance, she went to a Sale-Shop, equipt herself in the Habit of a Man, or rather Boy, for being very short, she seem'd in that Dress not to exceed twelve or thirteen Years of Age at most.

Thinking herself not sufficiently disguised even by this, she made her fine Flaxen Hair be shaved, and covered her Head with a little brown Wig; which wrought so great a Change in her, that had her own Father happened to have met her he would scarce have known her after this Transformation.

But it was not her Intention to run that Hazard, nor had she taken all these Pains to live conceal'd in London.—She always knew she loved the Captain, but knew not till now with how much Violence she did so; or that for the Sake of being near him, she could forgo all that ever had or ought to have been dear to her.

I will not detain your Attention with any Repetition of those Conflicts which must necessarily rend her Bosom, while going about the Execution of a Design, the most daring sure that ever Woman form'd.—You will naturally conceive them when I acquaint you what it was.

Not able to support Life without the Presence of him who had her Heart, she seem'd with her Habit to have thrown off all the Fears and Modesty of Womanhood.—The fatal Softness of our Sex alone remained; and that, guided by the Dictates of an ungovernable Passion, made her despise all Dangers, Hardships, Infamy, and even Death itself.

She went directly to Gravesend, where her Lover's Ship lay yet at Anchor, waiting his Arrival, who was gone into the Country to take leave of some Relations. This she knew, and resolved, if possible, to get herself entered on board before he came, being unwilling he should see her till they were under sail.—Not that, as she has since declar'd, she had any Thoughts of discovering herself to him in case he knew her not, but that if he should happen to do so, she might avoid any Arguments he might make use of to dissuade her from an Enterprise she was determined to pursue at all Events, and even against the Inclination of him for whose Sake she undertook it.

She was a great Admirer of an old Play of Beaumont and Fletcher's, call'd *Philaster; Or, Love lies a Bleeding.*—The Character of Bellario, who, disguised like a Page, followed and waited on her beloved Prince in all his Adventures, strangely charm'd her, and she thought, as her Passion was equal to that of any Woman in the World, it would become her to attest it by Actions equally extravagant; and in the midst of all those Shocks, with which Reason and Modesty at some Times shook her Heart, felt a Pleasure in the Thoughts of attending her dear Captain, being always about him, doing little Services for him, and having an Opportunity of observing his Behaviour on all Occasions.

As she had often heard the Captain talk of his First Lieutenant with a great deal of Friendship, she thought him the most proper

Person to address; accordingly she waited till he came on Shore, and went to his Lodgings, where being easily admitted, she told him she had a great Inclination to the Sea, but as her Age, and Want of Skill in the Art of Navigation rendered her unfit as yet for any Service, excepting that of attending some or other of the Officers, she begg'd to be received in the Station of a Cabin-Boy.—She added, that she had heard such extraordinary Praises of the Captain's Humanity and Gentleness to all belonging to him, that she had an extreme Ambition to attend on him, if such a Favour might be granted her.

The Lieutenant eyed her attentively all the Time she was speaking, and was seized with a something which he had never felt before, and at that time was far from being able to account for; and this secret Impulse it was that made him unable to refuse her Request, tho' he knew very well that a sufficient Number of Boys had been already enter'd. He told her, however, that he could not give her an Assurance of being employed about the Captain's Person till he had spoke to him concerning it, but that since she seemed so desirous of it, he would use all his Interest with him on that Score; and added what she knew as well as himself, that he was absent at that Time, but was expected to arrive the same Day.

Aliena was highly content with the Promise he made her, and not doubted but when she was once in the Ship with him, she should find out some Stratagem or other to make him take Notice of her, and also to ingratiate herself so much with him, as to occasion him to take her under his own Care, even though it should be her Fate at first to be placed with any of the inferior Officers.

She thank'd the Lieutenant a thousand Times over, and was ready to fall at his Feet in Token of her Gratitude; but entreated he would continue his Goodness so far as to order her to be put on Board, lest he should, in the Hurry of his Affairs, forget the Promise he had made, and they should sail without her. To which he answer'd, that she had no need to be under any Apprehensions of that Sort, for he would send his Servant with her to a House where there were several Boys of the same Station, and he believed much of the same Age, and that the Long-Boat would put them all on Board that Evening.

This entirely eased all her Scruples, and she was beginning afresh to testify the Sense she had of the Favour he did her, when some Company coming in to visit the Lieutenant, he call'd his Man, and sent him to conduct her to the House he had mentioned.

There she found several Youths ready equipt for their Voyage, and whose rough athletic Countenances and robust Behaviour became well enough the Vocation they had taken upon them, but rendered them very unfit Companions for the gentle, the delicate Aliena.

The Discourse they had with each other, the Oaths they swore, and the Tricks they played by way of diverting themselves, frighted her almost out of her Intention; but she was much more so when they began to lay their Hands on her to make one in their boisterous Exercises. The more abash'd and terrify'd she look'd the more rude they grew, and pinching her on the Ribs, as Boys frequently do to one another, one of them found she had Breasts, and cry'd with a great Oath, that they had got a Girl among them.—On this they were all for being satisfy'd, and had doubtless treated her with the most shocking Indecency, had not her Cries brought up the Woman of the House, who being informed of the Occasion of this Uproar, took Aliena from them, and was going to carry her into another Room, in order to learn the Truth of this Adventure, when the Lieutenant entered, and found his new Sailor all in Tears, and the rest in a loud Laugh.

The Cause of all this was soon explained to him, but the greatest Mistery was still behind, nor did he find it very easy to come at; for tho' Aliena confess'd to him, and to the Landlady, after they had taken her into a private Room, that she was a Woman, yet who she was, and the Motive which had induced her to disguise herself in this Manner, she seem'd determin'd to keep from their Knowledge, and only begg'd that as her Design had miscarried, by her Sex being so unfortunately discovered, they would permit her to go without making any further Enquiry concerning her.

But this Request the Lieutenant would by no Means comply with; he now no longer wonder'd at those secret Emotions which had work'd about his Heart at first Sight of her, and avow'd the Force of Nature, which is not to be deceiv'd, tho' the Senses may, and frequently are.

He now indulg'd the Admiration of her Beauty, much more than he would give himself the Liberty of doing while he thought her what her Habit spoke her, and look'd so long till he entirely look'd away his Heart.—He was really in Love with her, but was either asham'd of being so for a young Creature, whose Virtue and Discretion he had no Reason to have a very high Idea of, or was awed by that Respect which is inseparable from a true Affection, from declaring himself. To whichever of these Motives it was, I will not take upon me to determine, but he was entirely silent on that

Head, and only told her in a gay Manner, that as he had entered her on her earnest Desire, he could not consent to discharge her without knowing something more of her than that she was a Woman.—*Nay,* added he, *even of that I am not quite assured:—I have only the Testimony of two or three Boys, who in such a Case are not to be depended upon:—I think that I ought, at least, to satisfy myself in that Point.*

In speaking these Words he offered to pluck her towards him, and the vile Woman of the House, who had no Regard for any thing but her own Interest, in obliging her Customers, guessing the Lieutenant's Designs, and perhaps thinking them worse than they were in reality, went out of the Room and left them together.

This, indeed, quite overcame all the Resolution of Aliena; she thought she saw something in the Eyes of the Lieutenant that, even more than his Words, threatened her with all a Maid of Honour and Condition had to dread; and after having struggled with all her Might to get loose of the hold he had taken of her, threw herself at his Feet, and with a Flood of Tears, and broken trembling Voice, conjured him to have Pity on her and suffer her to depart.—*If ever,* said she, *you were taught to revere Virtue in another, or love the Practice of it yourself, if you have any Kindred whose Chastity is dear to you, for their Sakes, and for your own, commiserate a wretched Maid, whom Chance and her own Folly alone have thrown into your Power.*

These Words, the Emphasis with which they were deliver'd, and the Action that accompany'd them, made the Lieutenant, who, as it luckily prov'd for her, was really a Man of Honour, shudder as she spoke them.—He rais'd her from the Posture she had been in with more Respect than indeed, considering all Things, she could in Reason have expected; desir'd she would not be under any Apprehensions of his behaving to her in a Manner she could not be brought to approve; but in return for that Self-denial, he still insisted she would make him the Confidante of the Motive which had oblig'd her to expose herself to the Dangers she had done.

Alas, Sir, answer'd she, still weeping, *as for the Dangers you mention, and which I have but too cruelly experienced, I never had once a Thought of them; and as for any I might encounter from the Inclemency of the Winds and Waves, I despised them.—Whatever Hardships I should have sustain'd in the Prosecution of my intended Enterprise, would have afforded me more Pleasure than Pain, had Fate permitted me to have undergone them.—Nay, Death itself had been welcome, had it seiz'd me on Board that Ship my Heart was bent to live or die in.—But endless Grief and Misery is now my Doom, since deny'd the last, the only Satisfaction this wide World could give me.*

Yet pardon me, continued she, *if I cannot let you into the Secret of who I am, or what induced me to this strange Ramble.—Let it therefore content you to know I am not of the lowest Rank of People;—that my Reputation is not altogether my own, since my Family will be Sufferers by my Fault, if known; and also that how much soever my disguising myself in this Manner may subject me to your Censure, yet my very Soul shrinks at Dishonour, and that this Action, which alone can be alledg'd against me, is a greater Disguise to my real Principles, than my Habit has been to my Sex.*

The Lieutenant listen'd with all the Attention she wish'd; every Syllable she uttered sunk into his Soul.—His Love, his Admiration, his Astonishment, increased every Moment; but tho' he began to feel more pure Flames for her, than those he testify'd at his first Information she was a Woman, yet they were too ardent to permit him to let her go from him without giving him some probable Hopes of ever seeing her more. He gave a Turn indeed to his Manner of treating her, yet still gave her to understand, he would not part from her without being made privy to every thing he wish'd to know.

To this poor Aliena answer'd little but with Tears; and while he continued pressing, she evading, a Sailor came in to acquaint him the Captain was arrived; on which he hastily took leave, but before he left the House charg'd the Landlady, as she valued his Friendship, not to let the seeming Boy stir out of the Room.

This Aliena was ignorant of, till imagining herself at Liberty, she was going down Stairs, in order to quit a Place where she had nothing but Ruin to expect, she was met by the Woman of the House, who obliged her to turn back, and then lock'd her into a Room, telling her she must stay till the Return of the Lieutenant.

Now had this unfortunate Creature full Liberty to reflect on the Mischiefs she had brought upon herself.—Night came on, and every Moment came loaded with new Horrors.—The Lieutenant return'd not, but as she was in continual Apprehensions of him, she resolved not to pluck off her Cloaths, nor even venture to lie down on the Bed, lest she should fall into a Sleep, and by that Means be rendered incapable of resisting any Violence that might be offer'd to her.

All Night long did she walk about the Chamber in an Agony of Mind which stands in need of no Description, nor can be reach'd by any.—Had the Window look'd into the Street, she would certainly have jump'd out, but being backwards, her Escape would have been no farther than the Yard of the same House, which, as she was wholly ignorant of the Passages, left her no room to hope she could get through without Discovery.

A thousand different Ideas rose in her almost distracted Brain.—She fear'd the Lieutenant, and saw no way to avoid him, but by the Protection of the Captain, and how to acquaint him with any thing of what had pass'd she knew not;—at last she bethought herself of attempting to do it even by the Lieutenant himself; and accordingly when he came, as he did pretty early in the Morning, she said to him with all the Courage she could assume,

Sir, You insist on knowing who I am, which I am determined to die rather than comply with.—There is but one way, by which you have a Chance of gratifying your Curiosity.—Be the Bearer of a Letter from me to your Captain.—He knows me, and if he thinks fit will inform you of every thing.

The Lieutenant on this began to guess somewhat of the Truth, and agreed to do as she desir'd, and immediately call'd for Pen, Ink, and Paper for her; which being brought, she was not long writing these Lines.

To Captain ————

Unable to support your Absence, I followed you in Disguise, desirous of no other Happiness than to enjoy conceal'd your Sight.—An unlucky Accident has discover'd me.—Your First Lieutenant, whose Prisoner I now am, can tell you by what Means.—For Heaven's Sake deliver me from his Power, that I may either return to my Father, if he will receive me after this Adventure, or die with Shame of it in some obscure Corner of the World.

She subscrib'd no Name, nor was there indeed any Occasion for doing it to one so well acquainted with the Characters of her Handwriting; the Lieutenant suffered her to seal it without once asking to see the Contents, and gave his Word of Honour to deliver it the same Hour into the Captain's Hands, and bring whatever Answer should be return'd.

He now, 'tis certain, began to see a good deal into this extraordinary Affair.—He no longer doubted but Love of the Captain had been the Cause, but, 'tis highly probable, imagin'd also that more had pass'd between that Gentleman and his fair Charge than they in reality were guilty of.

The generous Concern he had for her Youth and Beauty, however, made him impatient to see in what Manner her Lover would receive this Billet; he therefore hurry'd away to his Lodgings, where he was strangely surpriz'd to find a great Crowd of Officers and other People about the Door, and on his going up Stairs saw the Captain, and three Gentlemen, whom he knew not engaged in a very warm Dispute.—The Cause of it was this:

The Family of Aliena had no sooner miss'd her than strict Search was made for her all over the Town.—Accident at last discovered where she had exchanged her Habit, and the Disguise she had made Choice of made them naturally conjecture on what Design she was gone; but not being able to imagine that so young and artless a Maid should have undertaken an Enterprize of this bold Kind, concluded she must have her Advisers and Exciters to it, and who but the Captain could they suspect of being so.—They were, therefore, assured in their own Minds, that some private Correspondence had been carry'd on between them since his pretended taking Leave.—Incensed against him, as had their Thoughts been true they would have had the highest Reason, they complain'd of the Insult, and obtained an Order to search the Ship, and force her from this supposed Betrayer of her Honour.—To this end, they brought proper Officers with them to Gravesend, and had the Assistance of others belonging to that Place.

Before they proceeded to Extremities, however, they went to the Captain's Lodgings, being told on their Arrival he was not yet gone on Board.—At first the Father, an Uncle, and a Cousin of Aliena's, who all came down together, remonstrated to him, in Terms tolerably mild, how ungentlemanlike an Action it was to delude a young Girl of Family, and to whom he had made an honourable Courtship, to quit her Friends, and accompany him in so shameful a Manner; but finding he deny'd all they accused him of, as well he might, they began to grow extremely rough.—The Uncle, who had some Interest at the Board of Admiralty, told him he would shake his Commission, and many such like Menaces. Which the Captain, knowing his Innocence, was little able to endure, and their mutual Rage was expressing itself in the highest Terms when the Lieutenant enter'd.

This Gentleman listen'd for some Moments to what was said, without speaking, and easily perceiving, by the Repartees on both Sides, the Meaning of what at his first Entrance seem'd so astonishing.—*Hold Gentlemen,* cry'd he to the Kindred of Aliena,

*your Passion has transported you too far, and I dare say you will
hereafter own to be guilty of an Injustice you will be ashamed of,
when once the Truth comes to be reveal'd.—I believe,* continued he, *I
am the only Person capable of clearing up this Mistery; but before I
do so, beg leave to give a Letter to my Captain, put into my Hands
this Morning, for the safe Delivery of which I have pawn'd my
Honour.*

Not only the Captain, but those who came to accuse him were
surpriz'd at what he said; but the former taking the Letter hastily out
of his Hands, and having read it with a great deal of real Amazement,
which I have heard them all allow was very visible in his
Countenance, walk'd several Times about the Room with a confus'd
Emotion; then paus'd,—then walk'd again, and paus'd again, as if
uncertain how he should behave in an Exigence which, it must be
own'd, demanded some Deliberation; the Father and the Uncle of
Aliena still crying out he must produce the Girl, and growing
clamorous, Spleen, Pettishness, or a Value for his own Character
more than for that of the Woman he had once pretended to adore,
made him throw the Letter upon the Table in an abrupt Manner, and
at the same time bad them go in search of the Person they came in
quest of; adding, that what was wanting in the young Lady was
owing to her Want of proper Education, rather than to any
Insinuations or Crafts he had practised on her.

The Father, finding it his Daughter's Hand, read it with a Shock
which is not to be express'd; and having given it to his Brother,
cry'd, *Where,—who is this Lieutenant, into whose Power my poor
unhappy Girl has fallen?*

I am the Person, said the Lieutenant, *and but to clear my Captain
from any Imputation of a base Design, should not have spoke what I
now find myself obliged to do.*

He then related in what Manner Aliena came to him, the
Earnestness with which she begg'd to be enter'd on Board; and in
fine, neither omitted nor added to any thing of the Truth.

This struck the Kindred of Aliena into the utmost
Confusion.—Every thing prov'd the Innocence, and as even I, dear
Ladies, who am her Friend must own, the Folly of this unhappy Girl;
all blush'd and hung down their Heads oppress'd with conscious
Shame.—The Captain pity'd the Consternation they were in, and his
Heart, I cannot but think, throbb'd for the Condition of
Aliena.—*Come,* said he to his Lieutenant, in as gay a Manner as the
Circumstance would admit, *let us go visit the Lady who it seems is*

your Prisoner, and see what Ransom will be demanded for her.

The Lieutenant made no other Answer than a low Bow, and immediately conducted them, where they found the unfortunate Aliena walking about the Room in her Boy's Cloaths, distracted in her Mind at what Reception her Letter would find from the Captain, but little thinking of the new Guests who now enter'd her Chamber.

Oh, dear *Spectator*, think and judge what this poor Soul must feel, at the Sight of her Lover, her Father, and the nearest of her Kindred thus at once presented to her.—What might have excused her to the one, rendered her criminal to the other; nor could the soft Impulse of Love, coincide with what she owed to Duty, and the Decorum of Reputation.

At seeing them thus altogether, she fell into Faintings, from which she was recover'd but to relapse again, and the first Words she spoke were — I am ruin'd for ever.—*You, Sir*, said she to her Father, *can never, I am sure, forgive the Dishonour I have brought upon our Family.—And you*, pursued she, turning to the Captain, *what can you think of the wretched Aliena! This very Proof I have given you of my Love, the extremest, the tenderest Love that ever Heart was capable of feeling, even you may censure as not consistent with the Prudence and Decorum of my Sex.—Oh wretched!—Wretched am I every way, by all deservedly abandoned.*

The Condition they saw her in disarmed her Kindred of great Part of the Indignation they had before been full of, and hearing the Captain testify abundance of tender Concern for the Hazards to which she had expos'd herself for his Sake, they withdrew to a Window, and after a short Consultation, desir'd the Captain to go with them into another Room; which Request he readily complying with, the Father of Aliena told him, that as he had courted his Daughter, and so far engag'd her Affections as to be induced by them to take a Step so contrary to Duty and Reputation, he thought it would become him to silence the Reproaches of the World by marrying her before he embark'd.

The Captain not returning an immediate Answer to this Proposal, gave Opportunity to the Uncle and Cousin of Aliena to second what the Father had said; and they made use of many Arguments to convince him, that in Honour and Conscience he ought not to depart and leave her to be exposed to Calumny for an Action of which he had been the sole Cause.

To all which, as soon as they had done speaking, the Captain reply'd, that he desired no greater Happiness in Life than being the

Husband of Aliena, provided the Duties of his Post had not called him so suddenly away; but as he must not only be immediately snatched from her Arms, but also be absent thence for so long a time, he thought it inconsistent, either with Love or Reason, to leave her a Wife under such Circumstances.—That if her Affection was as well rooted as she said it was, she would doubtless have the Patience to wait his Return, and that if he heard nothing on her Part which should oblige him to change the Sentiments he at present had, he should then himself be a Petitioner for her Hand.

On this they told him, he had no Reason to suspect the Sincerity of her Love, she had given but too substantial a Proof of it, by the mad Exploit she had undertaken.

Do not think me ungrateful, answer'd he hastily, *if I say it is a Proof of the Violence of it, which I see with more Grief than Satisfaction; because Actions of this Kind are judged by those who view them with different Eyes, as somewhat romantic, and occasion a good deal of idle Ridicule among the laughing Part of the World.—But*, continued he, *as Constancy more than Vehemence of Affection is requisite to render the conjugal State a happy one, it is Time alone can assure me of Felicity with the Lady in question.—For which Reason I must not think of entering into any Bonds of the Nature you mention till after my Return.*

This Answer, determinate as it was, did not make them give over; but all they urged was preaching to the Wind, and the more they seemed to resent his Refusal, the more obstinately he persisted in it; and they were obliged to leave Gravesend, taking with them the disconsolate Aliena, no less dissatisfy'd in their Minds than when they came into it.

How changed is now the Fate of this young Lady!—The Idol once of her Acquaintance, the Pity now of some, and the Contempt of others.—The Search made for her in Town after her Elopement made the Affair no Secret. Every one talks and judges of it according to their different Humours; but few there are who put the best Construction.—Sensible of this, she rarely stirs Abroad, and at Home is treated in a Manner quite the reverse of what she was accustomed to be before this Accident.—Her Father and Brothers look on her as a Blemish to their Family, and her Sisters take every Opportunity to reproach her.—The Captain has never wrote to her since he went, tho' several Letters from him have been receiv'd by others.—In fine, 'tis impossible to paint her Situation so truly miserable as it is.—All I can say gives but a faint Idea of it; yet such as it is, I flatter myself, will be sufficient to induce you to make her Innocence as public as possible, by inserting this faithful Account of the whole Affair.

I am also pretty confident that the Good-nature which seems to sparkle through all your Writings, besides the common Interest of our Sex, will make you a little expatiate on the ungenerous Proceeding of the Captain.—The more Honour he may have in other Respects, the less he is to be excused in regard to Aliena; since it was that very Honour which betrayed her into a fatal Confidence of his Love and Sincerity.

Had he been possess'd of a much less Share of Passion for her than he had profess'd, or had she even been indifferent to him, Gratitude, methinks, should have made him marry her, since there was no other Way to heal the Wounds she had given her Reputation for his Sake.

But I will not anticipate your Judgments on this Head, and after begging Pardon for this long Letter, conclude with assuring you that
      I am, LADIES,

            Your sincere Well-wisher,
Red-Lyon-Square,   And most humble Servant,
March 29, 1745   CLARIBELLA.

Of all the Letters with which the *Female Spectator* has been favour'd, none gave us a greater Mixture of Pain and Pleasure than this.—'Tis difficult to say whether the unhappy Story it contains, or the agreeable Manner in which it is related, most engages our Attention; but while we do Justice to the Historian, and pity the unfortunate Lady, in whose Cause she has employ'd her Pen, we must be wary how we excuse her Faults so far as to hinder others from being upon their Guard not to fall into the same.

...It is certain that nothing can be more astonishing than that so young a Creature, bred up in the strictest Principles of Virtue, and endued with the Perfections Claribella ascribes to her, could all at once throw off every Consideration of what she owed herself,—her Family, and her Sex, to expose herself to such wild Hazards, the least of which was worse than Death.

To us it seems plain, that how much Wit soever she may be Mistress of in Conversation, she is altogether incapable of making any solid Reflections.—There must be a romantic Turn in her Mind, which may have been heighten'd by reading those extravagant Fictions with which some Books abound.—This Claribella seems to think herself, by her mentioning the

Fondness her fair unhappy Friend testify'd for the Character of Bellario.—
As she thought it an amiable one, it is not therefore to be wonder'd at that
she copy'd after it.

If Poets would consider how great an Effect their Writings have upon
the Minds of young People, they would surely never paint whatever is an
Error in Conduct in too beautiful Colours, nor endeavour to excite Pity on
the Stage for those Actions, which every where else justly incur both
Punishment and Contempt; but too many of them, as well ancient as modern, have seem'd to employ their whole Art in touching the Passions,
without any Regard to the Morals of an Audience; as a very judicious
Italian Author once said of them:

> *Oltramontani non sono zelanti delle buone regele de Modestia &*
> *de Prudenza.*

That is, 'Those on the other Side the Mountains make no Scruple of
breaking the good Laws of Modesty and Prudence.'

A gentle, generous, tender Soul we are ready to allow her, but must at
the same time say, that such a Disposition where it happens to be join'd
with a weak Judgment, is extremely dangerous to the Person possess'd of
it; because it often transports such a one to Excesses, by which the best
Virtues may become Vices.

This was evidently the Case in regard of Aliena.—Her Love for the
Captain, as his Addresses were honourable, was natural, and nothing in it
which could arraign her Prudence or her Modesty.—The Grief she was
under at the Necessity of parting with him for so long a Time, and even her
soft Desires of being united to him before their Separation, had something
amiable in them. Had she stuck there, and preserved her Heart and Person
till his Return, and he had afterwards proved ungrateful or inconstant to
such Love and Sweetness, no Reproaches could have been equal to his
Crime; but I am sorry to say, that by giving too great a loose to those
Qualities, which kept within due Limits had been worthy Praise and Imitation, she forfeited all Pretensions to the Esteem of the Man she lov'd, as
well as of those least interested in the Affair.

The *Female Spectator* must not therefore be so far sway'd either by her
own Good-nature, or the Desires of Claribella, as to attempt framing any
Excuse for those very Errors in Conduct which these Monthly Essays are
intended only to reform.

From Volume III, Book XIV, 65-95

☙ 16 ❧

The Lady's Revenge

Whether these Monthly Essays answer the great End proposed by them, of conducing in some Measure to that Rectification of Manners which this Age stands in so much need of, we cannot yet be able to determine; but of this we are certain, by the Letters we receive, that Wit, and the Love of Virtue are not altogether banish'd the Realm. The following, as well as many we already have had the Pleasure of transmitting to the Public, is a Proof of it.

To the FEMALE SPECTATOR.

MADAM,

As I perceive you intersperse your moral Reflections with such Adventures as promise either Instruction or Entertainment to your Readers, I take the Liberty of enclosing a little Narrative, which I can answer is a recent Transaction, and the Truth of it known to a great many others as well as myself.

I shall make no Apology for any Blunders in Stile, having drawn it up as well as I could, and leave the Correction and Amendment to your more elegant and judicious Pen, which I am well convinced can smooth the harshest Expression, and extract even Gold from the coarsest Metal.—I am, with the most perfect Admiration and good Wishes for your Undertaking,

      MADAM,
           Your very humble Servant,
Kensington,   And Subscriber,
April 16, 1745.   ELISMONDA.

* * *

The LADY'S REVENGE

Among the Number of those gay Gallants who pride themselves on being distinguish'd at all public Places, none had more Reason to boast of the modish Accomplishments than Ziphranes. He sung, danc'd, dress'd well;—had the Knack of setting off, to the best Advantage, his Family, his Fortune, and his Person.—Knew how to trace his Ancestors long before the Conquest; to discover some particular Perfection in every Acre of his Land, and to give all his Limbs and Features such Gestures as his Glass inform'd him would be most becoming: in fine, he was what we Women call a mighty pretty Fellow. For as the Poet too justly says of us:

> *Our thoughtless Sex is caught by outward Form*
> *And empty Noise, and loves itself in Man.*[1]

As he either found or thought himself admir'd by all the Ladies he conversed with, he in Return seem'd to admire them all.—Many Friendships were broke, and great Annimosities have arose on the Score of this great Almanzor[2] in Love, who triumph'd wherever he came, without giving any of the fair Contenders for his Heart leave to think she had the Power of entirely subduing it.—If one seem'd to have the Advantage over him Today, she was sure of yielding it Tomorrow to some other Beauty, who again lost it in her Turn.—Nay, sometimes in the same Hour he would press one Lady by the Hand, whisper a soft thing in the Ear of another, look dying on a third, and present a Love Sonnet of his own composing to a fourth.

In this Manner did he divide his Favours till he became acquainted with Barsina, a Lady of a good Fortune and very agreeable Person.—She lived mostly in the Country, and when she was in Town kept but little Company, and seldom appear'd in any public Place.—She was, indeed, more reserved than any one I ever knew of her Age and Circumstances; and tho' she had an Infinity of Wit, chose rather to be thought to have none, than to expose it by speaking more than she thought consistent with that Modesty, which she set the higher Value upon, as she saw others value it so little.

It was, perhaps, as much owing to this Character of Reserve as to any other Perfection in her, tho' few Women can boast of greater, that made the Conquest of her Heart more flattering to the Vanity of Ziphranes, than any he had yet gain'd.—But be that as it may, he approach'd her with a different kind of Homage to what he had ever paid to any other Woman;

and not only gave her that Proof of his serious Attachment, but also a much greater, which was this: He entirely gave over his Gallantries to every former Object of them, and confined his Addresses to her alone, to the Astonishment of all his Acquaintance, who spoke of it as a Prodigy, and cry'd, *Who would have believ'd it — Ziphranes is grown constant!*

This Change in his Behaviour, join'd with a secret liking of his Person, and the Sanction of a near Relation's Perswasion, who had introduced him to her, and thought they would be a proper Match for one another, engag'd her to receive him in quality of a Lover; tho' long it was before he could prevail on her to acknowledge she did so through any other Motive than meerly in Compliance with the Request of a Person so nearly allied to her.

To make Trial of his Perseverance, she pretended Business call'd her into the Country; he begg'd Leave to accompany her, but that not being permitted, he follow'd to her Retirement, took Lodgings as near her as he could, and visited her every Day, renewing the Declarations he had made in Town, nor would return till she had fixed the Day for coming also.

As she came in the Stage-Coach, she could not prevent him from doing so too, if she had been affected enough to attempt it. Yet could not all his Assiduity, his Vows, his Protestations, meet any farther Reward than the bare Acceptance of them.

By Degrees, however, he gain'd further on her, and got the better of that cruel Caution which had given him so much Trouble; and she at last confess'd, that she thought him worthy of every thing a Woman of Honour could bestow.

With what Rapture he express'd himself at hearing these long wish'd-for Words any one may judge, by the Pains he had taken to induce her to speak them.—He had now nothing to do but to press for the Confirmation of his Happiness, and in the most tender Terms beseech'd her to settle a Day for that Purpose; to which she blushing answer'd, he must depend for that on the Gentleman who first brought them acquainted, and had always been so much his Friend.

This he seem'd very well satisfy'd with, as she doubted not but he would, and as she knew the Person she mention'd had greatly promoted the Interest of his Love; and she now began to set herself to think seriously on Marriage, as of a State she should soon enter into.—Some Days, however, pass'd over without her hearing any thing of the Matter, than that Ziphranes told her, that he had been to wait on her Cousin, but had not the good Fortune to meet with him at home.

Prepossessed as she was in favour of this Lover, it seem'd a little strange to her, that the Vehemence of the Passion he profess'd, should not influence him to watch Night and Day for the Sight of a Person to whom

she had refer'd the Grant of what he had seemed so ardently to desire.—
Besides, she very well knew there could have been no Difficulty in finding
him, had the other attempted it in good earnest; and this, with the Imagination that she observed somewhat of a less Tenderness than usual in his
Looks and Behaviour to her, fill'd her with very perplexing Agitations.

A Week was hardly elaps'd, since she made him that soft Concession
above recited, when he sent to acquaint her, he was extremely indisposed
with a Cold, and could not have the Pleasure of waiting on her.

This Message. and the Manner in which it was deliver'd, heighten'd her
Suspicions, that she had deceiv'd herself in an Opinion either of his Love
or Honour.—*I am betray'd*, cry'd she in a good deal of Agony of Spirit, *it
is owing to the Coldness of his own Heart, not any the Inclemency of the
Season has inflicted on him, that he absents himself.*

She kept her Vexation conceal'd however, and tho' her Relation had
visited her several Times since she had seen Ziphranes, she never once
mentioned any thing concerning him, till that Gentleman one Day, in a gay
Humour, said to her, *Well, Cousin, how thrive my Friend's Hopes?—When
are we to see you a Bride?* On which, before she was aware, she cry'd *I am
not the proper Person to be ask'd that Question.—What does Ziphranes
say?*

*I cannot expect that Confidence from him, which you so near a Relation
deny*, answer'd he; *but indeed I wanted to talk a little seriously to you on
that Head:—I am afraid there is some Brûlée between you, for I have met
him two or three Times, and he rather seems to shun than court my Company.*

To hear he was abroad at the Time he had pretended Sickness, and that
he had seen the very Person to whom she had consign'd the disposing of
herself, without speaking any thing to him of the Affair, was sufficient to
have opened the Eyes of a Woman of much less Penetration and Judgment
than she was.—She was at once convinced of his Falsehood and Ingratitude, and the Indignation of having been so basely imposed upon was
about to shew itself, by telling the whole Story to her Cousin, when some
Ladies that Instant coming in to visit her prevented it.

No Opportunity offering that Night to disburthen the inward Agony she
was inflam'd with, by reason her Cousin went away before the rest of the
Company took Leave, she pass'd the Hours till Morning in a Situation
more easy to be conceiv'd than describ'd.

She would have given the World, had she been Mistress of it, to have
been able to have assign'd some Reason for so sudden a Change in a
Person, whose Love and Constancy she had as many Testimonies of as
were in the Power of Man to give.—The more she reflected on his past and

present Behaviour, the more she was confounded; and how far soever he had insinuated himself into her Heart, she suffered yet more from her Astonishment than she did from her abused Affection.

The Greatness of her Spirit, as well as her natural Modesty and Reserve, would not permit her either to write, or send to know the Meaning of his Absence; and her Cousin not happening to come again, she had none on whose Discretion she could enough rely to make a Confidant on in an Affair, which she look'd upon as so shameful to herself; and endur'd for three Days longer a Suspence more painful than the Certainty which the fourth produced had the Power of inflicting.

As soon as she rung her Bell in the Morning, her Maid brought a Letter which she told her was left for her very early, by a Servant belonging to Ziphranes.—*Ziphranes* cry'd Barsina, with a Hurry of Spirits which that Moment she had not Command enough over herself to be able either to repel or to conceal, —*What is it he can say?*

To BARSINA.

MADAM,
Since I had last the Honour of waiting on you, a Proposal of Marriage was made to me, which I found is very much to my Convenience to accept, and I did so the rather, as I knew there was too little Love on your Side to render it any Disappointment:—I thought myself obliged to acquaint you with it before you heard it from any other Hand; and wish you as happy with some more deserving Man as I hope this Morning will make me:—I shall always continue to think of you with the greatest Respect, and am,
    MADAM,
        Your most humble,
        And most obedient Servant.
        ZIPHRANES.

What she felt on reading this Letter any Woman who, without Love, has the least Pride or Sense of Resentment may judge; but as Barsina had certainly once a very great Share of Regard for this perfidious Prophaner of the most ardent Vows and Protestations, her Affliction must be violent indeed, at the first News of his Inconstancy.

But whatever it was, with her usual Prudence, she confin'd it to her own Breast, and tho' that Day, and several succeeding ones, she heard of nothing but Ziphranes's Marriage, and the Wonder every one express'd at the Suddenness of it, as well as that it was to any other than herself; yet did she so well stifle all the Emotions of her Soul, that none could perceive she was the least disturb'd at it.

His ungenerous Behaviour had doubtless turn'd her Heart entirely against him.—She soon grew to despise him much more than ever she had loved; but then the Thought how much she had been deceiv'd in him, and that he had it in his Power to boast that he had made an Impression on her, gave her the most poignant Anguish.

In fine, all the Passion she now had for him was Revenge, and by what Method she should inflict a Punishment, in some measure proportionable to his Crime, took up her whole Thoughts; and at last having hit on one to her Mind, was not long before she accomplish'd it.

She knew he was accustomed to walk every Day in the Park, and being informed that since his Marriage he continued to do so, she made it her Business to throw herself in his Way; and meeting him according to her Wish, accompany'd only with an old Gentleman, who did not seem to be a Person of any very great Consequence, she went directly up to him, and told him she desir'd to speak with him, on which the other immediately took Leave.

Ziphranes was so confounded at the Sight of her, that he was scarce able to return the Salutation she gave him with the Complaisance of a Gentleman; which she perceiving, to add to his Mortification, told him she did so, but added with a great deal of seeming Gaiety, that he had no Reason to be under any manner of Concern; for tho' his quitting her for another was extremely cruel, he had it in his Power to attone, and it was for that End she came to seek him.

All this, which he could not but look on as Raillery, was very surprizing to him from a Woman of her serious and reserved Temper.—And his Confusion both at that, and meeting her, was still so great, that he could not answer it in kind as he would have done, had he been more Master of himself, and it was but with a stammering Voice he at last drawled out, that he should rejoice to oblige her in any thing he could.

What a Force has conscious Guilt!—How mean, how cowardly does a base Action render one! He who found it easy to commit the Crime, trembled at the Reproaches it deserv'd:—Barsina felt a gloomy Satisfaction in her Mind at the Pain he was in, but that was little to what her Resentment demanded; and it was necessary to ease his present Disquiets, in order to have it in her Power to inflict on him others of a more terrible Nature.

She therefore assumed as much Softness in her Eyes and Voice, as a Person not accustomed to Dissimulation could possibly put on, and with a half Sigh, *Well, Ziphranes, I accuse you not,* said she, *Love I know is an involuntary Passion, and besides I have heard say there is a Fate in Marriage which is not to be withstood:—I only think the long Acquaint-*

ance we had together ought not to have been so abruptly broke off:—I might have expected you would have taken one tender Leave of me at least!

He was beginning to make some pitiful Excuse or other for his Behaviour in this Point, but she would not suffer him to go on:—*Say nothing of it*, interrupted she, *what is done is past Recall; but if you would have me think you ever meant me fair, or that all the Vows you made were but to ensnare and triumph over my artless Innocence, you must comply with the Request I now make you, which is to let me see you once more at my Lodgings:—You may depend on hearing no Upbraidings:—I desire no more than to take a last Farewel, and if you gratify me in this, which I know you will think, and I confess, is but a Whim, I give you my solemn Promise never more to trouble you.*

Such an Invitation, and deliver'd in this Manner from a Mouth, whom he had Reason to believe would have been filled with Expressions of a vastly different Sort, might very well amaze him.—He thought her Behaviour, as indeed it was, a little out of Nature, and quite the reverse of that Reserve and perfect Modesty she had formerly treated him with; but to whatever Source this Change in her was owing, he could not be so unpolite as to refuse what she desir'd of him, and it was agreed between them that he should breakfast with her the next Morning.

Accordingly he came; she received him with great Civility, but somewhat more serious and more like herself than the Day before.—Chocolate was served up, and the Maid attending while they breakfasted, Barsina entertain'd him only with Discourses on ordinary Affairs.—When they had done, she order'd a Bottle of Cyprus Wine to be set upon the Table, and made a Sign to her Servant to leave the Room.

Now being alone together she fill'd out two Glasses, and presented one to Ziphranes, but he desir'd to be excused, telling her he never drank any Sort of Wine in a Morning.—*You must break through that Custom for once*, said she smiling; *and to engage you to do so, as well as to shew I have not the least Animosity to the Lady who has supplanted me in your Affections, the Toast shall be Health and Happiness to your Bride. This, sure, you will not offer to refuse.*

With these Words she put the Glass a second Time into his Hand, *Well, Madam*, answer'd he, *it would not become me to disobey you, since you so much insist upon it:—I will do myself the Honour to pledge you.*

She then drank the above-mention'd Health, and he having drain'd his Glass to the same, *Now I am satisfy'd*, cry'd she; *tho' my cruel Stars deny'd me the Pleasure of living with you, we shall die together, at least:—I drank my happy Rival's Health sincerely, and may she enjoy long Life, and many prosperous Days, if she can do so without Ziphranes, but for a little, a very little longer shall she triumph with him over the forsaken Barsina.*

What is it you mean, Madam! said he hastily. *That you have drank your Bane,* answer'd she: *The Wine I gave you, and partook of myself, was mix'd with the most deadly Poyson, nor is it in the Power of Art to save the Life of either of us.*

You would not do so sure! cry'd he: *What could I do but die,* reply'd she, *when your Inconstancy had made Life a Burthen not to be borne? and to have dy'd without you would have been mean and poor, unworthy of my Love or my Revenge: Now both are gratify'd.*

'Tis a Question whether these last Words reach'd his Ears, for before she had quite given over speaking, he started up and ran out of the Room like a Man distracted, uttering a Volley of Curses on her, and on himself, as he went down the Stairs.

What Effect the Draught had on Barsina, and what kind of Reflections enter'd her Head, when left to think seriously on what she had done, the Reader shall hereafter be inform'd at full; but we must now follow Ziphranes, who had not the least Inclination to die, and see how he behav'd in a Situation so terrible to him.

The Moment he got within his own Doors he sent for a Physician, told him he had swallowed Poyson, and that he had Reason to fear it was of the most mortal Kind; tho' by whom administer'd, and for what Cause, he kept a Secret, not to alarm his Wife.—Oyl was the first Thing judged necessary, great Quantities of which he took; but nothing appearing but what any Stomach thus agitated might disgorge, more powerful Emetics were prescrib'd; but even these had no other Effect than to throw him into fainting Fits.—Yet low and weak as he was, he continually cry'd out, *Have I yet evacuated the Poyson?* and being answer'd in the Negative, told the Doctor and Apothecary that they were ignorant Fellows, and he would have others sent for.

It was in vain, the one assured him that there was not in the whole *Materia Medica* a more efficacious Medicine than what he had prescrib'd; or that the other alledg'd, his Shop afforded the very best Drugs in Town; he still called out for better Advice, and accordingly two others of the same Faculty were sent for.

These said that it was possible the Poyson might be lodg'd in some of the *secretory Passages*, and therefore the former Prescription, which could reach no farther than the *Primae Viae*, wanted its due Effect.—That there was a Necessity for the whole *Viscera* to be cleansed;—that every *Gland* must be deterg'd;—all the Meanders of the *Mesentery* penetrated;—not a Fibre, or Membrane, even to the Capillary Vessels, but must suffer an Evacuation;—and the whole Mass of Nervous Fluid also rarify'd; and that after all this was over, he must go through a Course of Alteratives, which should pass with the *Chile* into the *subclavian* Vein, in order to purify the Blood and abrade the Points of any sharp or viscous Particles which the Poyson might have thrown into it, and were not to be eradicated by any other Methods.

This, and a great deal more learned Cant, which it was impossible for any one not practised in Physick either to understand or remember, our Patient listened to with the utmost Attention, and looking on this second Doctor as an Esculapius,[3] told him, he rely'd upon the great Judgment he found he was Master of, and put himself wholly under his Direction.

Glisters, Cathartics, and Diaphoretics in abundance were now prescrib'd, all which Ziphranes readily submitted to, and went through their different Operations with a consummate Resignation, till, to avoid Death, he was brought even to the Gates of it; and when reduced to such a Condition as not to be able to move a Finger, or speak articulately, it was thought proper, in order not to lose so good a Patient, that some Intermission of his Tortures should be permitted, and in their room Balsamic Cordials, and all manner of Restoratives administer'd.

As Youth, and a good Constitution help'd him to sustain the Asperity of the first Medicines, so it also greatly added to the Efficacy of these latter ones, and he was in a few Days able to sit up in Bed, and take nourishing Food, pretty frequently, tho' in small Quantities.

The Fears of his own Death dissipated, he began to have a Curiosity to know what was become of Barsina, and accordingly sent privately to enquire after her in the Neighbourhood where she lived.

The Person charged with this Trust, brought him Word that she was dead, and had been buried in a very private Manner about three Weeks past; and that some of those he had questioned concerning her, spoke, as if 'twas whisper'd she had been guilty of her own Death; but as to that they could not be positive, tho' they were so as to her Decease; and that they saw her Coffin put into a Hearse and Six at five o'Clock the very next Morning after they heard of her Death, attended by one Mourning Coach with only her Maid in it, and that it was supposed they carry'd her out of Town.

This Intelligence made him hug himself for the Precautions he had taken, to which alone he thought he owed the Preservation of his own Life; but then at the same time he shudder'd at the Reflection of the Danger he had escaped.

He did not, however, enjoy any Calm of Mind but for a short while, a Friend of his who came to visit him unluckily happened to mention Doctor Mead's Treatise on Poysons, which maintaining that there was a Possibility for the Venom to lurk in some Parts of the Body, for many Years after it was thought to be entirely expell'd; and then break out with a Fierceness which no Art could subdue, the poor unhappy Ziphranes presently imagined that might be his Case, and could not be at rest till he had again consulted his Physician.

Few People chuse to argue against their own Interest; Ziphranes had been too liberal of his Fees for the Doctor to offer any thing in Opposition to this Tenet; but on the contrary favour'd it obliquely by asking him if he did not sometimes feel little Twitches in his Head, his Back, or about his Heart? Which he answering with great Concern that he did (as indeed it was impossible he should not, after the violent Operations he had undergone) *Alas! Alas!* cry'd the Empyric, shaking his Head, *these are bad Symptoms;—You must have more Physic:—I am afraid indeed the Venom is not quite expunged.* And then run on a long Discourse on the Nature and Subtilty of some Poysons, till he had terrify'd his Patient almost out of his Senses.

Whether the same Medicines as were before prescrib'd, or others of a different Kind were now administer'd, I will not pretend to say; but whatever they were, they brought him into such a Condition that his Life was despair'd of; and the Doctor was obliged indeed to have recourse to all his Art to save him.

But not to be too tedious in so disagreeable a Part of my Story, I shall only say, that Fate had not yet decreed to call him hence.—He once more recovered, and seemed to want only Change of Air to re-establish his former Health.

As he was thought too weak to travel so far as his own Country Seat, which was near a hundred Miles from London, Lodgings were hired for him at a little village call'd Casehaughton, the Air of which was judged extremely proper for his Condition by his Doctor, as being neither thick nor too pure for one so much weaken'd as he had been.

He soon experienced the good Effect of it, or of having entirely left off even the most palatable Compositions of the Apothecary's Shops.—And in a few Days was able to walk about the Gardens, every Morning bringing him an Increase of Strength, of Appetite, and Spirits.

In fine, he grew in a very small Time so perfectly well, that he was beginning to think of returning home, when an odd and surprizing Accident happened to throw both his Mind and Body into fresh Disorders, equal, at least, I may say, to any he had before experienced.

He was indulging the pleasing Meditations of his Recovery, one Evening, in a fine Lane at a little Distance from the Village, when as he was walking on he saw a Lady dress'd all in white, leaning over a Gate that opened into some Fields belonging to a Gentleman in that Part of the

Country.—He thought nothing of this Adventure, but pass'd forward, when being advanc'd within twenty or thirty Paces of the Gate he imagin'd he beheld the Figure of Barsina, her Shape, her Stature, her Face, the very She in every Part.—He started back and stopp'd, all Horror and Amazement; but unwilling to be deceiv'd by Similitude, summon'd up all his Courage, and still look'd attentively, till the Object of his Terror turned full upon him, which before it had not, and crying out *Ziphranes!* immediately vanish'd from his Sight, or rather his Sight forsook his Optics, for he fell into a Swoon the Instant he heard his Name pronounced, and by a Voice so exactly the same with that of Barsina, that he was certain it could proceed from no other than her Ghost.

Unluckily for him he had gone out this Evening entirely alone, which since his Illness he had never done before; and had not the Diligence of one of his Servants, who fearing, as the Night was drawing on, the Air might be prejudicial to him, made him come in search of him, he had probably lain in that Condition till some worse Accident had befallen him.

The Fellow seeing him prostrate and motionless, at first thought him dead, but rubbing his Temples, and partly raising him, perceiv'd his Mistake, and with much ado brought him to himself; the first Words he spoke seem'd strangely incoherent, for he talk'd of nothing but Ghosts and Death, and said it was not his Fault that she killed herself.—Recollecting his Senses, however, by Degrees, he ceased these Exclamations, but ask'd his Man if he had seen nothing, to which he answering that he had not; *No*, cry'd Ziphranes wildly again, *'tis only myself that both alive and dead must be persecuted by her.*

He was at last perswaded to go to his Lodgings where he immediately went to Bed, but made his Servant sit in the Room near his Bed-side, who was amaz'd to find that instead of sleeping he talk'd all Night to himself in so odd a Manner, that the other believ'd him delirious, as indeed he was; the Fright he had sustain'd had thrown him into a high Fever, and the next Morning the Physician was sent for once more.

In his Ravings he discovered to every Body that came near him all that had pass'd between Barsina and himself, and how not content with attempting to poyson, her Spirit had appear'd and call'd to him.—Nay, so strongly did the Remembrance of what he had seen work on his distemper'd Mind, that he frequently imagin'd he heard her Voice crying out to him, *Ziphranes!*

In this unhappy Situation let us leave him for a while, and return to the Authoress of it, the injured, but well reveng'd Barsina.

After she found herself forsaken for another, at a Time when she thought herself most secured of her Lover's Affections, she bewail'd not the Loss with Tears, but bent her whole Thoughts on gratifying her Resentment for the Affront.—To this end she affected to appear so passive, neither upbraiding his Infidelity, nor discovering any Surprize at it, till she prevail'd with him, as I have already related, to come to her Lodgings, when she indeed frighted him to some Purpose. The Wine she gave him was just as it came from the Merchant, unmix'd with any poisonous Drugs, but as she judg'd it happen'd.—Conscious he deserved all the Vengeance she could inflict on him, he easily believed she had in reality done as she said, and the Terrors he was in, which he in vain strove to conceal under a Shew of Rage, as he went from her, gave her the highest Satisfaction.

She made her Kinsman and her Maid privy to the Plot she had laid, and between them they found Means to get Intelligence how he behav'd, and the cruel Operations he submitted to in order to get rid of the supposed Poison, all which gave her a Diversion beyond what can be express'd.

Not thinking him yet sufficiently punish'd, she order'd it to be given out she was dead, and to strengthen the Report, caus'd a Coffin to be carry'd from the House she lived in, attended by her Maid.—The Reader knows already the Effect this Stratagem produced, therefore it would be impertinent to make a Repetition.

To prevent all Possibility of his being undeceiv'd, she retired to a Place where she was not at all known, and happen'd to be near that very Village where Ziphranes went for the Recovery of his Health.

Chance in the very Choice of her Situation assisted her Revenge, when she was beginning to grow weary of prosecuting it any farther.—As she admitted no Company but her Cousin, who had provided that Recess for her, and sometimes came down to visit her, she frequently walk'd about the Fields belonging to the House without any Body with her; and as if every thing concurr'd to favour the undesign'd Deception, she happen'd to have a white loose *Robe de Chamber* on, when in one of those little Excursions she saw, and was seen by her perfidious Lover.—As she had not heard he was so near a Neighbour, the unexpected Sight of him made her shriek out *Ziphranes*, without any Design of renewing his Terrors; nor did she immediately know the Effect it had upon him, for she flew back into the House with all the Speed she could, not caring to run the Hazard of what Treatment she might receive from him in a solitary Place, by way of Retort for the Plagues she had given him.

The next Day, however, afforded her sufficient Matter to have gratify'd her Spleen, had any remain'd in her against a Man, now too much her Contempt to be any longer the Object of her Hate.—Every one's Mouth was full of the News, that a Gentleman had seen a Spirit over the Gate by the Lane, and that he was run mad upon it.

Impossible was it for her to refrain being merry at the first Part of this Intelligence; but mean and base as he was, she could not avoid affording him some Share of Pity as to the last.—She resolv'd, however, not to give herself any farther Trouble concerning him, and having gratify'd the just Resentment she had against him, even more than she had expected to do, returned to Town, and appear'd with all her former Serenity and Good-humour.

Tho', as I have already observed, she never kept a great deal of Company, she was yet seen by enough to have it known every where that she was alive.

The whole Transaction afterwards got Wind, 'till it was in the Mouth of all their Acquaintance.—Those who loved Barsina highly approved of the Method she took to punish his Inconstancy, and even the Friends of Ziphranes could not condemn it.

It was some Time before he could be brought to believe what he was told from every Quarter, and even when his Fever left him, and he grew perfectly restored, as to his Bodily Health, yet still his Mind continued in a very disturb'd Situation; and after being with great Difficulty convinced of the Truth, the Raillery he found himself treated with wherever he came, on the Subject of poisoning, and having seen a Spirit, so much soured his Temper, that from being that gay, polite, entertaining Companion I at first describ'd him, he is now one of the most morose ill-natur'd Men in the World.

Disregarded by his Wife, ridiculed by his Acquaintance, and uneasy in himself, he lives an Example of that Vengeance which Heaven seldom fails to take on Perjury and Ingratitude; and even Barsina, tho' the Instrument of inflicting it, almost pities his Condition, and confesses the Consequences of her Stratagem, are more severe than she either wish'd or intended.

I heartily wish, however, that all Women who have been abandoned and betrayed by Men, either through a determin'd Baseness, or Caprice of Nature, would assume the Spirit she did, and rather contrive some Means to render the ungrateful Lover the Object of Contempt, than themselves, by giving way to a fruitless Grief, which few will commiserate, and which greatly adds to the Triumph of the more happy Rival, if she can be call'd happy, whose Felicity consists in the Possession of a Heart that has once been false, and consequently can never be depended upon.

* * *

This Story, for which Elismonda has the very sincere Thanks of all the Members of our little Society, gave us a double Pleasure in the reading, not only for the agreeable Manner in which it is related, but also, as we were before acquainted with some Part of it from common Report, we were glad to be inform'd in the Particulars of so extraordinary an Adventure, by a Person, who, it is easy to be seen, is well acquainted with even the most minute of them.

The Force of Imagination has employed the Pens of many learned Authors; and indeed there cannot be a Subject more worthy the Consideration of a philosophic Genius, as it is common to every one, and makes a great Part of our Happiness or Misery.—It not only enhances all our Pains and Pleasures, but is of that prolific Nature as to produce, from one single Hint, a thousand and ten thousand subsequent Ideas.—It also imposes upon our Senses, or to speak more properly, renders them subservient to its own creative Faculty, so as to make us call them in for Witnesses to Things that never were; and we really believe we hear, see, or touch what is most remote from us, and oftentimes what is not, nor cannot be in Nature.

It is not therefore to be wondered at, that the Plot contrived, and so artfully executed by Barsina, had such an Effect on Ziphranes. A Man of more solid Judgment than his Character denotes, might have been deceiv'd, by the same Means, into the Horrors he testify'd; and also having once receiv'd them, suffered their Dissipation with as much Difficulty.

In this respect the Body discovers a more quick Sensation than the Mind.—After enduring any exquisite Torture, such as the Stone, Gout, Sciatica, and many other Persecutors of the Human System, the Moment as the Fit is over how does the afflicted Person cry out, in a Transport of Joy, *That he is eased! That he is in Heaven!* and soon loses the Memory of his former Pains.—Whereas those Agonies that have once invaded the Mind are hard to be erased, and when one is even convinced that the Cause of them is entirely vanish'd, they still leave a heavy Languor on the Spirits, which continues for a long Time, and sometimes is never wholly dispersed.

The Reason of this is plain; as the Body being endued only with sensative Faculties can suffer no longer than it feels, but the Mind, of which Memory is a Part, cannot be wholly at rest, till Reason, which tho' sure, is slow in its Operation, exerts its Power to chace all dark Ideas thence....

Indeed, when we have once got the better of that Melancholly which past Ills have left behind, and begin to grow thankful for recovered Peace, we then are doubly happy, and enjoy the present Blessings with a much higher Relish; as after a long Famine every thing is a Delicate.

But this can only be when the Misfortunes we have sustain'd have not been brought upon us by any base Action of our own, and we have rather suffered through the Faults of others than ourselves; then, and never but then, we look back with Pleasure on the Tempests we have escap'd, give all due Praises to protecting Heaven, and laudably exult in our own good Fortune.

As for Ziphranes, he can indulge no such pleasing Meditations, and I do not think it at all strange, either that he should so easily believe his Condition as bad, or even worse, than it was represented to him, or that he was so hard to be convinced that the Danger was over, even when those about him found it their Interest he should do so.

In fine, wherever there is Guilt there will be Fear.—We naturally expect what we are conscious we deserve.—So true are Dryden's Words:

Fear ever argues a degen'rate Mind.[4]

It must be own'd Barsina acted her Part admirably well; yet still the first Scene of this Tragi-Comedy was only her's;[sic]—the rest was performed by his own Apprehensions, which gave Scope to the Physicians to exert their Talents for making the most they could of him.

In ordinary Distempers, indeed, nothing is more frequent than for People to take a Load of Drugs, improperly called Medicines, till they destroy that Life they are endeavouring to preserve; but in the Case of Poison the common Opinion is, that it must be immediately expell'd, or not at all; and doubtless to give him one sudden Shock was all the Lady intended by her Stratagem, or could have expected from it; it succeeded, however, in a Manner which made not only his Guilt, but the Meanness and Cowardice of his Mind, exposed, so as to render him an Object of public Contempt; and had he even fallen a Sacrifice to the Force of his own Imaginations and the Practices of his Physicians, I cannot look on Barsina, but the Crime he was guilty of, as the primary Occasion of his Death; to which, as she did not design it, she could have been no more than innocently accessory.

I am glad, notwithstanding, for her Sake, that it happened otherwise, because had he dy'd in reality, I know not but there might have been People malicious and cruel enough to have suggested that the Wine she gave him was actually poisoned, and that she had secured herself by taking an Antidote, from any Effect the partaking it with him would otherwise have produced.

Had no worse ensued than barely the spreading about Insinuations of this Sort, it would have been a Circumstance very disagreeable to a Woman of the Character we find her in all respects so tenacious of preserving.

I also believe, tho' Elismonda has been silent on that Head, that she would have repented, even to a Degree of Affliction, what she had done, had the short Punishment she intended him prove of that fatal Consequence it was so near accomplishing.

It therefore must be acknowledg'd that this Adventure adds one demonstrative Proof to the Numbers which are every Day produced, how ready we are to judge of every Action by its Success.—From the greatest down to the most minute Affair, the Praise or Blame depends on the Event.— Heaven and Fate, which alone sees the secret Springs of every Heart, and either forwards or controuls our Purposes, can alone determine how far they are laudable, or the contrary....

We therefore join to congratulate the amiable Barsina, for an Event which so abundantly answer'd all her Purposes, and at the same time secured her Reputation from Censure.

From Volume III, Book XIV, 102-24

Explanatory Notes:

1 Our thoughtless Sex...Man.: not identified.

2 Almanzor was the hero of Dryden's *The Conquest of Granada*, or *Almanzor and Almahide*, published in 1672.

3 Esculapius, (or Aesculapius) the Greek god of medicine.

4 Fear ... Mind.: from Dryden's translation of Virgil's *Aeneid,* (1697) Book IV line 17 (the actual text reads: 'Fear ever argues a degenerate kind.').

ᖫᖫᕁ 17 ᖫᖫᕁ

The Female Spectator's Advice not followed

A Letter has been left for us at our Publisher's from Mrs. Sarah Oldfashion, the first Correspondent the *Female Spectator* was favoured with; but we do not think proper to insert this, because the Contents can be of no Manner of Service to the Public.

She reproaches me bitterly for the Advice I gave her to send Miss Biddy into the Country, where she fell passionately in Love with the Groom of a neighbouring Gentleman, and has privately married him.—To this I think myself obliged to answer, that she has not followed my Advice, but her own.—Whoever will give themselves the Trouble to turn back to the Fifth Book of the *Female Spectator*, will find I was totally averse to her sending the young Lady into a Place, where she could meet with no Diversions to compensate for the Want of those she left behind.—The good old Gentlewoman confesses also, that, instead of ordering she should be in-dulg'd in all those innocent Sports a rural Life affords, she gave a strict Charge to the Person who had the Care of her, to keep her continually at Work, and threatened herself with very severe Punishments, if she did not embroider the Hanging of a very large Drawing-Room before the Summer was elapsed.

This was taking a very improper Method, indeed, to make her forget the dear Delights of Ranelagh, and the fine Things which doubtless were said her, not only there, but in all other public Places.

Nor can I by any means approve of compelling young Ladies of Fortune to make so much Use of the Needle, as they did in former Days, and some few continue to do.—There are enough whose Necessities oblige them to live wholly by it; and it is a Kind of Robbery to those unhappy Persons to do that ourselves which is their whole Support.—In my Opinion, a Lady of Condition should learn just as much of Cookery and of Work, as to know

149

when she is imposed upon by those she employs in both those necessary Occasions, but no more.—To pass too much of her Time in them may acquire her the Reputation of a *notable House-wife*, but not of a Woman of *fine Taste*, or any way qualify her for polite Conversation, or of entertaining herself agreeably when alone.

It always makes me smile, when I hear the Mother of several fine Daughters cry,—*I always keep my Girls at their Needle.*—One, perhaps, is working her a Gown, another a Quilt for a Bed, and a third engaged to make a whole Dozen of Shirts for her Father.—And then, when she has carried you into the Nursery, and shewn you them all, add, *It is good to keep them out of Idleness, when young People have nothing to do, they naturally wish to do something they ought not.*

All this is very true; but then there are certainly Avocations to take up the Mind, which are of a more pleasing as well as more improving Kind.— Such as those I mentioned, and I will appeal to any young Lady, under the above-mentioned Confinement, if she had not rather apply to Reading and Philosophy than to Threading of Needles.

It is not enough, that we are cautious in training up Youth in the Principles of Virtue and Morality, and that we entirely debar them from those dangerous Diversions in Fashion, and which have been the Ruin of so many, in order to make them remember that Education we have given them, and to conduct themselves according to it when they come to be their own Managers; we should endeavour to make them wise, and also to render Virtue so pleasing to them, that they could not deviate from it in the least Degree without the utmost Repugnance....

It is not encouraging the natural Haughtiness of a young and beautiful Girl, and flattering her with the Opinion that she deserves every Thing, and may command every Thing, that will stem the Torrent of Inclinations, if it once fixes on a Man beneath or unworthy of her; but inspiring her with those just Notions, which will prevent her from giving way at first to any Inclinations unbefitting her Rank and Station in Life.—In fine, it is cultivating her Genius, improving her Understanding, finding such Employments for her as will rectify her Mind, and bring her to that good Taste, which will not suffer her to approve of, or be pleased with any Thing that is indecent or unbecoming, even in the most minute, much less in any important Thing.

From Volume III, Book XV, 176-9

ᎯᏇ 18 ᏨᏳ

A Letter from Leucothea,
and an Accident Occasioned by a Ram

To the FEMALE SPECTATOR.

Dear Female Moraliser,

You have not a Reader in the World more inclined to wish you well than myself; yet I must tell you, that I am a little angry with you, and so are several others of my Acquaintance, that you confine all your Satire to our Sex, without giving one Fling at the Men, who, I am sure, deserve it as much to the full, if not more than we do.

I defy the most strict Examiner to find any one Folly in us, that they do not abound with in equal Degree:—If we have our Milleners, [sic] Mantua-makers, and Tire-women to take up our Time, have they not their Taylors, Barbers; aye, and their Face-menders too, to engross as much of theirs?—Are there not as many Implements on the Toylet of a Beau, as there can be on one of the greatest Coquet among us?—Does he not take the same Pains to attract, and is as much fond and proud of Admiration?—Are not the Men in general affected with every new Mode, and do they not pursue it with equal Eagerness?—Are there any of the fashionable Diversions (call them absurd as you will) that they do not lead into by their Example?—If we affect a little of the Rusticity of a Country Maid in our Walk and Motions, do not they shoulder into all public Places with the Air and Mein of a German Hussar?—If we sometimes put on the *Romp*, I am sure they act the Part of the *Russian* to the Life.

I will tell you how I was served the other Day in the Mall.—There were five of us perfectly well dress'd; for my Part I had a new suit of Cloaths on, I had never wore before, and every body says is the sweetest fancied Thing in the World:—To speak Truth we took up

151

the whole Breadth of the Walk; unfortunately for me, I happened to be on the outside, when a Creature, who I afterwards heard was a Dettingem Hero,[1] came hurrying along, with a Sword as long as himself, hanging dangling at his Knee, and pushing roughly by me, his ugly Weapon hitched in the pink'd Trimming of my Petticoat, and tore it in the most rueful Manner imaginable.

I am so happy as not to be enough concern'd for any of that Sex to give myself any Sort of Pain, how ridiculous soever they make themselves:—I only laughed at the Khevenhuller Cock of the Hat,[2] so much the Fashion a little Time ago, and the fierce Arm-a-Kembo Air in a Fellow that would run away at the Sight of a Pot-gun. As the Poet says,

All these Things moved not me.[3]

But as my whole Sex, and myself in particular, have been aggrieved by Swords of this enormous Size, and the Manner in which they are worn, I could not help communicating my Thoughts to you on the Occasion, which I beg you will not fail to insert in your next Publication.

If you are really as impartial as you would be thought, you will add something of your own, to make the Men ashamed of appearing in a Country which, thank Heaven, is at present at Peace within itself, as if they were in a Field of Battle, just going upon an Engagement.

A Touch also upon some other of their Follies and Affectations I am very confident will be extreamly agreeable to all your Female Readers, and in a particular Manner oblige her who is,

With the greatest Good Will,
   MADAM,
     Your humble, and
Pall Mall   Most obedient Servant,
May 30 1745   LEUCOTHEA.

P.S. Just as I had finished the above, a young Lady came to visit me, and, on my shewing her what I had wrote to you, desired I would hint something about the Men loitering away so many Hours at Coffee-House Windows, meerly to make their Observations, and ridicule every one that passes by; but as this Subject is too copious for a Postscript, and I am too lazy to begin my Letter anew, if you bestow a few Pages on the Folly of such a Behaviour, it will add to the Favour of giving this a Place.—Adieu for this Time, good *Female Spectator*, if any Thing worth your Acceptance falls in my way hereafter, you may depend on hearing from me.

I own myself under an Obligation to the good Wishes of this Correspondent; but must take the Liberty to say she is guilty of some Injustice in her Accusation:—Vanity, Affectation, and all Errors of that Nature are infinitely less excuseable in the Men than in the Woman, as they have so much greater Opportunities than we have of knowing better.

If therefore I have directed my Advice in a peculiar Manner to those of my own Sex, it proceeded from two Reasons, First, because, as I am a Woman, I am more interested in their Happiness: And secondly, I had not a sufficient Idea of my own Capacity, to imagine, that any Thing offered by a *Female Censor* would have so much Weight with the Men as is requisite to make that Change in their Conduct and Oeconomy, which, I cannot help acknowledging, a great many of them stand in very great need of.

As to the Grievance she complains of, it is a common Observation, that in Time of War the very Boys in the Street get on Grenadier Caps,[4] hang wooden Swords by their Sides, and form themselves into little Battalio's. —Why then should she be surprized that Boys of more Years, but not older in their Understanding, should affect to look like Warriors for the Queen of Hungary, and equip themselves as much as possible after the Mode of those who fight the Battles of that famous German Heroine.

Many have already made a Campaign in her Service, and possibly it is in the Ambition of others to do so, if the War continues, as in all Likelihood it will, and they are now but practising the first Rudiments of Fierceness, as the Curtsy precedes the Dance.

One of the distinguishing Marks of a bad Taste in either Sex, is the Affectation of any Virtue without the Attempt to practise it; for it shews that we regard only what we are thought to be, not what we really are:—A rough boisterous Air is no more a Proof of Courage in a Man, than a demure, prim Look is of Modesty in a Woman.

These long Swords, which give so much Offence to Leucothea, might be, perhaps, of great Service at the late Battle of Fontenoy,[5] because each would serve his Master for a Crutch upon Occasion; but here, at London, in my Opinion, and according to my Notion of Dress, they are not only troublesome to others, but extreamly unbecoming, because unnecessary to those that wear them.

I believe, however, that if the Ladies would retrench a Yard or two of those extended Hoops they now wear, they would be much less liable, not only to the Inconveniencies my Correspondent mentions, but also to many other Embarassments one frequently beholds them in when walking the Streets.

How often do the angular Corners of such immense Machines, as we sometimes see, though held up almost to the Arm-pit, catch hold of those little Poles that support the numerous Stalls with which this populace City abounds, and throw down, or at least indanger the whole Fabrick, to the great Damage of the Fruiterer, Fishmonger, Comb and Buckle-Sellers, and others of those small Chapmen.

Many very ugly Accidents of this Kind have lately happened, but I was an Eye-witness from my Window of one, which may serve as a Warning to my Sex, either to take Chair or Coach, or to leave their enormous Hoops at Home, whenever they have any Occasion to go out on a Monday, or Friday, especially in the Morning.

It was on one of the former of those unhappy Days, that a young Creature, who, I dare answer, had no occasion to leave any one at Home to look after her best Cloaths, came tripping by with one of those Mischief-making Hoops, which spread itself from the Steps of my Door quite to the Posts placed to keep off the Coaches and Carts; a large Flock of Sheep were that Instant driving to the Slaughter-House, and an old Ram, who was the foremost, being put out of his Way by some Accident, ran full-butt into the Foot-way, where his Horns were immediately entangled in the Hoop of this fine Lady, as she was holding it up on one side, as the genteel Fashion is, and indeed as the Make of it requires.—In her Fright she let it fall down, which still more encumbered him, as it fix'd upon his Neck;—she attempted to run, he to disengage himself,—which neither being able to do, she shriek'd, he baa'd, the rest of the Sheep echo'd the Cry, and the Dog who follow'd the Flock, bark'd, so that altogether made a most hideous Sound.—Down fell the Lady, unable to sustain the forcible Efforts the Ram made to obtain his Liberty;—a Crowd of Mob, who were gathered in an Instant, shouted.—At last the Driver, who was at a good Distance behind, came up, and assisted in setting free his Beast, and raising the Lady; but never was Finery so demolished.—The late Rains had made the Place so excessive dirty, that her Gown and Petticoat, which before were yellow, the Colour so much revered in Hanover, and so much the Mode in England at present,[6] were now most barbarously painted with a filthy Brown;— her Gause Cap half off her Head in the Scuffle, and her *Tete de Mutton*[7] hanging down on one Shoulder. The rude Populace, instead of pitying, insulted her Misfortune, and continued their Shouts till she got into a Chair, and was quite out of Sight.

From Volume III, Book XV, 179-86

Explanatory Notes

1 Dettingem Hero: War of the Austrian Succession. Austria, England, Holland, and others, against Prussia, France, Spain, Bavaria, and others. English forces, under George II, forced their way out of a box at Dettingen (27 June 1743) badly damaging the French. It was the last engagement in which an English king took part in person.

2 Khevenhuller...Hat,: Kevenhuller (or Khevenhuller) was the name of an Austrian general (1683-1744). The term was applied to a broad-brimmed military hat pointed before and behind and rising to a point at the crown, and with the brim turned (ie, 'cocked').

3 All...not me.: Source unknown: nearest identification is from the New Testament, Acts 20:24: 'But none of these things move me'.

4 Grenadier Caps: originally a 'grenadier' was a soldier who threw grenades, but by the eighteenth century the name 'grenadiers' was applied to a company of the tallest and finest men in the regiment. Nowadays the word is retained only for the Grenadier Guards, the first regiment of house-hold infantry. The 'cap' was a mitre-shaped headdress of cloth or fur, this being more appropriate to the action of throwing the grenades than was the contemporary broad-brimmed hat.

5 Fontenoy: a village in the Low Countries, defended by the French where the English troops, led by the young Duke of Cumberland (second son of George II), fought gallantly, but were eventually defeated, in May 1745.

6 Mrs Haywood is making a political point here: she was at that time 'anti-whig', and therefore against the government led by Sir Robert Wal-pole. The Hanoverians, Georges I and II, had the support of the whigs, whose Liberal successors still use yellow as the party colour.

7 *Tete de Mutton* [French: tête de mouton – 'sheep's head']: A head-dress of close frizzly curls worn by women at that time.

🖎 19 🖎

On the Cruel Behaviour of some Step-Mothers

To the ingenious Authors of the FEMALE SPECTATOR.

LADIES,

As it was easy to perceive from the Beginning, that your Works were intended to correct all ill Habits, whether natural or acquired, particularly those which are a Disturbance to Society; I have been impatient for every new Publication of the *Female Spectator*, in Hope it would touch on the ungenerous and cruel Behaviour some of our Sex are guilty of after they become Step-Mothers.

Nothing, in my Opinion, can be more incongruous, than for a Woman to pretend an Affection for her Husband, yet treat his Children with all the Marks of Hatred; yet this is so common a Thing, that we shall scarce find one, whose Father has made a second Venture, without having Reason for Complaint of the sad Alteration in their Fate, even though the Person, who is put in the Place of her that bore them, has all those Qualifications which, in the Eye of the World, may justify the Choice made of her.

It must certainly be a mean Envy of the Dead, or a ridiculous Distrust of the Living, that can make a Wife look with an evil Eye on those Tokens of Tenderness her Husband bestows on the Children he had by a former Marriage; and I am amazed any Man, who perceives this Disposition in his Wife, can depend either on her having a sincere Affection for himself, or that she will discharge any Part of the Duty expected from her to those he has put under her Care.

I wonder, therefore, any Woman can be so impolitic as to shew her Ill-nature in this Point, since if the Husband have one Grain of Tenderness to those that owe their Being to him, he cannot but be

156

extremely offended at it.—If Dissimulation can ever be excused, it certainly might in a Circumstance of this kind; since good Usage, though not flowing from the Heart, would render the Persons, who experienced it, easy in their Situation.

But how shocking is it for a young Creature, accustomed to Tenderness, and arrived at sufficient Years to know the Value of that Tenderness, to be, all at once, obliged to submit to the insolent and morose Behaviour of a Person, who was an entire Stranger in the Family till Marriage set her at the Head of it!—A Son, indeed, has less to apprehend, because the Manner of his Education renders him less at Home, and consequently not so much exposed to the Insults of a barbarous Step-Mother; yet does he often suffer in the Want of many Things, by the sly Insinuations and Misrepresentations she makes of his most innocent Actions to perhaps a too believing Father. But a poor Girl, who must be continually under the Eye of a Person, invested with full Power over her, resolved to approve of nothing she does, and takes Delight in finding Fault, is in a Condition truly miserable.—Want of proper Encouragement prevents her making the Progress she might do in those Things she is permitted to be instructed in, and then she is reproached with Stupidity, and an Incapacity of learning, and very often, under this Pretence, all future Means of Improvement are denied to her.

Then as to her Dress; that is sure to be not only such as will be least becoming to her, but also such as will soonest wear out, to give the artful Step-Mother an Opportunity of accusing her of ill Housewifry and Slatterness.

It is impossible to enumerate the various Stratagems put in Practice to render a Young Creature unhappy.—First, she is represented as unworthy of Regard, and ten to one but afterwards made so in reality by her very Nature being perverted by ill Usage.

But this is a Circumstance which, I dare say, Ladies, you cannot but have frequently observed much more than I can pretend to do, though you have not yet thought fit to make any mention of it.—It is not, however, unbecoming your Consideration, as it is so great a Grievance in private Life, and is sometimes attended with the worst Consequences that can possibly happen in Families.

How many young Ladies, meerly to avoid the Severity and Arrogance of their Mother-in-laws, have thrown themselves into the Arms of Men whose Addresses they would otherwise have despised; and afterwards, finding they had but exchanged one Slavery for another, either broke through the Chain by the most unwarrantable

Means, or pined themselves almost to Death under the Weight of it!

Others again, who have had a greater Share of Spirit and Resolution, or, perhaps, were so happy as not to be tempted with any Offers of Delivery from their present Thraldom to go into a worse, have thought themselves not obliged to bear any Insults from a Person whom only a blind Partiality had set over them.—These, returning every Affront given them, and combating the Authority they refuse to acknowledge, have armed the Tongues of all their Kindred, on the Mother's Side at least, with the sharpest Invectives.—The Family has been divided,—at Enmity with each other, and the House become a perfect *Babel*.

I was once an Eye-witness of an Example of this kind, where I went to pass the Summer, at the Country-Seat of a Gentleman, whose Family, till his second Marriage, was all Harmony and Concord; but soon after became the Scene of Confusion and Distraction, through the Aversion his Wife immediately conceived against his Children, who being pretty well grown up, repaid in kind every Indignity she treated them with.—This, on her complaining of it, highly incensed the Father; he reproved them with the utmost Severity, which yet not satisfying the Pride of his new Choice, she converted her late Endearments into Reproaches, no less severe on him than them.—The young Family had the Good-Will and Affection of all the neighbouring Gentry, who failed not to remonstrate to him the Injustice of their Step-Mother.—Blind as his Passion at first had rendered him, he began at last to be convinced, and fain would have exerted the Power of a Husband to bring her to more Reason; but he soon found she had too much been accustomed to command, to be easily brought to obey.—She turned a kind of Fury,—made loud Complaints to all her Relations, who espousing her Cause against him and his Children, there ensued such a Civil War of Words, that all disinterested Persons, and who loved Peace, avoided the House.—I, for my Part, left it much sooner than I intended, as I found there was no possibility of being barely civil to one Party without incuring the Resentment of the other; and, indeed, being exposed to such Marks of it, as I did not think myself under any Obligation to bear.

I have since heard most dismal Accounts from that Quarter.—The eldest Son, who had a small Estate left him by his Grandmother, independant of his Father, retired to it; and falling into mean Company, was drawn in to marry a Girl very much beneath him, and of no good Character as to her Conduct.—The second, no more able to endure the perpetual Jars at Home than his Brother had been, came to London, where he was perswaded to go into the Army, and fell, with many other brave Men, at the fatal Battle at Fontenoy.—One of the Daughters threw herself away on a Fellow that belonged to a Company of strolling Players; another married a Man of neither Fortune nor Abilities to acquire any; and a third of a Disposition yet more gay, indulged herself, by way of Relaxation from the Domestic Persecutions, in going so often to an Assembly held at a neighbouring Town, that she was seduced by a young Nobleman to quit the Country before the Family did so, and come up to London with him, where she soon proved with Child; was afterward abandoned by him, and in that dreadful Condition, ashamed and fearful of having any recourse to her Father or Friends, entered herself for Bread into one of those Houses which are the Shops of Beauty, and was let out for Hire to the best Bidder.

So many Misfortunes happening, one on the Back of another, in his Family, has almost broke the Heart of the old Gentleman, and are rendered the more severe to him, as his Wife lays the Fault of them entirely on his having formerly used his Children with too much Lenity, and he is now thoroughly convinced that the Miscarriages they have been guilty of are wholly owing to the Cruelty of her Behaviour, which drove them from his House and Protection.

Dear Ladies, be so good to insert this in your next Publication, and as I am certain you cannot be without a great Number of Instances of the like Nature, if you would please to add some few of them by way of corroborating the Truth of this, and setting forth the ill Effects of using unkindly the Children of a Husband by a former Marriage, I am of Opinion it would be of great Service towards remedying this general Complaint.

I do assure you, I have been instigated to troubling you with the above by no other Motive than my good Wishes for the Preservation of Peace and Unity in Families, and the same will, I doubt not, have an Effect on yourselves, and influence you to draw your Pen in Defence of those who stand in need of such an Advocate against the Barbarity of Step-Mothers; in which Confidence I take the Liberty to subscribe myself,

With the greatest Respect,
LADIES,

Haymarket,　　　　Your most humble, and Most obedient Servant,
June 16 1745　　　　　　　PHILENIA

P.S. LADIES, The Hardships I have mentioned are still more cruel when exercised on Infants, who are incapable of making any Sort of Defence for themselves; and that Step-Mother who makes an ill Use of her Power over such helpless Innocence, ought, methinks, to be obnoxious to the World, and shun'd like a Serpent, by all those of her own Sex, who are of a different Disposition, till, ashamed of what she has done, she repairs the past by future Kindness.—But I flatter myself you will not leave this Point untouched, and it would be Folly to anticipate any Meaning you are so infinitely more capable of expressing in Terms proper to reach the Soul.—Adieu, therefore, good Ladies, pardon this additional Intrusion, and believe me, as above,

Sincerely Yours, &c. &c.

It is impossible to converse, or indeed to live at all in the World, without being sensible of the Truth Philenia has advanced; and every one must own, with her, that there cannot be a more melancholy Circumstance than what she so pathetically describes.—Every Tongue is full of the Barbarity of Step-Mothers; nor is there any Act of Cruelty more universally condemned by the World, or which doubtless is more detestable in the Sight of Heaven, than that we sometimes see practised upon Children, by those Women whose Duty it is to nurture and protect them.

Yet ought we not to think that all Step-Mothers are bad because many have been so; nor suffer ourselves to be prejudiced by a Name without farther Examination: I am very certain it is impossible for a Woman of real Sense and Virtue in other Things, to be guilty of a Failure in this:—I do not say she will feel all that Warmth of Affection for her Husband's Children, by another Wife, as she would do for those born of herself; but she will act by them in the same Manner, and if there should be any Deficiency in the Tenderness she has for them, it will be made up with a double Portion of Care over them.—Conscious of the Apprehensions they may be under on her Score, and how liable to Suspicion is the Character she bears, she will be industrious to remove both the one and the other, and behave in such a Manner, as to make them and the World perceive no Difference between their Way of Life under their natural Mother or their Mother-in-law.

...For my Part, it has ever been a Matter of the greatest Astonishment to me, that any Woman can have Courage enough to venture on becoming a Mother the first Day of her Marriage.—It would be endless to repeat the many Impediments in her Way to Happiness in such a Station, and if she has the good Fortune to surmount them, it ought to be recorded as a Prodigy.

From Volume III, Book XVI, 190-202

20

A Cruel Father

To the FEMALE SPECTATOR.

MADAM,

The good Advice you have given our Sex, and the Tenderness you have always expressed for our well doing in the World, emboldens me to become one of your Correpondents, though, Heaven knows, little qualified to write to a Person of so polite a Taste, much less to appear in Print.

The Matter, however, will, I hope, excuse the Manner in which I express myself both to you and to the World; and as I have no other View in publishing my unfortunate Story, but to prevent others from being subjected to the same Fate, and giving you an Opportunity to expatiate on a Cruelty too much practised, and too little condemned by the Generality of People, I cannot, I think, be blamed, with any Shew of Justice, for so doing.

Without any farther Apology then, Madam, permit me to acquaint you, I am the only Daughter of a Person, who, by his own Industry, and great Success in Trade, has accumulated a very large Fortune; my Mother dying when I was very young, he made up that Loss to me by an extraordinary Care both of my Person and Education; the latter of which was indeed beyond what is ordinarily allowed by Persons of his Station to their Children, especially Daughters; but as I was his all, and he declared against a second Marriage, therefore was to inherit whatever he should die possessed of, he told every body that he would bring me up so as not to let me be a Disgrace to my Fortune.

In this Resolution he persevered, till I arrived at the Age of Fifteen, or thereabouts, when I first began to perceive an Alteration. —Though Wealth continued to flow in upon him, and no

161

Disappointments happened in any of his Undertakings, he grew extremely parsimonious, and at last quite covetous.—He retrenched the Number of his Servants, the Dishes on his Table, and even denied himself a Bottle of Wine in an Evening, a Thing he was wont to say he could not live without.

Amidst this new Oeconomy it is not to be doubted but that I had my Share.—My usual Stipend for Pocket Money was lessened, had new Cloaths but seldom, and of a cheaper Sort than formerly, and was now never suffered to go to a Play, Opera, or any other public Diversion; not that he disliked them on any other account than the Expence, but every Thing that exceeded the common Necessaries of Life he now looked upon as so many Extravagancies.

This, Madam, you may perhaps imagine was a very great Mortification to me, and it would, indeed, have been so, had I not been taken up at that Time, as it happened, with Thoughts which left me no room to consider on any thing beside.

The Son of a Leicestershire Gentleman, who, whenever he came to Town, lodged at our House, found something in me that he thought worthy of the most serious Attachment, and I, for my Part, had never seen any Man before him whose Idea was capable of giving me either Pain or Pleasure in the least Degree.

In fine, having a mutual Affection for each other, it was easy for him to prevail on me to permit him to acquaint both our Parents with it.—The Supposition of my being a great Fortune made *his* listen with a very favourable Ear to the Proposal, and *mine* had no Objection to make, as the young Gentleman was Heir to a very good Estate, and had withall a fair Character from all that knew him.

That Love which before we had kept a Secret from all the World, was now avowed to all our Friends and Acquaintance; and none among them but thought the Union between us, which was soon expected, would be extremely agreeable on all Accounts.

For us, we thought of nothing but indulging the gayest Hopes of future Felicity, and had not the least Notion of any Disappointment in an Affair which was so well approved of by those who had the Disposal of us.

But, alas! we soon found we had but deceived ourselves, and that the enchanting Prospect before our Eyes was no more than an Illusion, which only served to make the coming Misfortune less easy to be borne.—The material Point to make us happy was yet wanting, though we had never once considered it.—Our own Wishes, our Ambition centered only in the Possession of each other, and we looked no farther.

As we had conversed together some Time, the Father of my Lover thought it proper to ask mine what Portion he intended to bestow on me, that he might order his Lawyer to draw up Articles, and make a suitable Settlement on me. To this my Father answered, that there was no need of being at that Trouble; that as I was to have all he had after his Decease, he did not think of parting with any Sum of Money by way of Portion before, which he might have occasion for in Trade, and the other could not want, having so good an Estate.

How much the Gentleman was surprized at so unexpected a Reply, I leave you to guess.—They had, it seems a long Debate upon it however; but the one thinking it unreasonable his Son should marry on such Terms, and the other being determined not to bestow any Money with me, they broke off the whole Affair, both mutually exclaiming against the Injustice of the other.

My Lover was now forbid by his Father, ever to see or write to me any more, and I was told I ought to despise him, for all the Passion he pretended to have for me, was only for the Portion he expected to receive with me.

I own to you, Madam, that at first this gave some Alarm to my Pride, but the dear injured Youth soon convinced me of his Fidelity, and disinterested Tenderness he felt for me, by making use of all the Arguments in his Power to prevail on me to be married in private; and when he found I would by no Means consent to that, offered to lead me publicly to the Altar, though he should by so doing incur the eternal Displeasure of his Father, and be deprived of all he was born to possess.

This Proposal seemed more extravagant than the other, and young as I was, and as much as I loved, and still do love, I could not think of gratifying that Love at the Expence of rendering myself, and the Person so dear to me, unhappy in every Circumstance in Life perhaps for ever.—I obliged him, therefore, to be content with seeing me at a Friend's House, where we sometimes meet by Stealth, till Heaven should be pleased to make some Alteration in our Fate, by turning one, or both our Parents Hearts.

A solemn Promise past, however, between us, never to listen with an assenting Ear to any Offers of Marriage that might be made to either, but preserve, through all Temptations whatever, both Heart and Hand for one another.

This is now near three Years since, in which Time several very advantageous Matches have been proposed to him, all which he has rejected with a Firmness, which well testifies both his Honour and his Love.

But now, dear *Female Spectator*, comes the severest and most shocking Part of my Misfortune:—It was not enough for my cruel Father to tear me from the only Man I ever did, or ever can love.—It was not enough that he reproached me in the most bitter Terms for not joining with him in railing against a Person, who, my Soul knew, merited the most exalted Praises.—It was not enough to withdraw all that Fatherly Affection he was accustomed to treat me with, and for these long three Years treat me rather as an Alien than a Child.—All this, I say, was not sufficient, without entailing a Misery upon me, which but with my Life I never can be eased of.

In a word, Madam, he has provided a Husband for me, to whom, if I consent not to be a Wife, am to be turned out of Doors, without the least present Support, or Hopes of any even at his Death.—That instead of the Blessings of a Father, I must receive only Curses both living and dying. My Heart shudders while I am writing this, at the dreadful Remembrance of what he has said to me on this Occasion; and at the Impossibility there seems of my any way avoiding doing what will render me not only wretched to a Degree beyond what any Words can represent, but equally wicked by becoming perfidious and ungrateful to the dear and worthy Object of my first Vows.

Several of our Relations perceiving my Aversion to this hateful Match, have used their utmost Interest with my Father not to force my Inclinations; but he continues inflexible, and their Sollicitations rather serve to make him hasten my Misfortune than to ward it off; because as he says he will not be teized on a Subject he is determined to persist in.

The grand Motive is, that the Person to whom my ill Stars have rendered me amiable, desires no Money with me, and has it besides greatly in his Power to be serviceable to my Father in his way of Business.

These are the Merits for which he is preferred.—These make him in the Eyes of an avaritious Parent appear a suitable Match; though to give his Character impartially, and without any of the Reasons I have for an Aversion, the most indifferent and disinterested Person must allow, that his Form is very ungraceful, that he has the Misfortune of being lame in one Arm, that his Countenance is sour, and that he is almost three Times my Age.—I say nothing of his Humour, because I am not sufficiently acquainted with it to be a Judge; but the World does not seem to think very favourably of it.

A Cruel Father

I do not mention this, Madam, as having any Sway over my Mind, for were he instead of the most disagreeable, the most lovely Man Heaven ever formed, I should detest him equally, if attempting to invade that Constancy I have promised to my first Love.

Yet, Wretch that I am, I am upon the Point of doing what the most false and perfidious of my Sex could but do;—and in that Light shall I appear to all who know the Professions of eternal Love I have made to him whom I am now about to render miserable for ever.—My Wedding Cloaths are making (wou'd to God it were my winding Sheet) and I must, in a few Days, be forced into a Bridal Bed by far more dreadful to me than the Grave.

The only Ease under this heavy Affliction I can enjoy is, in the Hope my Story will influence you to say something in your perswasive Manner that may have its due Weight with other Parents, (for I despair of mine being moved, even with an Angel's Eloquence). Unhappy as I am, I wish not to have any Sharer in the same Fate, though I am afraid too many have and will. That the Number may decrease, however, is the sincere Prayer of,

GOOD MADAM,
Cheapside,   Your most unfortunate Servant
October 2, 1745.   MONYMA.

P.S. Next Thursday is the Day appointed for my Doom, if it be possible for me to survive till then.—Think of me with Compassion, 'tis all can now be done for me.

Hearts the least sensible of the Woes of others cannot but be touched with the most tender Commiseration for Monyma's Condition, nor can any reasonable Person seriously reflect on the Conduct of her Father in this Affair without passing the severest Censure on it.

Unaccountable is it, as well as unnatural, that Parents, who in general are fond of their Children while they are very young, can afterwards resolve to make them for ever miserable, only to gratify some sordid Interest of their own.

Most indeed of those who thus force the Inclinations of their Children, being past all Sense of the softer Passions themselves, think they are acting for their Good, while they oblige them to sacrifice Love to Ambition; but the Father of this young Lady carry'd his Avarice to a much higher than one shall ordinarily hear of.—It seemed not to be so much what the World calls Interest, for her Sake, as for his own Selfishness in keeping his Money, that he forced her from a Man so dear to her, and compelled her to give herself to another equally hateful.

Detestable Propensity, to what does it transport us? Every noble, generous, or humane Sentiment is dead within us, when once it takes Possession of the Soul.—Nay, we seem even abandoned by common Sense, and act not only in direct Opposition to our Pretences, but likewise run counter to what we think or desire within ourselves.

…But to return to the unhappy Monyma, The *Female Spectator* sincerely wishes her Case had been sooner communicated. All Remonstrances on the one Side, or Advice on the other, would now come too late, if her Fate was really decided at the Time she mentions in her Letter.

Otherwise there is no one Member of our Club, not even Euphrosine herself, who is the most perfect Pattern of an implicit Obedience I ever knew, but is of Opinion, that Monyma, circumstanced as she was, and under a former Engagement, might have refused entering into a second without incurring any just Censure from the World.

We should not have advised so far indeed as for her to marry her young Lover; for that would have been to have flown directly in the Face of Paternal Authority, and a Breach of Duty which no Exigence could have rendered excuseable; but we think, at the same time, that she might easily have been absolved for persisting in her Refusal of the other.

By debarring herself from pursuing her Inclination she would sufficiently have discharged all that Filial Duty demanded from her; and by continuing resolute, to suffer any thing rather than yield herself to one for whom she could have no Inclination, she would have given a shining Testimony of Love and Constancy to him who seems so well to deserve it from her.—Whereas, by acting in the Manner she has done, she has not only involved herself, but the Object of her Affection, in Miseries, which, in all Probability, will be as lasting as their Lives.

I know very well it may be said, by some over discreet Persons, that she had no other Course to take, and doubtless she was of that Opinion herself, that if her Father had made good his Menace, and turned her out of Doors, she must have been exposed to Insults, Reproaches, and all the Ills that Poverty brings with it.—But I can scarce think her Condition would have been so desperate, even had her Father in reality abandoned her; she has doubtless Relations and Friends, some of whom [would] certainly have taken Pity of a young Creature that stood in need of their Assistance, by no other Crime than her strict Adherence to Love and Honour; or if, as indeed there are not many Instances of natural Affection in this Iron-hearted Age, all Hopes of this Kind had failed, that Education she confesses to have had, might certainly have furnished her with some Means or other of Support.

Neither can we believe, without being uncharitable, that her Father would not in Time have relented, at least so far as to take her home again, if not been brought to consent to the Terms required of him for her more perfect Happiness.

But when the indissoluble Union of Marriage is once formed, how disagreeable soever it may be at first, it is the Business and the Duty of each, thus joined, to render themselves, and Partner for Life, as easy as possible:—All After-Reflections,—all Struggles, serve only to render the Misfortune more grievous, and add new Weights to a Load already but too galling.

We therefore hope Monyma's good Sense will enable her to endeavour a Forgetfulness of every thing that may occasion a Melancholly in herself, or a Dissatisfaction to her Husband:—Virtue, Religion, Reputation, Reason, and Interest all concur to exact it from her; and in fulfilling their Dictates, she can only expect to find any true Ease or Consolation.

And this is all we have it in our Power to offer on her Account.

From Volume IV, Book XX, 98-112

On the Distinction between Good Manners and Good Breeding

[The following narrative appears after a letter from a 'correspondent' and subsequent comments on the part of the Editor, to illustrate the distinction between *Good Manners* and *Good Breeding* – the Editor asks the Reader to excuse her mentioning 'the Country where it happened or the Names of the Persons concerned in it']:

A certain Nobleman, who for his great Courtesy, Affability, and seeming Sweetness of Disposition, was the very Idol of the Populace, and the Delight of all those who were admitted to a nearer Conversation with him...had the Misfortune to fall under the Displeasure of his Sovereign, through the subtle Insinuations of the then Prime Minister, who being a wicked and weak Man, except in a low mean Cunning, in which it must be owned he excelled, hated all who either had any real Merit, or were judged to have it.

He was not, indeed, absolutely forbid the Court, but looked so coolly upon all belonging to it, that he seldom went there; and this absenting himself gave his Enemy many Opportunities of misrepresenting him, and putting a false Colour on every thing he did.

It happened one Day that a Gentlewoman, who had frequent Occasions of waiting on the Prime Minister, on account of a Business she was then solliciting, being desired to stay in one of his Parlors till a Person was gone, with whom they told her he was at present engaged, she saw soon after a Chair with the Curtains close drawn, brought by the Door of the Room where she was sitting, and in a few Minutes a Gentleman come out of a Closet where the Prime Minister usually received People who came to him on any private Affairs, and threw himself into it with the greatest

Precipitation, as if fearful of being seen, even by the Servants of the Person he came to.

So uncommon a Sight as a Chair being brought quite through the House, joined with the extreme Caution of him that went into it, a little surprized her; but she made no great Reflections on it at that Time, being presently admitted to the Presence of the Prime Minister; but before she had concluded what she had to say to him, his Valet de Chambre came in, and told him one of the Fathers of the Church desired to speak with him; on which he went hastily out, leaving her alone in the Closet.

As she sat ruminating on her own Affairs, and far from any Curiosity for knowing those of other People, her Eye, without her designing it to do so, chanced to glance on a Parchment which had been tied, but now lay half unrolled upon a Table near her, on the Top of which she could not help seeing these Words, *Articles of Impeachment for High Treason.* This somewhat startled her, and she could not refrain looking a little farther, where she read the Name of that Nobleman above-mentioned, and below that of another Person who she had heard was his most bitter Enemy.

She not doubted, but that the Prime Minister and this other were hatching some Mischief towards the noble Lord; and as she had some small Acquaintance with him, and had the highest Estimation for his Character, it aggravated the Indignation which she could not but have felt at the Injustice attempted to be practised, had it been against a Person she had thought less worthy.

She had no Time to examine into the Body of the Scroll. The Prime Minister returned, and after some Discourse with him on the Business which had brought her thither, she took her Leave, but with an Agitation of Mind, which required no less Presence of Mind than she was Mistress of to conceal.

On her Return Home, and ruminating on what she had seen, she thought it her Duty to apprize the Nobleman of the Danger he was in, to the end he might be armed against it. For this Purpose she wrote to let him know she had a Discovery of something, which it was highly necessary for his Interest, and even Safety, he should be immediately acquainted with, and added, that if he would be at Leisure she would wait on him that same Evening to explain the Matter.

To this he returned a very complaisant Answer; but added, that being obliged to sup with some Friends at a Villa he had some Distance from Town, he would order his Secretary to attend her, and entreated she would communicate the Secret to him, which, he said, might be done with the same Safety as to himself.

The Gentleman accordingly came, and in Compliance with the Request made to her by his Lord, she related to him the whole of what she knew; and withal, that she imagined, that the Gentleman she had seen go away in the covered Chair, was no other than him whose Name she had seen in the Parchment, as the Person who attempted to prove the Articles therein inserted.

The Secretary seemed greatly astonished, and she thought dismayed at the Intelligence she gave him. But, after having paused a little, *There is nothing ill*, said he, *that is not to be expected from the Malice and implacable Hatred of the Prime Minister; but as to the Supposition you mention of the Person who went out in that private Manner, being the same whose Name you saw in the Parchment, it is altogether groundless; for I am very certain he is not in this Kingdom, and that my Lord has taken effectual Measures to keep him where he is.*

As the Lady had only bare Conjecture on her Side, though backed with Probability enough, she offered no more in defence of it, and the Secretary went away; but, as she afterwards heard, took Post-Chaise immediately to his Lord, to acquaint him with what she had told him, which convinced her how material he even then thought it, though he would not seem to do so.

The Nobleman, however, in this Point was less capable than his Servant of disguising himself, as being more deeply interested; and sent him again the next Day with many fine Compliments, and Expressions of the utmost Gratitude, to which was annexed a Request of her using all her Efforts to come at the Truth, and find out, if possible, the Person in the Chair; adding, that whatever Pains or Expence she should be at in unravelling this important Mystery, they should certainly be amply recompensed.

As she knew and truly hated the Prime Minister's base Arts, had a Veneration for the good Qualities of the Nobleman who requested this Favour of her, and doubtless had some Sparks of Curiosity herself, she readily assured the Secretary, that nothing in her Power should be wanting to satisfy his Lord's Desire; on which he renewed his Compliments, and said he would attend her in a few Days; beseeching, that if she succeeded in her Enquiries before he came, that she would send to him.

The various Stratagems to which she was obliged to have recourse, in order for this Discovery, would be too tedious to recount. It shall suffice to say, that she gained her Point in less than a Week's Time, and found she had not been deceived in her first Thought, and that the Person who took so much Care to keep himself concealed, was the very individual He, whose Name she had seen as the grand Accuser of the noble Lord.

The next Request made her in his Name by the Secretary, who came to her every Day, was to find out where this Incendiary was lodged, which with a great deal of personal Fatigue, and no small Expence of Money, she at last attained the Knowledge of; but what cannot a sincere Zeal, Curiosity, and some Mixture of Self-Interest accomplish! Though born and bred to very great Expectations in Life, a Multiplicity of cross Accidents had rendered her not of the Number of the Rich, though above the Contempt of Want; and, as she had much to hope from the Favour of so great and honourable a Person, it doubtless added to her Diligence and Industry in serving him.

The Promises made her were indeed very great, and the Gratitude of the Nobleman exceeded in Shew even her own Imagination. After she had acquainted him where his Adversary was to be found, he sent his Secretary to tell her, that he should always acknowledge that he owed to her, if not his Life, his Honour, and whatever else was valuable in this World, and that he would, in a very few Days, convince her of the Sense he had of the Obligation she had conferred upon him, by making her Fortune as perfectly easy as she had made his Mind.

The Service she did him was certainly as great as ever Man received, for by this early Intelligence he found Means to circumvent all the Plots his Enemies were laying against him, reconciled himself to the good Graces of his Sovereign, bought off his grand Accuser from the Interest of the Prime Minister; so that the Thing was intirely dropped, and never more attempted.—But to return to the Lady.

Some Weeks after her knowing the Nobleman was again in Favour past over, without her hearing any thing from him, or his Secretary, to the former of whom she wrote a Letter, expressing the Satisfaction it gave her, to find the good Effect of what she had done.

This was the most modest Method she could take of reminding him, and one would think should have been sufficient to have made him ashamed of having stood in need of it; but when one can bring oneself to do a base, or an ungenerous Action, one shall always easily find Ways to evade the Scandal of it.

He sent a very civil, though cool Message, by the Person who delivered the Letter into his Hands, importing that he had been extremely busy of late, but would not fail of ordering his Secretary to wait on her in a short Time.

She had too much Penetration not to discover there was more of the Courtier than the honest Man in this Behaviour, and after having vainly waited the coming of his Secretary for several Weeks, at last resolved to make a Visit to the Nobleman, and know her Doom from his own Mouth.

But in imagining she could do so, she was wholly mistaken; on having sent up her Name, instead of being admitted to his Presence, as was usual, before she had conferred this Obligation on him, his Valet de Chambre brought down an Excuse, that he was engaged in Company, and should be glad to see her any other Time.

Resolving to see the Event, she went again the next Day, and was then told he was indisposed.—She repeated her Visit on the third, he was still out of Order.—On the fourth had the same Answer, though she was no sooner got Home all these Times than she saw him in his Chariot pass by her own Door.

This was sufficient to convince her, that the Benefit received was no longer thought worthy acknowledging; however, she went three or four Times afterwards, but he was then always from Home, so that she found the Servants had a general Order to refuse her Admittance whenever she came.

...Thus ended all her Expectations and Dependance on this Score.— Thus was testified the Gratitude and Honour of a great Man, who, on the Account of his Good Breeding and Affability, had acquired so high a Reputation of being possessed of every other excellent Qualification.

Not but he had in Effect done many generous Actions; but then it was where he was certain it would be either for his Interest or Character, by their being known and publicly talked of. Now here he had no such Motive.—As the affair transacted by this Lady was of a secret Nature, and, if divulged, would have incurred the Displeasure of the Prime Minister, he had nothing to apprehend from her Resentment on the Forfeit of his Promise to her, nor could expect any thing to gratify his Ostentation from her Good Will, had he fulfilled it. So that one may easily infer, that all his fine Qualities were superficial, meer Shew, and studied Artifice, and that he had really neither Honour, Gratitude, Good Nature, nor even common Honesty, or Integrity; in fine, though he was a perfect Master of *Good Breeding*, he was utterly void of all *Good Manners*.

That true Benevolence and Sweetness of Disposition which we call *Good Manners*, is, without all Doubt, the first and best of Virtues, because all the others are, in effect, no more than meer Consequences which necessarily attend upon it.—None who are possessed of it are capable of doing a premeditated bad Action:—I say *premeditated*, because the Faults of Inadvertency are liable to us all, and will not only be repented of, but repaired, when Consideration resumes its Place.

From Volume IV, Book XXIV, 334-43

22

Last Words

It is a very great Reflection, and I am sorry to say too just a one, upon the English Nation, that we have more Suicides among us in a Year, than in any other Place in an Age.—Whence can this unnatural Crime proceed, but from giving way to a Discontent which preys like a Vulture upon our very Vitals on every Accident that displeases us, fills us with black and dismal Thoughts, and at length precipitates us into the utmost Despair!

Like all other ill Habits this must be suppressed in the beginning, or it will grow too mighty for Controul, if in the least indulged.—To that end we should never put the worst Colours on Things, but rather deceive ourselves with imagining them better than they are.

Of this I am perfectly convinced, both by Observation and Experience, that an easy and unruffled Mind contributes very much to the preventing many ill Accidents, and to extricate us out of those Difficulties we are actually involved in: Whereas a Person of a fretful and discontented disposition is bewildered, as it were, amidst his Troubles. His Thoughts are in a Maze, and Reason has no Power to point him out the Path he ought to take for his Redress.

Besides, as I have already hinted, every Disappointment is not a real Misfortune, though blinded by our Passions we may think it so. I know a Gentleman, who, by the strangest Accidents in the World, was twice prevented from going a Voyage which had the Prospect of great Advantage to him. He thought himself the most unhappy Man that ever was, and could not help complaining in all Companies, how averse Fortune was to his Desires; but in a short Time after, News arrived that both those Ships, in which he had intended to embark, were lost, and every Soul on Board them had perished in the Waves. This compelled him to acknowledge himself happy in the imaginary Disappointment, and bless the Goodness of that Divine Power, he had so lately, under the Name of Fortune, accused of Cruelty.

Another, who was passionately in Love with a very beautiful young

Lady, behaved himself in the most extravagant Manner on a Rival's being preferred by her Father.—All his Acquaintance trembled, lest some Act of Desperation should ensue; and it is much to be feared, they would not have been mistaken, if in two or three Days after the Loss of all Hopes on her Account, he had not providentially discovered she had been made a Mother two Years before by one of the Helpers in the Stable.

A Lady of my Acquaintance, who was brought near the Brink of Distraction for the Death of a Husband to whom she had been married but two Months, and tenderly loved, soon found a Consolation for her Loss, in the Discovery that he had been an Impostor, had not an Acre of Land in the World, though he pretended himself in Possession of a large Estate; and what was yet worse, that he had been contracted to a Woman who was about to sue him for half the Fortune he had received with her; and that if he had lived but a very little Time longer, she must have been inevitably ruined.

The least Observation may convince us in daily Instances, that what we most desire, is in reality our greatest Happiness to miss; but tho' all see, and confess it in the Affairs of others, few can be perswaded it is so in their own, till Time and Accidents open the Eyes of Reason.

Blind to our own Good, as to our Faults, we hurry on precipitately to whatever Phantom Fancy sets before us,—adore it as a Deity,—sacrifice our *all* to it, and push from us with Vehemence and Contempt, the friendly Hand that aims to pull us back, though by Heaven itself directed.

I am not insensible that to be of a Disposition not over anxious nor eager in the pursuit of any Thing, is looked upon to savour too much of the Stoic, and by some is accounted even Dulness, Stupidity, and Sluggishness of Nature; it may indeed betray a Want of that Vivacity which is so pleasing in Conversation, and renders the Person who possesses it, more taken Notice of than otherwise he might be; but then, if those who argue in this Manner, would give themselves the Trouble to reflect how dear sometimes People pay for exerting that Vivacity, or rather, as the French term it, a *brusque* Behaviour, none would wish to exchange the solid, serious, and unmoved Temper for it.

I am always extremely concerned, when I see People place their whole Happiness in the Attainment of any one Aim.—I scarce ever knew it to succeed without being productive of very great Mischiefs.—We are so little capable of judging for ourselves, that when the Almighty, offended with our Presumption, gives his Fiat to our Wishes, they seldom come uncharged with Ills, which we then pray as earnestly and with much more Reason to be delivered from.

Upon the whole, therefore, we ought to look on all the little Calamities of Life as things unworthy of wholly engrossing our immortal Part.—*Virtue* and *Wisdom* are the two only Pursuits where Ardency is reconciled with Reason. For the acquiring these, we cannot indeed be too eager. All the Zeal, all the Warmth we testify for them is laudable. The more we are possessed of *them*, the less we shall feel of any *other* Wants. Besides, we have this Reflection to encourage our Endeavours, that whoever is happy enough to arrive at any Degree of Perfection in the *one*, cannot fail of being in a great measure possessed of the *other* also.

...But now it is Time to quit the *Spectatorial* Function, and thank the Public for the extraordinary Encouragement these Lucubrations have received; to those who have favoured us with their Correspondence, and who express a Desire of having the Work continued yet a longer Time, our Gratitude is particularly due. Though on a Consultation of our Members, it is judged more for the Advantage of our Reputation, to break off while we are in the good Graces of the Town, than become tedious to any Part of it.

As we have more than once expressed our Intention of concluding with this Book, the Authors of several ingenious Letters, which came too late to be inserted, will not, we hope, think themselves neglected; since, as the Number of our Correspondents has every Day greatly multiplied, it is likely the *Female Spectator* might be prolonged till we ceased to be, if a *Finis* to the Undertaking were not to be put, till either Matter failed us to write upon, or kind Assistance to it failed from other Hands.

But though we think convenient to drop the Shape we have worn these two Years, we have a kind of hankering Inclination to assume another in a short Time; and if we should do so, Notice shall be given of it in the public Papers, flattering ourselves, that those who have testified their Approbation of the *Female Spectator*, either by their Subscriptions, or Correspondence, will not withdraw their Favour from the Authors, in whatever Character we shall next appear.

Close as we endeavoured to keep the Mystery of our little Cabal, some Gentlemen have at last found Means to make a full Discovery of it. They will needs have us take up the Pen again, and promise to furnish us with a Variety of Topics yet untouched upon, with this Condition, that we admit them as Members, and not pretend to the World, that what shall hereafter be produced, is wholly of the *Feminine* Gender.

We have not yet quite agreed on the Preliminaries of this League, but are very apt to believe we shall not differ with them on Trifles, especially as one of them is the Husband of Mira.

In the mean time, should any one, from this Hint, take it into their Head, to publish either Book or Pamphlet, as wrote by the Authors of the *Female Spectator*, it may be depended on that whether we do any Thing ourselves or not, we shall advertise against whatever shall come out that Way, and lay open the Imposition.

End of the TWENTY-FOURTH and last BOOK
(378-84)

SELECTED BIBLIOGRAPHY

Primary Sources

The Female Spectator, Vols I-IV printed and published by T. Gardner at Cowley's Head, opposite St Clement's Church in the Strand (1745-6).

The Female Spectator, being selections from Mrs Eliza Heywood's [sic] periodical (1744-6), chosen and edited by Mary Priestley (London, 1929).

The History of Miss Betsy Thoughtless, Vols I-IV (London), printed by T. Gardner and sold at his Printing-Office at Cowley's Head, facing St Clement's Church in the Strand and sold by all Booksellers in Town and Country, M, D, CC, LI.

Pope, Alexander, *The Dunciad*, James Sutherland (ed.) (London, 1943, 1963).

The Daily Post (1744-6; Burney Papers, Brtish Library).

The General Advertiser (1744-6; Burney Papers, British Library).

The Gentleman's Magazine (December 1744).

The London Magazine (1744-6).

The Westminster Gazette (1745-6; Burney Papers, British Library).

The Whitehall Evening Post: or London Intelligencies (24-6 February 1756; Burney Papers, British Library).

Whicher, G., *The Life and Romances of Mrs Eliza Haywood* (New York, 1915).

Secondary Sources

Adburgham, Alison, *Women in Print* (London, 1972).

Baker, David Erskine, *Biographica Dramatica* (London, 1812).

Cross, Wilbur, *The History of Henry Fielding* (Yale, 1915).

Dictionary of National Biography (London, 1891).

Eighteenth Century Short Title Catalogue (London 1983-).

Hodges, James, '*The Female Spectator*: A Courtesy Periodical', in *Studies in the Early English Periodical* (University of North Carolina Press, 1957).

Koon, Helene, 'Eliza Haywood and the *Female Spectator*', in the *Huntington Library Quarterly*, No. 42 (1978-9).

Macaulay, Lord, *The History of England* [1848] (reprinted London, 1962).

National Union Catalog (London, 1980).

Notes and Queries (January 1973, June 1991).

Rogers, Pat, *Henry Fielding, a Biography* (New York, 1979).

————— *The Augustan Vision* (London, 1974).

Schofield, Mary Anne, *Quiet Rebellion: The Fictional Heroines of Eliza Fowler Haywood* (Washington, DC, 1982).

————— *Eliza Haywood* (Boston, 1985).

Spencer, Jane, *The Rise of the Woman Novelist, from Aphra Behn to Jane Austen* (Oxford, 1986; 1987).

Spender, Dale, *Mothers of the Novel* (London, 1986).

Watt, Ian, *The Rise of the Novel* (Harmondsworth, 1957; 1961).

Weinreb, Ben, and Hibbert, Christopher (eds), *The London Encyclopaedia* (London, 1983).

Willey, Basil, *The Eighteenth Century Background* (London, 1940; 1986).

Williams, Basil, *The Whig Supremacy (1714-1760)*, vol. XI, in *The Oxford History of England*, Sir George Clark (ed.) (Oxford, 1939; 1985).

INDEX

[Compiled from the original indexes placed at the end of each volume]